A Journey to the Land of the Saints

spiritual reflections and communal prayers
following the pilgrimage of
Saint Brendan the Navigator

by
Timothy J. Ray

with selections from
The Voyage of Saint Brendan,
translated by John J. O'Meara

TO THE MEMORY OF MY PARENTS

who taught me to embrace the unknown
in every journey

Table of Contents

Selections from *The Voyage of Saint Brendan*,
with companion reflections and exercises

A Journey to the Land of the Saints:
a sequence of prayer services

Returning Home

Resources for Prayer and Worship

Preface

the Celtic journey of an Ignatian pilgrim

Like the voyage of Saint Brendan and his companions they emulate, these materials reflect a personal pilgrimage — a journey of prayer and self-exploration now over a decade-long. Traversing years both turbulent and rewarding, these reflections provided a calm focal point to my spiritual life and I now wish to give testimony to some of what I have learned along the way.

My voyage with Brendan and his Celtic companions began during a seminal conversation at a Jesuit retreat house in northwest England. At the end of a thirty-day retreat using *The Spiritual Exercises of Saint Ignatius*, a small group of my fellow retreatants and I were discussing the spiritual influences that guided us from our different religious and national backgrounds toward this shared experience of prayer. One member of our group — an English evangelical Christian — spoke with particularly strong passion about his visit to the "holy island" of Lindisfarne in northeast England. He also spoke very highly of the writings by the Anglican vicar on the island, David Adam. Intrigued by his fervor, and since I had a few quiet days in which to read before beginning a sabbatical course in Ignatian spiritual accompaniment, I went to a room in the retreat house where books for sale were displayed to find one of David Adam's books.

The only book by David Adam that I could find that day was *A Desert in the Ocean*, a reflection on an ancient Celtic poem called "Brendan's Prayer on the Mountain". It was a small paperback, and I bought it expecting some pleasant reflections during what promised to be a calm interlude before my studies began. But, shaped by the powerful spiritual and emotional experiences at the heart of my recent retreat, my reading of this book proved to be an intense experience in which I connected Brendan's prayer to the Ignatian values at the heart of my own spiritual life.

Over the coming months of my renewal course, I read most of David Adam's other books — similar reflections on Celtic prayers and hymns or collections of his own Celtic-inspired prayers — but I kept returning to the parallels between Brendan's approach to pilgrimage and the Ignatian ideals being discussed in my workshops, classes and seminars. So, at the end of my studies, I spent Holy Week on Lindisfarne and took this opportunity to speak with David Adam in a few brief but powerful conversations on the resonances between the Celtic ideal of spiritual wandering and the apostolic openness of Ignatian spirituality. These conversations initiated a broader process of prayer and spiritual reflection but, before I say more, you should take a moment to consider the version of Robert Van de Meyer's translation of "Brendan's Prayer on the Mountain" I first encountered in *A Desert in the Ocean*:

> *Shall I abandon, O King of Mysteries, the soft comforts of home?*
> *Shall I turn my back on my native land, and my face towards the sea?*
>
> *Shall I put myself wholly at the mercy of God, without silver, without horse, without fame and honour?*
> *Shall I throw myself wholly on the King of kings, without sword and shield, without food and drink, without a bed to lie on?*
>
> *Shall I say farewell to my beautiful land, placing myself under Christ's yoke?*
> *Shall I pour out my heart to him, confessing my manifold sins and begging forgiveness, tears streaming down my cheeks?*
>
> *Shall I leave the prints of my knees on the sandy beach, a record of my final prayer in my native land?*
> *Shall I then suffer every kind of wound the sea can inflict?*
>
> *Shall I take my tiny coracle across the wide, sparkling ocean?*
> *O King of Glorious Heaven, shall I go of my own choice upon the sea?*
> *O Christ will you help me on the wild waves.*

This powerful statement of faith helped me to see my own

---

* Cited in David Adam, *A Desert in the Ocean: God's Call to Adventurous Living* (London: Society for Promoting Christian Knowledge, 2000), page 9. David Adam excerpted this prayer from Robert Van de Weyer's *Celtic Fire* (London: Doubleday, 1990), which presents the prayer in prose.

spiritual ideals with new eyes. My approach to spirituality has always involved an openness to learn from other religious traditions but my encounter with Brendan's prayer penetrated deeper into the core principles of my life than in any of my previous reflections. Its openness to making a pilgrimage into the unknown echoed the willingness to surrender oneself fully to God's desires fostered through *The Spiritual Exercises of Saint Ignatius*, which I had completed just before reading David Adam's reflections in *A Desert in the Ocean*. During that intense month-long experience of prayer, I recommitted myself to the Ignatian ideals that shaped my life choices since early adulthood, both while a Jesuit and after leaving the order, so I was grateful to find a resource that might reinforce the foundations of my spiritual life. This was not entirely new terrain — my interest in the Celtic tradition extends back to my initial university studies — but I now actively sought out aspects of Celtic spirituality that paralleled and augmented my Ignatian beliefs and practices.

At first, I was learning a new language that helped me explain things that were already familiar. Ignatian and Celtic spiritualities share many of the same principles — a belief that God is found in all things, a Trinitarian view of creation, a commitment to developing a personal relationship with Christ, a sustained acknowledgment of God's blessings in our lives, and so on — but they use different words and phrases to explain these shared ideals. So, acquiring this broader vocabulary offered me the opportunity to explain Ignatian principles and practices in a more ecumenical manner, allowing me to reach out to individuals from different religious traditions and alleviating some of the concerns I encountered from non-Catholics about the "Roman" character of my spiritual direction work. Consequently, I became quite excited as my use of newly acquired Celtic language offered many practical advantages in developing an inclusive spiritual practice.

But, as is often the case when acquiring fluency in another language, the vocabularies of my old and new languages began to illuminate one another and broaden my worldview. I quickly discovered that the nuances of Celtic expression helped me better appreciate aspects of a spiritual tradition I thought I already understood while I recognized that Ignatian idioms revealed subtle aspects of the Celtic practices I was learning. As I began using both languages on a regular basis, I admired the many ways in which the Celtic and Ignatian spiritual terms and concepts elaborate and strengthen one another. Yet they never blurred together into a spiritual pidgin. Instead, the language and terminology of each tradition maintained its own integrity and allowed me to speak with greater clarity in a dynamic conversation that moved back and forth between Celtic and Ignatian vocabularies about new concerns — especially the Celtic approach to pilgrimage or "holy wandering" — as well as the ideals to which I have devoted most of my life.

Still, despite the harmonious interplay of these spiritual languages, my explorations encountered their share of frustrations. Unlike the Ignatian tradition, which has a 500-year-old living history of first-hand commentaries on its practices, the advocates and admirers of the Celtic spiritual tradition are attempting to revive an eclipsed tradition through the interpretation of surviving documents and folk traditions. These efforts have produced a multitude of books, articles and other materials seeking to explain and encapsulate the Celtic spiritual vision — including collections of original sources, scholarly studies of particular documents and practices, the creation of rules for new quasi-monastic communities and associations, and personal interpretations or elaborations on various Celtic themes. These materials also interpret the Celtic traditions in a variety of ways, ranging from traditional Christian understandings of spirituality to those rooted in New Age concerns. So, I soon found myself overwhelmed by the dissonant voices of the many different proponents of "Celtic Christianity".

But I realized that this plethora of resources echoed the diversity of spiritual opinions found among the original Celtic saints. The Celtic churches emerged around the abbeys of particular saints, each observing the rule of a particular abbot or abbess. So, while they may share many of their principles and practices, each community emphasized particular aspects of their traditions and fostered unique spiritualities — much like the history of spirituality in the broader Church. This insight helped me become more selective in my reading, leading me to focus principally on primary sources and studies of prayer and spiritual practice among the Celtic saints.

Another obstacle to my explorations emerged from the ways different authors treated the practice of pilgrimage in relation to the monastic traditions of the early Celtic churches. I found many traditional Christian interpretations of Celtic pilgrims relied on an understanding of monastic stability which, while certainly existing in some Celtic religious communities, only became prevalent in the monastic traditions that supplanted the spiritual practices of the early

Christianized Celts. So, while mentioning examples of "holy wanderers", many of these authors dismissed pilgrimage as an extension of the Irish tradition of heroic journeys or as an alleged disposition toward adventure among the Celts. Ironically, this heroic interpretation of adventurous pilgrimage was praised among many authors discussing Celtic spirituality through the lenses of contemporary social and spiritual concerns, but I discovered these authors devoted little attention to the contributions of this spiritual practice to the early Celtic churches or its significance in modern spirituality. Consequently, I found few authors who directly addressed my questions about the Celtic spirituality of pilgrimage and I often needed to draw upon my knowledge of other spiritual traditions to understand those resources I was able to find.

Since the Celtic spiritual traditions are often compared to those of the Orthodox Christian churches, I turned to my experiences with the ascetic practices of these other ancient churches to better appreciate the materials I found on Celtic pilgrimage. While preparing to enter the Jesuits during my university studies, I was asked if I would be interested in working with the Orthodox churches after entering the order. So, to answer this question, I met with a group of Jesuits in New York City who introduced me to the Orthodox understandings of theology and spirituality both by taking me to Christian Orthodox liturgies and by discussing various aspects of Orthodox theology and spirituality (especially *The Way of a Pilgrim*). While these discussions were brief and did not lead me further into the Orthodox tradition, they did introduce me to two practices that had a lasting impact on my spiritual life before becoming central to my exploration of Celtic spirituality — seeing pilgrimage as following a deeply personal spiritual path (rather than traveling toward a shrine sanctified by others) and using the Jesus (or Pilgrim's) Prayer while on this journey.

Also, to keep my reflections on pilgrimage from becoming too subjective, I relied on the Ignatian practice of discernment. Primarily through a daily review called the examen, this process seeks to understand the concrete expressions of God's presence in our lives — and our resistance to it — so we may cultivate increasing personal generosity in our service of Christ in the world. So, I included my reflections on pilgrimage as part of my activities in order to discern the activity of God in both my intellectual inquiries and daily life. Still, both in my experiences while a Jesuit and after leaving the order, I have come to understand that this ideal of a generous disposition before God

— returning love for the love God bestows on us — is not about achieving goals, apostolic or otherwise. It is about living one's life with a continuous openness to the desires of God and the needs of others around you, becoming a witness to God's love for the world and a beacon of hope to those living in it. With this in mind, I sought to understand how the Celtic practice of pilgrimage might help me reach that goal.

As my reflections congealed into a coherent understanding of witness-based pilgrimage — one that remains consistent both with its practice among the Celtic saints and the Ignatian ideal of generous service to Christ — I returned to Brendan as an archetype and lens for understanding the concrete choices of "holy wandering". As a model of the faith journey, the voyage of Brendan and his companions encapsulates all aspects of the pilgrim's experience. It begins when Brendan hears the original invitation to leave his "native land" through the various challenges faced with his companions on the voyage to his returning home to give witness to what he had experienced. Brendan's story also helps us understand those who choose to leave the familiar surroundings of home and country but never returned, having found God's presence in the place prepared specifically for them — what the Celtic saints called "the place of resurrection".

The ideal of apostolic pilgrimage epitomized by Brendan offers a valuable contribution to the discussion and revival of early Celtic spirituality in the contemporary Church but — as both the Celtic and Ignatian traditions attest — it is not something that should be explained. It must be experienced since, as Robert van de Weyer observes in "Grasping Water":

> *You cannot grasp water in your hand.*
> *It drops through your fingers.*
>
> *You cannot grasp truth in your mind.*
> *It drops through your thoughts.*
>
> *You can only possess water by drinking it,*
> *Taking it into your body.*
>
> *You can only possess truth by living it,*

Taking it into your heart. [*]

So, rather than give an explanation of the role of "spiritual wandering" among the Celtic saints or argue for the continuing significance this practice in our own times, these materials will guide you into a personal encounter with the unique form of spiritual testimony exemplified in the legend of Brendan's pilgrimage. It is my hope that in listening to the journey of Brendan — whether alone or with companions — you will experience the presence of God in your own life and the invitation to seek out your own particular place of resurrection.

---

[*]   Robert Van de Weyer, *Celtic Parables: stories, poems and prayers* (London: Society for Promoting Christian Knowledge, 1997), page 10.

Thanks and Acknowledgements

This book represents a personal journey that would not have been possible without the companionship of J. L. Chapman, Bernard Colonna, John Dale, Kathleen Deignan, Edward Egros, Rosalyn Knowles Ferrell, Ruben Habito, Patrick Henry, Per Mollerup, Susan Rakoczy, Brian Ramsay and David Teschner. To varying degrees, and for different lengths of time, the support and encouragement of these friends helped me persevere in this pilgrimage.

In a very special way, I also would like to thank James Swonger for his generous assistance in designing and creating the digital audio components of this project as well as for a friendship that began long before this journey with Brendan and his companions.

In addition, I am grateful for:
- the permission of Padraic Colum's estate to excerpt his "The Burial of Saint Brendan" from *The Poet's Circuits: collected poems of Ireland* (Dublin: Dolmen Press, 1981).
- the permission of *The Capuchin Annual* and the King estate to reproduce Richard King's image of Saint Brendan on the cover of this book.
- the permission of Dr. John J. O'Meara's estate to include selections from his translation of *The Voyage of Saint Brendan: Journey to the Promised Land* (Gerrards Cross, Buckinghamshire: Colin Smythe Limited, 1991) in this book. This version of Saint Brendan's travels helped inspire this project and its inclusion in this book enriches it.
- the permission of Robert Van de Weyer to excerpt his translation of "Brendan's Prayer on the Mountain" from *Celtic Fire* (London: Doubleday, 1990) and his "Grasping Water" from *Celtic Parables: stories, poems and prayers* (London: Society for Promoting Christian Knowledge, 1997).
. - the permission of the Division of Christian Education of the National Council of the Churches of Christ in the United States of America to present biblical citations in this book from the *New Revised Standard Version Bible: with the Apocrypha* (New York: Harper Bibles, 1989).

Finally, I would like to acknowledge the contributions to this book of Alexander Carmichael's compilation of Gaelic prayers in *Carmina Gadelica: Hymns and Incantations* (Edinburgh: Floris Books, 1992). This public domain collection provides an invaluable spiritual resource by gathering prayers passed from one person to the another for centuries while remaining relevant to each successive generation.

However, although these prayers offer highly intimate expressions of personal faith, the language of Alexander Carmichael's translations may occasionally distract modern readers from this fact. So, while preserving the poetic nature of these prayers, some of their language has been revised in the prayer services and in the materials presented in the resources section of this book to reflect contemporary English usage.

Preparing for your Journey with Brendan

Before beginning this journey with Brendan and his companions, you should consider the experience you want to have and the best ways to achieve this goal.

Preparing for your Journey with Brendan

some considerations on approaching this book

It is always wise to prepare for any journey. If you are planning on traveling alone, a guidebook will help you know what to look for in your travels as well as the ways to make your trip secure and pleasant. On the other hand, if you intend to travel with a guide, you may rely on his or her guidance in these matters. Still, in either case, you will need to consider who you want as traveling companions, how much time you will spend "sightseeing" on your tour and the items you need to bring with you to make yourself comfortable.

This book presents two distinct journeys following the pilgrimage of Saint Brendan, intended either to stand alone or to be coordinated to each other:

• The first section presents nine selections from *The Voyage of Saint Brendan*, translated by John J. O'Meara, accompanied by nine brief meditations on the spiritual themes of the passage. Each set of readings also suggests a psalm and an excerpt from the Gospel of Saint John as well as other exercises designed to help you prayerfully consider an aspect of Brendan's journey. For readers interested in the affinities between Celtic and Ignatian spirituality shaping this project, the footnotes in this section provide extended comments on these similarities. Used in the manner best suited to your personal desires and temperament, these materials form cohesive meditations on various aspects of Brendan's spiritual odyssey.

Note: As a further aid to your consideration of Brendan's journey, the excerpts from The Voyage of Saint Brendan *and their companion meditations are available in digital audio versions that may be downloaded by following directions in the resources at the end of this book.*

• "A Journey to the Land of the Saints" contains a sequence of ten prayer services adapted from the traditional Gaelic prayers collected in Alexander Carmichael's *Carmina Gadelica*. The selections from *The Voyage of Saint Brendan* and their companion meditations establish the themes for these services, which also include the Psalms and readings from the Gospel of Saint John suggested in the reflection exercises for each selection. In addition, depending on the desires of the community presenting them, these services offer the option of celebrating the Eucharist as well as the opportunity for members of the community to share their thoughts and prayers during the service.

Selections from *The Voyage of Saint Brendan*,
with companion reflections and exercises

It is important to remember that these readings offer an opportunity for prayer and should not be approached as a chore to be completed quickly or efficiently. Spiritual reading involves listening for God's voice and stopping when necessary to hear the unique thoughts and leadings that God wants you to hear. This requires you to allow time for slow, deliberate reading as well as for silent pauses when God invites you to ponder a specific moment or idea.

So, if you decide to reflect prayerfully on the excerpts from *The Voyage of Saint Brendan* and their companion meditations, take some time to look at the passages and consider how much time you will need to spend reading. Decide whether you want to read these materials together or to engage the events from Brendan's voyage separately, creating a pace for reading the episodes (and their companion meditations) that you will be able to sustain. You also should determine how you want to approach the reflection exercises at the end of the meditations. Then, dedicate a particular time in your day to being alone with God — choosing a time when you are usually both relaxed and alert — and remain consistent in your prayer by removing anything from this time that might distract you.

In addition to devoting a specific amount of time to reading, you should consecrate a private space for your prayer that fosters a quiet, meditative atmosphere. It should be comfortable and separated from your normal living area, either a small prayer room or a chair and table set aside in a secluded part of a larger room. It also would be helpful if this place had a lamp or other muted light source that could be used when reading and turned off when it is not needed. In addition, you may want to create a focal point in this space — a statue, icon or cross with a few candles — that will hold your attention in the moments of silence when you listen for God's voice while reading. Finally, you may want to develop personal rituals for entering and leaving this prayer space — simple and deliberate actions asking God to encircle the holy place you are entering as well as to protect you during your time in it.

Note: Three personal prayer rituals may be found in "On Holy Ground," which is in the resources section at the end of this book.

Having prepared the time and place for your spiritual reading, develop a pattern of prayerful behavior that allows you to move consistently through the voyage of Brendan and his companions. You should begin by telling God your needs and asking that he open you to understand his desires during your time together. Then, read the passage you have selected. You will want to be able to remain focused on the readings, but you will need to maintain a listening heart that is open to God's promptings while you read. So, allow time to pause, ponder and pray in a conversational voice whenever you feel prompted to do so. When you are finished, conclude with a brief prayer of gratitude for any insights or spiritual leadings you received during your time with God.

Note: You also might want to coordinate the readings to the prayer services using the cycle suggested in the introduction to the section containing the excerpts from Brendan's journey and their companion meditations.

Finally, to clarify the memories and insights of your prayer, it is important that you devote a portion of your journey to careful review — both of the specific times when you are praying and of the echoes of that prayer in your daily life. So, after each session of spiritual reading, take some time to note the emotional dynamics of your prayer and any special gifts that you received in your conversation with God. You also should commit ten to fifteen minutes every day to one of the prayerful reviews of your day (called examens) provided in this book. It is recommended that you select the one furthest from your prayer sessions so you maintain a perspective on your entire day, reviewing both your prayer and your life while making your journey with Brendan and his companions.

A Journey to the Land of the Saints:
a sequence of prayer services

This sequence of prayer services offers an experience of communal worship following Brendan's pilgrimage. While these prayer services are carefully structured, they offer a range of options designed to accommodate the particular needs of the various groups presenting them, from large congregations to small prayer groups. So, as you and your community prepare to make this journey together, you may find it helpful to have a series of preparatory discussions about your desires — both personal and communal — for these prayers as well as the type of spiritual atmosphere you want to foster during them since these concerns will help you determine when and where you want to pray.

The first concern you should address involves the intensity of your experience. The services may be presented in ten successive days or over ten weeks. In the first option, you will quickly encounter the various episodes in Brendan's journey to the Land of the Saints in an intense and prayerful liturgical retreat as you commit a week and a half to these prayers. In the second option, as the prayer services spread over ten weeks, you will not make such a significant commitment of time but you will find Brendan's pilgrimage shaping your prayer during the weeks in which you participate in these prayer services. The pace at which you conduct the services will encourage very different types of prayer, both when you are together as a community and when you return to your private devotions.

Your choice about the pacing of these prayer services also will have an impact on the number of people wanting to participate in them, helping you define many of the other issues related to the type of experience you wish to have as you pray together. The ten-day format requires a commitment to attend daily prayer services, something many people may find difficult. Consequently, this option may lead to much smaller — but more devoted — groups at the prayer services. The ten-week option may be appealing to a larger number of people but they may not be as committed to participating in the cycle as a smaller group. So, you need to decide the degree of spiritual intensity you desire from these prayer services as well as how much hospitality you wish to demonstrate to your larger community.

Once you have made these choices, you will need to determine the time and place best suited for your presentation of these prayer services. If you invite the community-at-large to your services, you will need to schedule them outside of working hours in a church or chapel large enough for the number of people you expect to arrive. On the other hand, if you decide to make this a more private prayer experience, you may schedule the services at the convenience of your group members in a smaller space such as a small chapel, a prayer room in a church or a room in a regular home set aside for the services. Whatever you decide, the place in which you choose to conduct the prayer services should have a meditative focal point — a Celtic cross, icon or statue — and muted lighting (perhaps dominated by candlelight) to help the participants pray in silence.

Note: After making these choices, you will need to decide how you want to approach music and silence, the presentation of readings and the Eucharistic prayer during the services. The introduction to the prayer services offers suggestions on all these issues.

Another concern you will need to address before conducting the services involves leadership and group participation. You may decide to appoint a single leader to conduct all of these services or you may decide to rotate this role among the members of your group. In either case, you may find it helpful to have a discussion about the amount of group participation you feel is most appropriate in the services — specifically how participants will share their thoughts after the Gospel reading (during the final service or possibly during earlier services) as well as how the personal prayers should be offered at the end of the services throughout the sequence. You will find it helpful to provide clearer boundaries for group participation as the number of people involved in the prayer services increase, so you also should consider the type of leadership role that fosters the communal experience you want to cultivate during your prayers.

Finally, as you present these prayer services, you also may choose to enrich the spiritual experience of your participants by inviting them to use the time between services for spiritual reading — using either the seven-day cycle of spiritual reading described in the introduction to those readings or the self-guided retreat presented in *A Pilgrimage to the Land of the Saints* (the extension of this book). In this way, the services become a gateway to a deeper experience of prayer as you follow the pilgrimage of Brendan and his companions. But, in making this decision, you should ensure that your spiritual experience is enriched — rather than overwhelmed — by this choice.

Once you have decided which kind of journey you want to make with Brendan and his companions, you should consider the resources provided in this book that will help you have a positive — and, hopefully, powerful — spiritual experience.

• If you are planning to contemplate the selections from *The Voyage of Saint Brendan*," you should reflect on the considerations at the beginning of that section and the "Resources for Prayer" at the end of this book. You also should decide how much time you will commit to these activities and create a special space in which to conduct them — alone or with others. By creating a suitable environment for your imaginary journey, you will heighten your awareness of the spiritual nuances in the story of Brendan and of the particular ways God chooses to speak to you through it.

• If you intend to conduct the prayer services in "A Journey to the Island of the Saints," you should review the considerations at the beginning of that section and the "Resources for Worship" at the end of this book. If any of the participants in your prayer services — whether individually or in a special prayer group — also choose to pursue the suggested cycle of readings for *The Voyage of Saint Brendan*," you should consider the resource materials for that option and determine any ways you might assist them. This simple act of generosity will enhance your own prayer in the communal services will be enriched.

Regardless of the path you choose to follow with Saint Brendan and his companions, rely on the Spirit of God to guide you in your imaginary travels and allow that Spirit to nourish your efforts — both personally and communally — to reach the Promised Land of the Saints.

Selections from
The Voyage of Saint Brendan[1]

translated by John J. O'Meara,
with companion reflections and exercises
by Timothy J. Ray

[1]   This section contains slightly abridged excerpts from Dr. O'Meara's *The Voyage of Saint Brendan: Journey to the Promised Land* (Gerrards Cross, Buckinghamshire, UK: Colin Smythe Limited, 1991). Ellipses (...) mark those places in the selections where words were removed. Also, when necessary, some words have been added [in brackets] to ease the transitions caused by these removals. While these excisions were made with the approval of Professor O'Meara's estate, any shortcomings produced by them remain Timothy Ray's responsibility.

prayerfully reading the story of Brendan

Instructions on downloading the digital audio files designed to accompany this section may be found in the resources section at the end of this book. These include the readings from *The Voyage of Saint Brendan* **and their companion reflections (presented in this section) as well as guided versions of two prayerful considerations of the day (called examens).**

These readings may be approached on their own or in conjunction with the prayer services from the following section. However you choose to follow Brendan and his companions on their pilgrimage, it is recommended that you not read more than one episode at a time.

If you would prefer to use these selections for private spiritual reading, you should decide whether to read (or hear) the following selections from *The Voyage of Saint Brendan* and their companion meditations at the same time or separately. After making this choice, you should determine how much time you will need to complete these readings — being certain that you leave space to listen for God's invitation to deeper reflection and prayer while you read. Then, consider how (or if) you want to approach the reflection exercises at the end of each episode before creating a personal program of reading and prayer that you will be able to sustain throughout your reflections on Brendan's journey.

If you would like to reflect on Brendan's journey in a reading group, you might use the following schedule as you proceed through the excerpts:

  • Day 1 — Consider the selection from *The Voyage of Saint*

Brendan
- Day 2 — Read and reflect on the companion meditation
- Day 3 — Reflect on the Psalm in the first reflection exercise
- Day 4 —Reflect on the Gospel in the first reflection exercise reading
- Day 5 — Consider the quotation in the second reflection exercise
- Day 6 — Complete the imaginative exercise in the third reflection exercise
- Day 7 — Share your reflections on these material with the reading group

If you would like to combine your spiritual reading with the sequence of prayer services presented in the second section, you should use the following week-long cycle:
- Day 1 — Attend or read the prayer service
- Day 2 — Consider the selection from *The Voyage of Saint Brendan*
- Day 3 — Read and reflect on the companion meditation
- Day 4 — Reflect on the Psalm in the first reflection exercise
- Day 5 — Reflect on the Gospel reading in the first reflection exercise
- Day 6 — Consider either the second or the third reflection exercise
- Day 7 — Engage in an open conversation with God about the earlier reflections

After deciding how you want to approach these readings, it would be helpful for you to consider the following issues:

Reviewing your Experience

After you finish your journey with Brendan and his companions, you will find it helpful to reflect on the spiritual benefits you received during your pilgrimage as well as the ways your prayers may have changed your relationship with God and other people. With this in mind, you should devote two prayer periods to considering the reflections on Saint Brendan and his companions found in the "Returning Home" section (after the self-guided retreat). Reflecting on the experiences of these saints after they finished their pilgrimage will help you understand the spiritual gifts you received from your own spiritual journey as well as suggest the ways to protect these graces as you integrate them into your daily life.

Considering the Extended Footnotes in these Readings
      The footnotes in this section provide citations for quotations from the Bible or from the writings of various authorities on Celtic Christianity used in the meditations. However, following these references, there are extended notes highlighting the echoes of the Celtic ideals discussed in these meditations that may be found in Ignatian spirituality. These observations (printed in italics) include remarks by the author, recommendations from Ignatius of Loyola's *Spiritual Exercises* and letters, and the reflections of eminent Ignatian spiritual directors. These extended reflections also offer references if you are interested in exploring these parallels between Celtic and Ignatian spirituality.

I • BARRIND'S STORY

The legendary journey of Saint Brendan, who came to be known as 'The Navigator', begins with an amazing story told one evening by a visitor to the saint's abbey.

(BARRIND'S STORY) Saint Brendan, son of Findlug, descendant of Alte, was born among the Eoganacht of Loch Léin in the land of the men of Munster. He was a man of great abstinence, famous for his mighty works and father of nearly three thousand monks.

When he was fighting the good fight, in a place called Clonfert of Brendan, there arrived one evening one of the fathers whose name was Barrind, a descendant of Niall.

When this Barrind was plied with many questions by the holy father, he wept, prostrated himself on the ground and stayed a long time praying. But Saint Brendan lifted him up from the ground and embraced him, saying:

'Father, why should we be sad during your visit? Did you not come to encourage us? Rather should you give joy to the brothers. Show us the word of God and nourish our souls with the varied wonders that you saw in the ocean.'

When Saint Brendan had finished his remarks, Saint Barrind began to describe a certain island, saying:

'My son Mernóc, steward of Christ's poor, left me and sought to live the life of a solitary. He found an island near Slieve League, called the Delightful Island. Then, a long time afterwards I heard that he had many monks with him, and that God had shown many wonders through him. So, I set out to visit my son. At the end of a three-day journey, as I was approaching, he hurried with his brothers to meet me. For the Lord revealed to him that I was coming. As we were crossing in a boat to the island the brothers came, like bees swarming, from their various cells to meet us.

Their housing was indeed scattered but they lived together as one in faith, hope and charity. They ate together and they all joined together for the divine office. They are given nothing to eat but fruit, nuts, roots and other greens. But after compline each remained in his own cell until the cocks crowed or the bell was struck. Having stayed overnight and walked round the whole island, I was brought by my son to the sea shore facing west, where there was a boat. He said to me:

"Father, embark in the boat and let us sail westwards to the island which is called the Promised Land of the Saints which God will give to those who come after us at the end of time."

'We embarked and sailed, but a fog so thick covered us that we could scarcely see the poop or the prow of the boat. But when we had spent about an hour like this a great light shone all around us, and there appeared to us a land wide, and full of grass and fruit. When the boat landed we disembarked and began to go and walk round that island. This we did for fifteen days — yet we could not find the end of it. We saw no plants that had not flowers, nor trees that had not fruit. The stones of that land are precious stones. Then on the fifteenth day we found a river flowing from east to west. As we pondered on all these things we were in doubt what we should do.

'We decided to cross the river, but we awaited advice from God. In the course of a discussion on these things, a man suddenly appeared in a great light before us, who immediately called us by our own names and saluted us, saying:

"Well done, good brothers. For the Lord has revealed to you the land, which he will give to his saints. The river there marks the middle of the island. You may not go beyond this point. So return to the place from which you departed."

"When he said this, I immediately questioned him where he came from and what was his name. He said:

14

"Why do you ask me where I come from or how I am called? Why do you not ask me about the island? As you see it now, so it has been from the beginning of the world. Do you feel the need of any food or drink or clothing? Yet for the equivalent of one year you have been on this island and have not tasted food or drink! You have never been overcome by sleep nor has night enveloped you! For here it is always day, without blinding darkness. Our Lord Jesus Christ is the light of this island."

'Straightaway we started on our journey, the man coming with us to the shore where our boat was. As we embarked in it he was taken from our eyes and we passed through the same darkness to the Delightful Island. When the brothers saw us they rejoiced with great joy at our arrival and complained of our absence for such a long time, saying:

"Why, fathers, have you left your sheep wandering in the wood without a shepherd? We knew of our abbot going away from us frequently somewhere or other — but we do not know where — and staying there sometimes for a month, sometimes for a fortnight or a week or more or less."

'When I heard this, I began to console them, saying to them:

"Think, brothers, only of good. You are living undoubtedly at the gate of Paradise. Near here is an island which is called the Promised Land of the Saints where night does not fall nor day end. Your abbot Mernóc goes there. An angel of the Lord guards it. Do you not perceive from the fragrance of our clothing that we have been in God's Paradise?"

The brothers then replied:

"Abbot, we knew that you were in God's Paradise in the wide sea; but where that Paradise is, we do not know. We have indeed often noticed the fragrance exuding from our abbot's clothes

15

when he returns from there after the space of forty days."

'I stayed on with my son for two successive weeks without food or drink. Yet our bodies were so satisfied that to others we seemed full of new wine. And after forty days I received the blessing of the brothers and the abbot and set off with my companions on the return journey to my cell. I shall go there tomorrow.'

When they heard these things, Saint Brendan and all his community prostrated themselves on the ground, glorifying God and saying:

'The Lord is just in all his ways and holy in his works. For he has revealed to his servants such great wonders. He is blessed in his gifts, for he has nourished us today with such a spiritual foretaste.'
...

When that night was over, Saint Barrind, having received the blessing of the brothers in the morning, set out for his own cell.

~ excerpted from The Voyage of Saint Brendan,
translated by John J. O'Meara, pp. 2-6

"Walking with the Celtic Saints"

When we walk with the Celtic saints — even if only for a very short while — we recognize that they do not see the world around us in quite the same way. In *Every Earthly Blessing*, Esther de Waal tells us that Christian Celts embraced an animated and optimistic view of the world. "It is not static or dead, but a dynamic, living, powerful universe, reflecting a power which comes ultimately from God," she writes, before continuing, "Men and women establish a relationship with this universe, speaking to it, listening, trying to create a harmony — for they are at its center."[2] While we may be tempted to see the world as chaotic and indifferent to our concerns, the Celtic saints felt assured of the innate harmony of the world around them as God lovingly cared for the unique needs of every living being (both human and nonhuman) in his grand plan of creation.

Certainly, the Celtic community was not the first to recognize God's presence in all things. This belief may be found in various psalms of the Old Testament, for instance, such as when Psalm 19 announces, "The heavens are telling the glory of God; and the firmament proclaims his handiwork."[3] Like the Celts, the ancient Hebrews felt God's guidance when they contemplated the beauty of the world and the intricate relationships it contains. They saw each living creature and natural event playing its own unique role in a cosmic drama, telling of God's desires for his creation — in the words of the psalmist, "their voice goes out through all the earth, and their words to the end of the world."[4] — telling of God's plans and laws for creation as they invite a response since "by them is [God's] servant warned; in keeping them there is great reward."[5] In their monasteries, praying the psalms on a daily basis, the

---

[2]   Esther De Waal, *Every Earthly Blessing: Rediscovering the Celtic Tradition* (Harrisburg, PA: Morehouse Publishing, 1999), page 64.

"Finding God in all things" is a central aspiration of Ignatian spirituality. In the final contemplation of his Spiritual Exercises, *as translated by Michael Ivens, (Leominster, Herefordshire: Gracewing, 2004) Ignatius directs the individual receiving the Exercises to "see how God dwells in creatures: in the elements giving being; in the plants giving growth; in the animals giving sensation; and in humankind granting the gift of understanding; and so how he dwells also in me, giving me being, life and sensation and causing me to understand. To see, too, how he makes a temple of me, as I have been created in the likeness and image of his Divine Majesty." (#235)*

Ignatius then suggests a prayer asking that God take and receive everything that the person is and has so he or she may participate in God's plan of creation.

[3]   Psalm 19: 1. All biblical citations in these reflections refer to the *New Revised Standard Version Bible: with the Apocrypha* (New York: Harper Bibles, 1989).

[4]   Psalm 19: 4.

[5]   Psalm 19: 11.

Celtic saints must have found tremendous encouragement and inspiration from the insights of their Hebrew forebears.

But the power of Celtic spirituality — especially its ability to lead its saints to abandon their homes and to venture out into the unknown — cannot be reduced to the ideas they acquired from others. It is the unique ways in which they grafted these external sources to their own traditions and experiences that allowed the Celtic saints to make such powerful testimonies to the presence of God in the world around us. Even before Christianity came to the Celtic lands, there was a deep reverence for the patterns of nature and a profound desire to live in harmony with its cycles. In pre-Christian times, the Celts' devotion to the natural world could be quite violent but the Christian belief in God's love for all of creation displaced this violence and gave the Celtic saints the strength to act with compassion and courage in the face of even the most hostile circumstances.

So, for Brendan and his companions, the conversation with Barrind was not simply an opportunity to hear of his adventures since their last meeting. Instead, they heard the voice of God inviting them to make the same journey as their friend. At the same time, they also understood that without God's on-going guidance and support it would be impossible to complete their journey. Brendan's confidence in making the radical choice to leave his community and country — a spiritual trait that marked the lives of many Celtic saints — relied on the continuing presence and protection of God in traversing a treacherous world, looking for the divinely-touched aspects of creation and avoiding those still hostile to that presence.

Brendan knew that finding God's presence in creation does not make this world perfect. It simply reminds us that we are not alone in it. Seeing God's activity in the ordinary things of daily life allows us to praise God while still remaining grounded in our day-to-day lives. But, more important, it also invites us to trust in God's continuing presence as we move into an uncertain future. Brendan and the other Celtic saints understood this, so it is important to recognize that the two primary forms of surviving Celtic prayer — the *lorica* (the shield prayer) and the *caim* (the encircling prayer) — both pray for protection. The early Celtic Christians understood that praising God in creation involves both gratitude for the blessings of the past and hope for God's protection and guidance in the future.

But the Celtic saints never forgot that these blessings and protections also are woven into the fabric of our lives by a humane and approachable God. In *The Celtic Way*, Ian Bradley says that, "To the Celts God was certainly to be approached with awe, reverence and wonder but he was at the same time an essentially human figure who was intimately involved in all his creation and engaged in a dynamic relationship with it."[6] In rediscovered poems and religious texts from the ancient past and in prayers preserved in folk traditions over the centuries, Celtic prayers never forget the love at the heart of God's relationship with creation as they ask for assistance and protection in facing the challenges of daily life. Also — whether it takes the form of angels or saints, Jesus or Mary, or even the Holy Trinity — the presence of God in the Celtic prayers always has a human face, a reminder that all men and women live as images of God in a world created for them.

These insights of the Celtic saints challenge us to listen for the voices of God's desire expressed in the world — and people — around us, and to be changed by what we hear. All too often, we think we know where we are going and why we are pursuing certain paths. But, more often than not, our choices have more to do with habits developed over time rather than with an intimate awareness of what it is that we truly need. Like the Samaritan woman at the well, shocked when a Jewish man interrupted her daily routine asking her to give him a drink, we see only what we are accustomed to seeing and do not recognize new possibilities until God transforms our perspective on the commonplace objects and activities of our daily lives.

When we keep our minds and hearts open to the presence of God all around us, we find ourselves surprised by opportunities we otherwise might have passed by. Quite often, we also recognize that

---

[6] Ian Bradley. *The Celtic Way* (London: Darton, Longman & Todd Ltd, 1993), pages 42-43.

Also at the end of his Spiritual Exercises, *Ignatius asks that a person "consider how God works and labors on my behalf in all created things on the face of the earth; that is, he acts in the manner of a person at work; as in the heavens, elements, plants, fruits, cattle, etc. giving being, conserving life, granting growth and sensation, etc." (#236)*

He concludes this contemplation by asking that the individual "see how all that is good and every gift descends from on high. Thus, my limited power descends from the supreme and infinite power above — and similarly with justice, goodness, pity, mercy, etc. — as rays descend from the sun and waters from a fountain." (#237)

God already prepared us to accept these new possibilities through the promptings we followed in the past — that the unknown future we fear is actually an extension of a plan that God has been unfolding throughout our lives. By taking a moment to carefully listen to what God has to say to us in these moments, we find ourselves renewed by the awareness that we are truly following the path intended for us. Again, like the Samaritan woman at the well, we find our truest self and purpose when we take the time to listen to what God has to say to us about our needs and our future — opening ourselves to recognize and accept the gifts being offered to us.

This is the nature of pilgrimage, whether by seeking God in the familiar situations of our daily lives or by responding to God's invitation to explore the spiritual possibilities of new and unknown places. The path of "holy wandering" involves a willingness to put aside our preconceptions and to listen for God's presence in all things, discovering the vitality of the world around us while recognizing our relationship to every other creature of God. It involves hearing the epiphanies God presents to us in each moment, offering us new beginnings on a path that God has already prepared for us. As each revelation changes us, we deepen in our understanding of God's activity in the world — including those places that see the most suffering and pain — as we learn more about our place in the plan of creation and what we may offer to it.

For prayer or reflection:
[1] Separately, consider Psalm 19: 1-14 and John 4: 3-26. Where do you find God's presence in the world around you? When was the last time you were surprised by that presence?
[2] In *Living Between Worlds*, Philip Sheldrake writes:
"The Celtic Christian attitude to nature involved a profound sense of the imminence of God. This reminds us that it is not nature as such that concerns the Celts. Nature was a kind of second sacred book, parallel to the Scriptures, that revealed the divine... Although there was an immediacy in the way a human relationship with nature was expressed, for example in some early medieval Irish poetry, nature was not really a value in itself. What the monastic poets sought and found

in the natural world was an image of the creator-God."[7]

Does the natural world speak to you about God? If so, what has it taught you? If not, how does God speak to you and what has he taught you?

[3] Take a moment to review Psalm 19:1-6, paying careful attention to the rhythms of the prayer. When you are finished, consider a natural object that you pass by every day — whether as large as a stream (with a complex ecosystem) or as small as a single flower (or leaf) — and contemplate the uniqueness and intricacy of this thing. Then, imagine God standing or sitting with you. In a casual and friendly manner, speak with God about how the object was created and sustained. Afterward, compose a prayerful poem (with rhyming or non-rhyming verses) linking God's presence and creative activity in this small fragment of nature to various aspects of your own life.

---

[7]   Philip Sheldrake, *Living Between Worlds: Place and Journey in Celtic Spirituality* (Boston, MA: Cowley Publications, 1995), page 73.

In Keeping in Touch: Posthumous Papers on Ignatian Topics *(Leominster, Herefordshire: Gracewing, 2007), Michael Ivens asserts:* "When Ignatius designates God as Creator and Lord of the material realities and the events and situations which make the category of 'all things', he is saying something more for these than that God created, willed or at least providentially permitted them. He is making a claim about God's here and now presence and action, and also about the ultimate purpose of all things. Thus as creator of all things and as Lord of all that happens within his creation God is in countless ways involved in our reality, in and through 'all things' working for us, caring for us, reaching out to us and revealing himself." (page 12)

II • THE BROTHERS VISIT HOLY ENDA
& AN UNINHABITED HOUSE

Inspired by Barrind's story, Saint Brendan decides to make his own pilgrimage to the Land of the Saints. So, he gathers some of his brother monks and begins his journey.

(THE BROTHERS ASSEMBLE) Saint Brendan, … when fourteen brothers out of his whole community had been chosen, shut himself up in one oratory with them and spoke to them, saying:

'From you who are dear to me and share the good fight with me I look for advice and help, for my heart and all my thoughts are fixed on one determination. I have resolved in my heart if it is God's will — and only if it is — to go in search of the Promised Land of the Saints of which father Barrind spoke. How does this seem to you? What advice would you give?'

They, however, having learned of the holy father's will, say, as it were with one mouth:

'Abbot, your will is ours. Have we not left our parents behind? Have we not spurned our inheritance and given our bodies into your hands? So we are prepared to go along with you to death or life. Only one thing let us ask for, the will of God.'

(VISIT TO SAINT ENDA) Saint Brendan and his companions, therefore, decided to fast for forty days — but for no more than three days at a time — and then to set out. When the forty days were over he said good-bye to the brothers, commended all to the man put in charge of his monastery, who was afterwards his successor there, and set out westwards with fourteen brothers to the island of a holy father, named Enda. There he stayed three days and three nights.

(THE BUILDING OF THE BOAT) Having received the blessing of the holy father and of all the monks that were with him, he set

out for a distant part of his native region where his parents were living. But he did not wish to see them. He pitched his tent at the edge of a mountain stretching far out into the ocean, in a place called Brendan's Seat, at a point where there was entry for one boat. Saint Brendan and those with him got iron tools and constructed a light boat ribbed with wood and with a wooden frame, as is usual in those parts. They covered it with ox-hides tanned with the bark of oak and smeared all the joints of the hides on the outside with fat. They carried into the boat hides for the makings of two other boats, supplies for forty days, fat for preparing hides to cover the boat and other things needed for human life. They also placed a mast in the middle of the boat and a sail and the other requirements for steering a boat. Then Saint Brendan ordered his brothers in the name of the Father, Son and Holy Spirit to enter the boat.

(THE UNINHABITED HOUSE) Saint Brendan then embarked, the sail was spread and they began to steer westwards into the summer solstice. They had a favourable wind and, apart from holding the sail, had no need to navigate.

After fifteen days the wind dropped. They set themselves to the oars until their strength failed. Saint Brendan quickly began to comfort and advise them, saying:

'Brothers, do not fear. God is our helper, sailor and helmsman, and he guides us. Ship all the oars and the rudder. Just leave the sail spread and God will do as he wishes with his servants and their ship.'

They always had their food, however, at evening time. When they got a wind, they did not know from what direction it came or in what direction the boat was going.

When forty days were up and all the victuals had been consumed, an island appeared to them towards the north, rocky and high. When they came near its shore they saw a high cliff like a wall

23

and various streams flowing down from the top of the island into the sea. Nevertheless they failed totally to find a landing-place where they could put in the boat. The brothers were greatly harrassed by the lack of food and drink. So each took up a vessel to try to catch some of the fresh water. When Saint Brendan saw this, he said:

'Do not do that. What you are doing is foolish. God does not yet wish to show us a place to land, and do you want to be guilty of plundering? The Lord Jesus Christ after three days will show his servants a landing-place and a place to stay, so that our harrassed bodies will be restored.'

When, then, they had circled the island for three days, on the third day about three o'clock they found an opening where one boat might enter. Saint Brendan stood up immediately and blessed the entry. It was a cutting with rock of remarkable height on either side, straight up like a wall. When they had all disembarked and stood outside on land, Saint Brendan forbade them to take any equipment out of the boat. As they were walking along the cliffs of the sea, a dog ran across them on a path and came to the feet of Saint Brendan as dogs usually come to heel to their masters. Saint Brendan said to his brothers:

'Has not God sent us a good messenger? Follow him.'

Saint Brendan and his brothers followed the dog to a town.

On entering the town they caught sight of a great hall, furnished with beds and chairs, and water for washing their feet. …

Then Saint Brendan spoke to the one who usually placed bread before the brothers:

'Bring the meal that God has sent us.'
This man stood up immediately, found a table made ready and linen and a loaf for each of marvellous whiteness and fish. When

all were brought before him, Saint Brendan blessed the meal and said to his brothers:

'Give praise to the God of heaven who gives food to all flesh.'

The brothers sat back, therefore, and glorified God. In the same way they found as much drink as they wanted. When supper was over and the office of compline said, he spoke:

'Rest now. There is a well-dressed bed for each of you. You need to rest, for your limbs are tired from too much toil.' …

In the morning when the brothers had hurried to the divine office and later had gone to the boat, they saw a table laid out just like the day before. And so for three days and three nights God prepared a meal for his servants.

~ excerpted from The Voyage of Saint Brendan,
translated by John J. O'Meara, pp. 7-12

"Finding Christ in All Things"

Any experienced traveler will say that proper planning is essential to the successful completion of a journey. So, it is not surprising to see Brendan and his companions gathering the necessary provisions for their travels as they build a vessel capable of withstanding the rigors of the open sea. But one aspect of their preparation remains unsaid, perhaps because they did not feel it necessary to express this overtly. They did not believe they were traveling alone — their pilgrimage was also a journey with Christ, who would accompany and protect them during their voyage — so they also prayed and fasted (as well as sought the blessings of others) to welcome his presence and to invite his guidance during their perilous pilgrimage.

Like their contemporaries, Brendan and his companions embraced a highly incarnational spirituality in which Jesus Christ was always close to them. "The Celts felt the presence of Christ almost physically woven around their lives," Ian Bradley writes in *The Celtic Way*, "They were conscious of being encircled by him, upheld by him and encompassed by him. This almost tangible experience of Jesus as a companion next to you, a guest in your house, a physical presence in your life was perhaps the most striking way in which Celts expressed their overwhelming sense of the divine presence."[8] Discerning the expressions of Christ's involvement in the world around them — and responding to these manifestations of God's love in their day-to-day lives — helped the Celtic saints to create communities of remarkable hospitality and to find the courage that helped them leave those communities as pilgrims and missionaries.

The Celts acknowledged Christ's presence in a wide variety of activities and roles, fostering attitudes that balanced familiarity and reverence. Images in many surviving Celtic prayers and artwork show the humanity of Jesus, often presenting him as a small child loved by his mother or as a worker engaged in the day-to-day tasks of ordinary people — demonstrating that Jesus both shared and understood our human experiences, whether of love, of labor or of pain. But other images of Jesus show him as the victor over death on the cross, triumphant manifestations of God's power to transcend the vicissitudes of our human experience. By embracing both sides of Christ's dual nature — his humanity and his divinity — the Celts recognized and accepted the loving presence of Christ in every facet of their lives, seeing him both as being "the humble Galilean fisherman who is a

---

[8]   Ian Bradley. *The Celtic Way*, page 33.

In Ignatius' Spiritual Exercises, *individuals are advised to pray for different graces while contemplating the earthly life of Christ: "inner knowledge of the Lord who became human for me so that I might the better love and follow him" (#104) during the contemplation of Christ's hidden and public life, "grief with Christ in grief, to be broken with Christ broken, for tears and interior suffering on account of the great suffering that Christ endured for me" (#203) during the Passion, and the "grace to feel gladness and to rejoice intensely over the great glory and joy of Christ our Lord" (#221) during the post-resurrection appearances.*

Using his or her imagination to walk with Jesus during his earthly life — as well as to contemplate aspects of his divinity — invites a person into the mystery of God and helps him or her discover the ways in which God's presence permeates his or her life and world.

constant friend and companion as well as being the redeemer of the cosmos."[9]

By finding distinct aspects of Christ in one another, the early Celtic Christians cultivated strong reciprocal relationships that expressed Christ's redemptive activity in the world. The sovereignty of the divine Christ encouraged deference toward those in authority with the expectation that these leaders would in turn be guided by the mercy and generosity Christ showed towards his own followers. This respect for Christ's heavenly authority also fostered humility and openness when speaking with one's *anamchara*, the "soul friend" responsible for nurturing the person's spiritual development through conversations bringing together personal confession and spiritual counsel. On the other hand, the generous humanity of the incarnate Jesus Christ animated companionship among peers and invited openness toward strangers. Rooted in palpable experiences of Christ in the world, these relationships gave powerful — and practical — witness to Christ's love.

This witness invites us to examine our own relationship with Christ. Most often, when we think of the Incarnation, we focus on God becoming human and suffering on our behalf to redeem humanity from its own sinfulness. But, parallel to this, there is a theological tradition that argues God would still become incarnate in the world even if humanity was not stained by sin because of the deep love expressed toward human beings throughout our history. It is this love — and a desire for us to participate freely in God's plan of creation — that allows Jesus Christ to say to his followers, "You are my friends if you do what I command you."[10] This companionship is a unique but intrinsic aspect

---

[9]   Ian Bradley, *The Celtic Way*, page 42.

At the heart of Ignatian prayer is a practice called the colloquy, which Ignatius introduces in his Spiritual Exercises *as "speaking as one friend speaks with another, or a servant with the master, at times asking for some favour, at other times accusing oneself of something badly done, or sharing personal concerns and asking for advice about them." (#54) In the Ignatian Exercises, this prayer usually appears at the end of imaginative contemplations which range in content from the most human aspects of Jesus's life (e.g., his childhood and adolescence, his conversations with the early disciples, etc.) to expressions of his divine nature. The use of the colloquy fosters a spiritual and emotional intimacy between the person praying and Christ in all his aspects.*

[10]   John 15: 14.

of Christian life as we are invited to transcend discipleship and to aspire toward friendship with the incarnate Christ.

To accept that friendship, we need to understand the manner in which the Incarnation transcends its historical manifestation. Like his crucifixion and resurrection, the ministry of Jesus is both a set of historical events and a continuing spiritual reality that ripples through human history as it brings about the promised Kingdom of God. Through the power of the Spirit of God, Jesus Christ calls new disciples in each generation — including our own. Just as it was with Jesus' first disciples, the circumstances of each individual's calling vary according to their personality and the purposes they will serve within Christ's plan, but each receives the same promise that Jesus made when commissioning his first followers, "Remember, I am with you always, to the end of the age."[11]

Accepting the invitation to serve and befriend Jesus allows us to live humbly in the promise and continuing presence of a loving Christ. Yet, we must never forget that we are welcoming God into our lives. From the ancient Hebrew psalms, we know that God's knowledge penetrates every aspect of creation, especially the deepest recesses of our own being. "Even before a word is on my tongue, O Lord, you know it completely. You hem me in, behind and before, and lay your hand upon me," says the author of Psalm 139, continuing, "Such knowledge is too wonderful for me; it is so high I cannot attain it."[12] Yet, after accepting God — as our Creator — knows every aspect of our being, the psalmist is able to implore, "Search me, O God, and know my heart; test me and know my thoughts. See if there is any wicked way in me, and lead me in the way everlasting."[13]

Receiving the guidance and companionship of God allows us to live our faith with confidence. This is particularly true as we deepen in our friendship with Jesus Christ. "Over the years we get to know him and he knows us, he becomes a familiar friend. It is this living relationship that makes any future Judgment far less threatening. We know him, we know his love and his forgiveness; he knows our weaknesses and our need for him." David Adam explains in *The Cry of the Deer*, "None of us knows exactly what lies ahead for us, but we can

---

[11]   Matthew 28: 20.

[12]   Psalm 139: 4-6.

[13]   Psalm 139: 23-24.

know who it is who is there to meet us."[14] It is this confidence that allows us to go out into the world without fear and also to recognize that we are indeed protected by our faithful friend and Lord.

We also realize that Christ's friendship extends to the rest of creation, changing our human relationships and opening us to others. We come to understand that a stranger is as important as our closest friend and that our companions are not simply those people we choose to be with but those who we meet along the paths of our lives. In time, this broadened sense of community even extends to nonhuman creatures as we discern the patterns of divine love woven into the intricate relationships of nature. Each time we recognize our kinship with others — whether human or nonhuman — and act towards them with generosity and compassion, we become signs of Christ's loving presence to those in need and symbols of hope to those in despair.

For prayer or reflection:
[1] Separately, reflect on Psalm 139: 1-17, 23-24 and John 1: 35-51. How do God or Christ offer you friendship in your life? How does their intimate knowledge of you help or hinder your ability to accept that friendship?
[2] Esther De Waal explains in *The Celtic Way of Prayer*:
    "The rise of the anamchara in the Celtic Churches was a natural

---

[14]   David Adam, *The Cry of the Deer: Meditations on the hymn of St Patrick* (London: Society for the Promotion of Christian Knowledge, 2000), page 63.

In Finding God in All Things: A Companion to the Spiritual Exercises of St. Ignatius *(Notre Dame, Indiana: Ave Maria Press, 1991), William Barry recognizes the promise and the challenge of befriending Christ when he says: "Many people have come to believe through their contemplation that Jesus desires their friendship and companionship even more than they desire his. And the desire is not utilitarian. That is, Jesus does not desire their friendship only because he needs workers in the vineyard. Jesus wants friends and companions. Just as he reveals himself to them, so too he wants them to reveal themselves to him. I underlined this point because I know from personal experience that it is so hard for us to believe that Jesus really wants our friendship, a friendship that is mutual." (page 96)*

development from the syncellus, the 'one who shared a cell' in the desert tradition, and to whom one confessed, revealing confidential aspects of one's life. The cell, wherever it may be found in the early years of the Church, whether in the Egyptian desert or in remoter areas of any of the Celtic countries, is the place of encounter with God and one's true self and the world, and thus the sharing of the cell is the sharing of one's inmost self, heart, and mind. Here is the truest and deepest form of friendship, what the desert guides called exagoreusis, the opening of one's heart to another which leads to hesychia, serenity and peace of heart."[15]

Are you comfortable in a friendship with someone who is not your peer? Are you able to recognize the wisdom that friend brings from experiences you do not yet share?

[3] Consider the nature of your own friendships. Do you have any friends with whom you may be completely open and honest, revealing your insecurities and failings? If so, take some time to contemplate the qualities that distinguish these friends. If not, consider the characteristics you hope for in an ideal friendship. Imagine speaking with Christ about these qualities, asking the various ways in which Christ offers these qualities to you. Then, address Christ in a litany (a

---

[15]   Esther de Waal, *The Celtic Way of Prayer: the Recovery of the Religious Tradition* (New York: Image Books, 1997), pages 134-135.

The early practice of Ignatian spiritual direction (which has been revived in recent decades) involves a one-to-one conversation. In its purest form, this dialogue occurs between the person giving the Spiritual Exercises *and the person receiving them. However, unlike the Celtic* anamchara, *the giver of the Exercises is not supposed to take a position of authority. Instead, the giver serves as a listener to a conversation that occurs between the person receiving the Exercises and his or her Creator.*

Ignatius points out, in the introductory notes to the Spiritual Exercises, *"It is more opportune and much better that in the search for the divine will the Creator and Lord communicate himself to the faithful soul, inflaming the soul in his love and praise, and disposing her towards the way in which she will be better able to serve him in the future. Hence the giver of the Exercises should not be swayed or show a preference for one side of a choice rather than the other, but remaining in the center like the pointer of a balance should leave the creator to deal with the creature, and the creature with the Creator and Lord." (#15)*

prayer listing petitions divided into groups sharing the same response) explaining the deepest concerns you wish you could share with a close friend but remain reluctant to say openly.

Note: An example of a litany may be found in the petitionary sequence used in the final prayer service on pages 219 and 220.

III • THE ISLAND OF SHEEP
& THE LEVIATHAN JASCONIUS

Saint Brendan and his companions set sail again after refreshing themselves on the island with the uninhabited house. Their travels take them to two other islands filled with wonders and surprises.

(A YOUTH BRINGS FOOD) The brothers then went with Saint Brendan to the shore of the island where their boat was. As they were embarking a youth came up carrying a basket full of bread and a jar of water. He said to them:

'Receive a blessing from the hand of your servant. A long journey lies ahead of you until you find consolation. Nevertheless neither bread nor water will fail you from now until Easter.'

Having received the blessing they began to sail out into the ocean. They ate every second day. And so the boat was borne through various places of the ocean.

(THE ISLAND OF SHEEP) One day they saw an island not far from them. When they began to steer towards it, a favourable wind came to their help, so that they did not have to exert themselves more than their strength could manage. When the boat stood to at the harbour, the man of God bade them all get out of the boat. He got out after them. When they began to go round the island they saw large streams of water, full of fish, flowing from various springs. Saint Brendan said to his brothers:

'Let us carry out the divine service here. Let us sacrifice the Spotless Victim to God, for today is Maundy Thursday.' ...

Walking round the island they found various flocks of sheep — all of one colour, white. The sheep were so numerous that the ground could not be seen at all. Saint Brendan called his brothers together and said to them:

'Take what you need for the feast from the flock.'

The brothers, hurrying according to the command of the man of God to the flock, took one sheep from it. When they had tied it by the horns, it followed the brother who held the rope in his hand as if it were tame to the place where the man of God was standing. Again the man of God spoke to one of the brothers:

'Take a spotless lamb from the flock.'

The brother hurried and did as he had been enjoined.

On Good Friday, while they were preparing for the service, a man appeared to them holding in his hand a basket full of bread, that had been baked under the ashes, and the other things that were necessary. When he placed these before the man of God, he fell prone on his face three times at the feet of the holy father, saying:

'How have I deserved, O pearl of God, that you should eat, on these holy days, of the labour of my hands?'

Saint Brendan lifted him up from the ground, embraced him and said:

'Son, our Lord Jesus Christ chooses a place for us where we can celebrate his holy Resurrection.'

The man replied:

'Father, here you will celebrate Holy Saturday. Tomorrow, however, God has ordained that you celebrate the Masses and the vigils of his Resurrection in the island that you see nearby.'

While he said this he prepared to serve the servants of God and do whatever was necessary for Holy Saturday.

When, on Holy Saturday, all was ready and brought to the boat, the man said to Saint Brendan:

'Your boat cannot carry any more. I, therefore, shall bring to you after eight days whatever food and drink you will need until Pentecost.' …

They [then] set out for the boat and began to sail, each party having blessed the other.

(JASCONIUS) When they approached the island, the boat began to ground before they could reach its landing-place. Saint Brendan ordered the brothers to disembark from the boat into the sea, which they did. They held the boat on both sides with ropes until they came to the landing-place. The island was stony and without grass. There were a few pieces of driftwood on it, but no sand on its shore. While the brothers spent the night outside in prayers and vigils, the man of God remained sitting inside in the boat. For he knew the kind of island it was, but he did not want to tell them, lest they be terrified.

When morning came he ordered each of the priests to sing his Mass, which they did. While Saint Brendan was himself singing his Mass in the boat, the brothers began to carry the raw meat out of the boat to preserve it with salt, and also the flesh which they had brought from the other island. When they had done this they put a pot over a fire. When, however, they were plying the fire with wood and the pot began to boil, the island began to be in motion like a wave. The brothers rushed to the boat, crying out for protection to the holy father. He drew each one of them into the boat by his hand. Having left everything they had had on the island behind, they began to sail. Then the island moved out to sea. The lighted fire could be seen over two miles away. Saint Brendan told the brothers what it really was, saying:

'Brothers, are you surprised at what this island has done?'
They said:

'We are very surprised and indeed terror-stricken.'

He said to them:

'My sons, do not be afraid. God revealed to me during the night in a vision the secret of this affair. Where we were was not an island, but a fish — the foremost of all that swim in the ocean. He is always trying to bring his tail to meet his head, but he cannot because of his length. His name is Jasconius.'

~ excerpted from The Voyage of Saint Brendan,
translated by John J. O'Meara, pp. 14-19

"Sharing in the Love of the Trinity"

For Christians, shaped in the belief that God feels a special affection for humans — enough to share their earthly experience — love must be at the center of faith. The author of the First Letter of John asserts, "God is love, and those who abide in love abide in God, and God abides in them."[16] This should remove fear from our lives, both in our own turbulent world and in the peaceable Kingdom of God, giving us the courage to return God's love through selfless service and to share it with others through generous acts of compassion knowing that "we love because he first loved us."[17] But this is not a one-time event. Our human frailty requires the continuing grace of God to sustain our faith when we fall into despair and to repeatedly reanimate our capacity for love.

Watching Brendan and his companions at the beginning of their journey, we see the trust and humility needed to accept and return God's expressions of love. As they come to their first landfall, they are guided — to no one's apparent surprise, by a dog — to a great hall which has been prepared for them and they eat a meal without ever asking who prepared it for them or if it was theirs to take. Again, when

---

[16]   1 John 4: 16.

[17]   1 John 4: 19.

they arrive at the island of sheep, Brendan orders the monks to select an animal from the flock and cook it for them without asking permission from the absent owner. After both of these events, neither Brendan nor his companions seem surprised as a mysterious person arrives bringing them additional food and supplies. Living in the expectancy of God's care, they accept the gifts that are given to them gracefully and without fear.

Yet, from the encounter with Jasconius, we can see that this gracious acceptance of God's love requires some cultivation. When the monks come across what appears to be a barren island, Brendan orders his companions to disembark so they may pray and rest on solid ground. Still, Brendan himself remains in the boat since he knows that they are not actually on land. He understands that God's generosity in allowing them to rest on the back of the leviathan could be overwhelming to his fellow monks, so Brendan does not reveal the true nature of the island until they have returned to the safety of their boat the following morning. But, later in their adventures, Brendan and his companions would meet Jasconius again and would even ride on its back as it moved through the ocean — overcoming their fear of the leviathan and recognizing God's gift of a place to pray and rest during their voyage.

The Celtic saints' devotion to the Holy Trinity nurtured this spiritual growth, fostering an appreciation of God's dynamic nature and activity in this world. The anonymous Thirteenth Century Welsh author of "Food of the Soul" asserts, "From the tender love which flames between the Father and the Son... come the sparks of the church triumphant, and from there they pass to the hearts of the faithful who are the Church militant here below." Inspired and nurtured by this love, men and women gain the courage to express God's love in the world around them since, "However small these sparks may be, they cannot be any less but only greater than the whole of creation since, although they are called sparks, they are not less than the whole of the fire from which they come, which is to say the Holy Spirit, who is no less than the unity of the Three Persons together."[18] By participating in the life of

---

[18]   "Food of the Soul" in *Celtic Spirituality*, edited by Oliver Davies with the collaboration of Thomas O'Loughlin (New York: Paulist Press, 1999), page 441.

the Trinity, the Celts learned to accept the gifts God presented to them each day and to share these tokens of love with others.

For the Celtic saints, God always offered new and surprising expressions of love that transformed the world and prepared its inhabitants to live in the kingdom of God. "Life was lived at two levels — the practical tasks of daily life are done for their own sake carefully and competently, but simultaneously they become signs of God's all-encompassing love. A thing is done well not only for itself but because of the part that it plays in God's world," Esther De Waal explains in *Every Earthly Blessing*, "It is through his world, in its totality, however mundane and down to earth, that God reveals himself. So the Celtic way of seeing the world is infused with the sense of the all-pervading presence of God. This is God's world, a world to be claimed, affirmed and honored."[19]

Early in his spiritual life, while writing the first drafts of the Spiritual Exercises, *Ignatius had a vision in which he perceived the Holy Trinity as three musical notes coming together in a single chord. This vision had profound implications for Ignatius' spirituality, shaping his understanding of creation and the redemptive mission of the Incarnation, as Michael Ivens notes in* Keeping in Touch: *"Ignatius' spirituality, both his personal and that promoted by the Exercises, is characterized by a Trinitarian consciousness... In Ignatius' Trinitarian theology the Trinity is seen not only as the final revelation of God's being in life, but of God's creating and saving action in the world. The action of the Trinity is understood as a pattern of descent and ascent by which all things come from the Trinitarian God and return to that God." (pages 47-48)*

[19] Esther De Waal, *Every Earthly Blessing*, page 15.

In An Ignatian Pathway: Experiencing the Mystical Dimension of the Spiritual Exercises *(Chicago: Loyola Press, 2011), Paul Coutinho encapsulates the core vision and purpose of Ignatian spirituality: "The whole of creation comes from God, goes back to God, and is in God. Creation finds its identity in God and the interconnectedness of all of life. This is the principle and the foundation of Ignatian spirituality. Ignatius believed that those who grow in the spiritual life will constantly contemplate how the Divine is present in every creature." (page 4) So, like ancient Celtic Christianity, Ignatian spirituality strives to recognize the signs of God's presence in every aspect of one's life — no matter how mundane. In Ignatian practice, this involves regularly reviewing one's consciousness of God in the events of daily life called the examen as well*

Since God's dynamic relationship with the world remains unchanged, this invitation to accept and share God's blessings — and to participate in the life of the Trinity — extends now to us. But, like Brendan's companions, we first must have the humility to learn how to trust in God's continuing love. For most of us, this may demand that we simplify our lives so we may better understand the presence of God in them. We now live in highly technological societies that often separate us from the natural world, so we may need to create reflective spaces where we can hear the rhythms of creation. We also tend to embrace very sophisticated understandings of the world that obscure the many acts of love — both by God and by other people — expressed around us. So, trusting in God's love also requires us to hear and embrace Jesus' admonition, "Truly I tell you, unless you change and become like children, you will never enter the kingdom of heaven."[20]

But accepting God's continuing blessings in our lives also requires a mature faith capable of approaching God confidently to care for us and those around us. Like Mary at the wedding feast in Cana, we know God's capacity to bring miracles into our lives — even when those around us do not — and we must be willing to ask God for help when we or our fellow creatures, whether human or nonhuman, are in need. We know that we cannot survive without God's blessings. The finite nature of our existence serves as a constant reminder of our vulnerability in an often-hostile world, but we still need to struggle against our tendency to believe that the prayers we offer for ourselves and others might become a burden on God's generosity. With the ancient Celts, we need to accept that "every moment of the day, every activity becomes a way to God"[21] since every event in our life becomes an opportunity to receive or return God's love.

---

as in the intense exploration of one's broader life and world during times of extended prayer or retreat.

[20]   Matthew 18: 3.

[21]   Esther De Waal, *Every Earthly Blessing*, page 15.

The primary goal of Ignatian spirituality is to become "contemplative in action," which, according to William Barry in Finding God in All Things, *involves being able "to contemplate [or find] God in our daily lives, in our activity." Barry further suggests that this changes the way individuals view their lives and the world around them since, "If we were contemplatives in action, we would approach everyone and everything with reverence." (Page 138)*

A fully developed faith allows us to live in the assurance of God's blessings — whether accepting them with childlike openness for ourselves or confidently coming to God for the needs of others. We can proclaim without hesitation, in the words of Psalm 27, "The Lord is the stronghold of my life; of whom shall I be afraid?"[22] But again, like Mary at Cana, we should be willing to approach others when they do not yet see the ways in which the Triune God might address their needs and desires. In these moments, we need to speak with humility about the many blessings we have already received as well as about the love God wishes to share with those around us. As instruments of God's presence, while reaching out to help others through acts of compassion and generosity, we should pray for ourselves "Teach me your way, O Lord, and lead me on a level path."[23] while saying to those who are suffering, "Wait for the Lord; be strong, and let your heart take courage... wait for the Lord!"[24]

For prayer and reflection:
[1] Separately, contemplate Psalm 27: 1-14 and John 2: 1-11. What are the blessings and miracles you encounter in your own life? How do these moments of joy strengthen you, allowing you to face the painful or difficult times in your life?
[2] In *The Celtic Way of Prayer*, Esther De Waal asserts:

"Everything that [the Celts] touched, every tool that they handled, was done with respect and reverence; every activity performed with a sense of the presence of God, indeed done in partnership with him. So life was lived at two levels. Each successive task performed seriously, carefully, with attention, and simultaneously becoming the occasion for finding the presence of God, and in particular the three members of the Trinity, since much of the work was routine and it could, therefore, be done rhythmically in the name of the Father, Son, and Holy Spirit."[25]

---

[22]   Psalm 27: 1

[23]   Psalm 27: 11.

[24]   Psalm 27: 14.

[25]   Esther De Waal, *The Celtic Way of Prayer*, pages 74-75.

Do you feel God's presence in your daily actions and activities? If so, how do you know that it is God that is present? If not, how would you welcome God's presence into your daily life?

[3] Take a moment to revisit the events of the last day, remembering your feelings as you completed each task or activity. Then, in your imagination, picture the Holy Trinity looking at these events and providing for your needs through them. Repeat this exercise for each day of the last week and contemplate the gifts or blessings you received from God during these days. Then, imagine yourself speaking to the Trinity — either as a group or through one person — about the struggles and achievements of the last week. Afterward, write a prayerful poem or litany expressing your gratitude for the gifts you received as well as your hopes, needs and desires for the coming week.

In Finding God in All Things, *William Barry highlights the Trinitarian dimension of being an Ignatian "contemplative in action" when he states:* "If we could only experience all blessings and gifts as descending to us from above, then we would be able to live in spiritual harmony. We would be 'indifferent to,' 'at balance toward,' all created gifts and blessings because we would have intimate knowledge that these are only pale, even though wonderful, reflections of the deepest desire of our hearts, 'from whom all blessing's flow.' To God, Father, Son, and Holy Spirit be honor and glory and praise for ever and ever." *(page 139)*

Like the ancient Celtic Christians, "contemplatives in action" experience the presence of God in every moment of their lives — making each activity and encounter a moment of blessing to be revered.

IV • THE PARADISE OF BIRDS

Stopping to rest on Easter, Saint Brendan and his companions come ashore on an island called The Paradise of Birds and join its unique community of prayer and praise until Pentecost.

(THE PARADISE OF BIRDS) When they were sailing near the island where they had spent the three days, and came to the western edge of it, they saw another island almost joining it, separated only by a small channel. There was plenty of grass on it; it had groves of trees and was full of flowers. They started circling it, looking for a landing-place. As they were sailing on its southern side they found a stream flowing into the sea and there they put the boat in to land. As they disembarked, Saint Brendan ordered them to draw the boat with ropes up along the river-bed with all their might. The width of the river was about the width of the boat. The father sat in the boat. So they carried on for about a mile, until they came to the source of the stream. Saint Brendan spoke:

'Our Lord Jesus Christ has given us a place in which to stay during his holy Resurrection.'

And he added:

'If we had no other supplies but this spring, it would, I believe, alone be enough for food and drink.'

Over the spring there was a tree of extraordinary girth and no less height covered with white birds. They covered it so much that one could scarcely see its leaves or branches. When the man of God saw this, he began to think and ponder within himself what it meant or what was the reason that such a great multitude of birds could be all collected together. He was so tormented about this that the tears poured out and flowed down upon his cheeks, and he implored God, saying:
'God, who knows the unknown and reveals all that is secret, you

know the distress of my heart. I implore your majesty to have pity and reveal to me, a sinner, through your great mercy your secret that I now look upon with my eyes. I rely not on what I deserve or my worth, but rather on your boundless pity.'

When he said this within himself and had taken his seat again, one of the birds flew from the tree, making a noise with her wings like a hand-bell, and took up position on the side of the boat where the man of God was sitting. She sat on the edge of the prow and stretched her wings, as it were as a sign of joy, and looked with a peaceful mien at the holy father. The man of God immediately concluded that God had listened to his plea, and spoke to the bird:

'If you are God's messenger, tell me where these birds come from or for what reason they are congregated here.'

She replied immediately:

'We survive from the great destruction of the ancient enemy, but we were not associated with them through any sin of ours. When we were created, Lucifer's fall and that of his followers brought about our destruction also. But our God is just and true. In his great judgment he sent us here. We endure no sufferings. Here we can see God's presence. But God has separated us from sharing the lot of the others who were faithful. We wander through various regions of the air and the firmament and the earth, just like the other spirits that travel on their missions. But on holy days and Sundays we are given bodies such as you now see so that we may stay here and praise our creator. You and your brothers have now spent one year on your journey. Six still remain. Where you celebrated Easter today, there you will celebrate it every year. Afterwards you will find what you cherish in your heart, that is, the Promised Land of the Saints.'

When she said this, she lifted herself off the prow and flew to the other birds.

When the hour of vespers had come all the birds in the tree chanted, as it were with one voice, beating their wings on their sides:

'A hymn is due to thee, O God, in Zion, and a vow shall be paid to you in Jerusalem.'

They kept repeating this versicle for about the space of an hour. To the man of God and his companions the chant and the sound of their wings seemed in its sweetness like a rhythmical song. Then Saint Brendan said to his brothers:

'Repair your bodies, for today our souls are filled with divine food.'

When supper was over they performed the divine service. When all was finished, the man of God and his companions gave repose to their bodies until midnight. Waking, the man of God aroused his brothers for the vigil of the holy night, beginning with the versicle:

'Lord, open my lips.'

When the holy man had finished, all the birds responded with wing and mouth, saying:

'Praise the Lord, all his angels; praise him, all his powers.'

So it was as for vespers — they chanted all the time for the space of an hour. …

In this way, day and night, the birds gave praise to the Lord. And so Saint Brendan refreshed his brothers with the feast of Easter until the octave day. …

Saint Brendan remained where he was until the beginning of the *octave of Pentecost. For the chanting of the birds revived their spirits. On Pentecost, however, when the man of God had sung Mass with his brothers, their steward came, bringing with him whatever was necessary for the celebration of the feast day. When they had sat down together for the meal, the steward spoke to them, saying:*

'You have a long journey ahead of you. Take the full of your vessels from the spring here and dry bread which you can keep until next year. I shall give you as much as your boat can carry.'

When all this had been finished, he received the holy father's blessing and returned to his own place.

After eight days Saint Brendan had the boat loaded with all the things the steward had brought to him, and had all the vessels filled from the spring. …

The brothers [then] stretched the sail and steered out into the ocean, while the birds chanted, as it were with one voice:

'Hear us, God, our saviour, our hope throughout all the boundaries of the earth and in the distant sea.'

~ excerpted from The Voyage of Saint Brendan,
translated by John J. O'Meara, pp. 19-25

"Accepting Forgiveness as a Loved Sinner"

Each of us bear a burden of sin that inhibits — if not completely prevents — our ability to accept the love God continues to offer. This ranges from the weight of truly horrible actions to the niggling doubts of those overcome by scrupulosity. Still, we all should feel hope as we visit the Paradise of the Birds with Brendan and his companions. After all, these birds stood by as their spiritual brethren warred against one another, choosing to remain neutral when God faced rebellion amongst his angelic host. They did no harm — certainly even the rebellion itself could not have harmed God — but they failed to stand in God's defense at a moment of cosmic crisis. Yet, despite their offense at such a critical moment, God did not condemn or abandon them. Instead, the birds received mercy and the opportunity to continue serving and praising God. As we consider how we allow our sinfulness to separate us from God, the singing of the birds should remind us of a love that transcends our ability to encompass it while remaining almost overwhelmingly intimate.

As Brendan and his companions listened to the birds they would have heard the echo of their own singing, remembering the psalms that speak of God's eternal love. In particular, they might have remembered the words of Psalm 33: "Truly the eye of the Lord is on those who fear him, on those who hope in his steadfast love, to deliver their soul from death, and to keep them alive in famine. Our soul waits for the Lord; he is our help and shield... Let your steadfast love, O Lord, be upon us, even as we hope in you."[26] Brendan and the Celtic saints lived in the expectation of God's redemptive love, knowing it would pick them up when they failed or faltered in their efforts to follow God and return them to the paths of praise and service they were called to travel.

Yet, this does not mean that the Celtic saints diminished the importance or impact of sin in their world. "The Celts had a very real sense of the reality and power of sin and evil but these were regarded as external forces rather than as innate features of human nature," claims Ian Bradley in *The Celtic Way*, "Along with the whole host of heaven, Christ had taken on these forces and defeated them and it was his victory and protection that was invoked in the breastplate prayers and the *caim* [or encircling prayer]."[27] Through his death on the cross,

---

[26]   Psalm 33: 18-22

[27]   Ian Bradley, *The Celtic Way*, page 65.

In the Spiritual Exercises, *Ignatius presents evil as a tangible, personal force that attacks each person's unique vulnerabilities to undermine his or her natural relationship with God as a redeemed and loved sinner, admonishing each individual to recognize and to struggle against these attacks by reviewing his or her life, asking for the grace to overcome these temptations when they become evident, and amending his or her life choices. Throughout the*

Christ shared — and, thereby, sanctified — the pain of human sin in an act of atonement for humanity. But, through his resurrection, Christ redeemed all of creation by vanquishing the powers of sin and death. These two actions transformed history, making our human experience an invitation to travel toward the kingdom of God in the company — and under the protection — of Christ as we struggle against the vestiges of sin in us and in the world around us.

In their efforts to overcome these lingering effects of sin, the Christian Celts developed guidebooks — called penitentials — listing various offenses and prescribing punishments and penances for each. But, "the Irish penitentials were designed to promote personal growth and development as much as to punish and correct," Ian Bradley observes in *Celtic Christian Communities*, "The penitentials did not provide simply punishments that fitted the crime but carefully calculated programs to change attitudes and behavior. The negative element must be replaced by a positive one as part of a progression away from sin and towards Christian perfection."[28] The Celts

---

Exercises, Ignatius reminds us that Christ defeated the power of sin through his cross but that individuals also risk losing hope when they succumb to temptation and sin. But, rather than chastise a person in despair or desolation because of his or her sins, Ignatius suggests "it is important not to be hard or curt with such a person but gentle and kind, to give courage and strength for the future, to lay bare the tricks of the enemy of human nature, and to encourage the exercitant (the person receiving the Exercises) to prepare and make ready for the consolation which is to come." (#7)

[28] Ian Bradley, *Celtic Christian Communities: Live the Tradition* (Kelowna, British Columbia: Northstone Publishing, 2000) page 92.

In Letters of St. Ignatius of Loyola *(Chicago: Loyola University Press, 1959), collected and translated by William J. Young, Ignatius counsels, "I am not going to save myself by the good works of the good angels, and I am not going to be condemned because of the evil thoughts and the weaknesses which the bad angels, the flesh and the world bring before my mind. God asks only one thing of me, that my soul seek to be conformed with his Divine Majesty. And the soul so conformed makes the body conformed, whether it wish it or not, to the divine will. In this is our greatest battle, and here the good pleasure of the eternal and sovereign Goodness." (page 25)*

In the Spiritual Exercises, *and through the examen (the prayerful review of each day), Ignatius hoped that men and women would become*

46

understood that sin was a deliberate offense against God and others that needed to be repented, but they also appreciated that it was a wound to be healed with care and compassion.

The Celtic saints also recognized that our human nature leads us either to diminish or to exaggerate the consequences of our own actions, even when we try to be completely honest with God in prayer. With this in mind, they developed the unique tradition of a "soul friend" — the *anamchara* — who served both as a confessor in absolving past sins and as a spiritual guide in advising future choices. This uniquely Celtic relationship has roots in the early monastic tradition in which an older monk shared his cell with a younger one — with the elder taking responsibility for the spiritual formation of the junior — and the pre-Christian Celtic tradition of Irish chieftains turning to druids for both spiritual and temporal advice. In the Celtic monastic communities, every monk or nun was expected to meet with their *anamchara* regularly. In this conversation, they would confess their sins and receive both penances to atone for these actions and advice to restore their confidence in approaching and praising God.

By our standards, the penances specified in the penitentials could be quite severe — requiring lengthy prayer vigils, rigorous fasting and even exile — but, in the caring hands of an *anamchara*, they challenged penitents toward greater devotion and love for God. In *Celtic Christian Communities*, Ian Bradley asserts that the Celtic saints "recognized the human capacity to slip back and the need for constant encouragement and stimulation to aid self-growth and development." Consequently, he continues, "The Irish penitentials replaced an essentially static approach to sin and guilt with a dynamic one based on the model and principle of pilgrimage. Penance became a process of repeated confession and absolution during the individual's journey

---

intensely aware of the many ways that God's love shaped each individual's life while also heightening the temptations and sins that might undermine the person's relationship with God. As Paul Coutinho suggests in An Ignatian Pathway, *"Ignatius wants the memory of the goodness and love of God to evoke in our hearts an intense abhorrence and disgust for our sinfulness. Then we will never go back to life apart from God." (pages 60-61) By recognizing the traps of sin and embracing the love of God evermore fully, the person becomes able to live a life of virtue in God's service.*

from cradle to grave."[29] Balancing chastisement with compassion, the Celtic institutions of repentance mirrored Christ's miracles as they repeatedly restored sight to sinners blinded by their own wrongdoing — both to God's desires for them and to the loving support offered to help them achieve their full potential.

For the Celtic saints and for us, the humble act of repentance also re-opens our eyes to the presence of Christ in our lives and in the world around us. Through his incarnation, Christ experienced every aspect of our humanity — even suffering for our sake pains and torments that we dare not imagine for ourselves. Yet, through the power of the Holy Spirit, he defeated the sinful powers of this world and transformed our history. So, with a compassion that transcends our capacity to encompass it, Christ continues to nurture and guide our "better angels" when we commit even the most heinous crimes against his love. The Celtic Christians understood this when they prayed for Christ's protection. The *lorica* (or breastplate prayers) and the *caim* (the encircling prayers) were not only invocations to summon Christ — they were reminders that he was already present and protecting them. In our modern world, which obscures so much of God's presence, we also

---

[29] Ian Bradley, *Celtic Christian Communities*, pages 94-95.

One of the earliest meditations in the Spiritual Exercises *requires a person to imagine Christ nailed on the cross in front of him or her, wondering "how it came about that the Creator made himself a human being and from eternal life came to temporal death, and thus to die for my sins" before requiring the person to ask "What have I done for Christ? What am I doing for Christ? What ought I do for Christ?" (#53) Later in the Exercises, these questions often intrude into the person's prayer as he or she walks with Jesus to his Passion and Death — evoking a profound sense of God's love and forgiveness as well as a passionate desire in the person to share completely in God's redemptive mission.*

As George Aschenbrenner explains in Stretched for Greater Glory: What to Expect From the Spiritual Exercises *(Chicago: Loyola Press, 2004): "Your sin's effect before your loving Creator is not some vague, cosmic confusion and sorrow... To stand in your responsibility before Jesus dying on the cross brings a sorrow that simmers in your heart and drops you to your knees. The suffering and death of God's son for your sin and his words of forgiveness are a clear revelation both of the frightful reality of sin and of a powerfully transforming forgiveness." (page 58)*

need to approach Christ with the same confidence.

But, as companions of Christ, we also need to reach out to others with the same love that has been shown to us. This requires us to forgive those who hurt us through their sinful actions, removing the burden of guilt and shame from them so they may become free to accept Christ's redemptive love. It also challenges us to be compassionate toward our fellow sinners by trying to heal the spiritual, psychological and material wounds caused by sinful choices in the world around us — whether in individual lives or in our shared communities. Finally, with the humility that comes from knowing our own human frailty, it invites us to take responsibility for our own sinful actions by seeking out anyone whom we have hurt to make amends and to make every effort to reconcile the conflicts in our world. In these ways, we become signs of Christ's selfless love to those around us while offering hope to a world that despairs in its inability to overcome the pain caused by self-centeredness and covetousness.

For prayer and reflection:
[1] Separately, ponder Psalm 33: 1-22 and John 9: 1-41. What feelings are evoked as you consider the difference between God's power and your own? How do you allow God to forgive and strengthen you? Where do you resist God's desire to heal you?
[2] Hugh Connolly observes in *The Irish Penitentials*:

"The symbols of Celtic Christianity, whilst at times harsh and severe, have the merit of reminding each Christian that they had to make their own journey. Thus, life was focused, life was purposed. In journeying toward Christ, Christians also journeyed deeper into themselves and began to forge their personal moral identity. They lived with the possibility of sin; but they also had a remedy for sin, and after each fall arose stronger and better equipped to forge a new moral life."[30]

---

[30]   Cited in Ian Bradley, *Celtic Christian Communities*, page 95.

The meditation of Christ on the cross early in the Spiritual Exercises *and the later contemplation of the Passion usually evokes a tremendous sense of shame as the person witnesses the humiliating and painful death of Christ.*

Do you believe that your sins can be healed? If so, how do you respond when God forgives your sins and returns you to your daily life? If not, what gives you the strength to carry the burden of your sins in your life? [3] In your imagination, see yourself standing at the foot of the cross as Christ dies for your sins. Take a moment to look at the cross and Jesus' appearance, registering any emotions you feel as you look upward. Consider the sins that you have committed and the people you have hurt through your sinful behavior. Then, write a litany or long poem confessing these sins to Christ, asking him to forgive each particular sin that comes to mind, to heal any damage you have done to those you wronged, and to give you strength in the future to avoid these sins.

But it is important that the person recognize and accept the gifts that God offers in these moments if he or she wants to live a life of service free from sin.

George Aschenbrenner contends in Stretched for Greater Glory, *"At the core of God's forgiveness in Jesus is a painful, humiliating purification. Like a fire cauterizing the egotistical wound of sin, the grace of forgiveness heals with hope for the future. Without the painful humiliation and purification, the forgiving grace cannot pierce deeply into your heart and remains more a surface solution without much hope for the future." (page 59)*

V • THE COMMUNITY OF AILBE

Leaving the Paradise of Birds, Saint Brendan and his companions wander on the oceans for many months before landing on another island where they are welcomed by the Community of Saint Ailbe.

(THE COMMUNITY OF AILBE) Then the holy father, with his group, was driven here and there for three months over the space of the ocean. They could see nothing but sky and sea. They ate always every second or third day.

One day there appeared to them an island not far away. When they were approaching the shore, the wind drew them away from landing. They, therefore, had to circle the island for forty days, and still they could not find a landing-place. The brothers in the boat implored God with tears to give them help. Their strength had almost failed because of their utter exhaustion. When they had persevered for three days in frequent prayer and abstinence, a narrow landing-place appeared to them, just wide enough to take one boat only; and there appeared before them there also two wells, one muddy and the other clear. The brothers then rushed with their vessels to drink the water. The man of God, watching them, said:

'My sons, do not do a forbidden thing, that is, something without permission of the elders who live in this island. They will freely give you the water that you now want to drink in stealth.'

When they disembarked and were wondering in which direction they should go, an elder of great gravity met them. His hair was snow-white and his face was shining. He prostrated himself three times on the ground. … But Saint Brendan and those with him raised him from the ground. As they embraced one another, the elder held the hand of the holy father and went along with him the distance of about two hundred yards to a monastery. Saint Brendan stood with his brothers before the gate of the monastery

51

and asked the elder:

'Whose monastery is this? Who is in charge of it? Where do the inhabitants come from?'

The holy father kept questioning the elder in various ways, but he could not get one answer out of him: he only indicated with his hand, with incredible meekness, that they should be silent.

As soon as the holy father realized that this was a rule of the place, he spoke to his brothers, saying: 'Keep your mouths from speaking lest these brothers be defiled by your garrulousness.'

At this remonstrance eleven brothers came to meet them with reliquaries, crosses and hymns, chanting the versicle:

'Rise, saints of God, from your dwellings and go to meet truth. Sanctify the place, bless the people, and graciously keep us your servants in peace.'

When the versicle was finished the father of the monastery embraced Saint Brendan and his companions in order. In the same way his community embraced the companions of the holy man.

When they had exchanged the kiss of peace, they led them to the monastery as the custom is in western parts to conduct brothers in this way with prayers. Afterwards the abbot of the monastery with his monks washed the feet of the guests. …

When this was done the abbot led them in great silence to the refectory. A signal was sounded, hands were washed, and then the abbot made them sit down. When a second signal sounded, one of the brothers of the father of the monastery got up and served the table with loaves of extraordinary whiteness and some roots of incredible sweetness. The brothers sat mixed with their guests in order. There was a full loaf between every two brothers.

The same server, on the sounding of the signal, gave the brothers drink.

The abbot for his part was urging on the brothers, saying with great glee:

'In joy and fear of the Lord, drink in love now water from the well from which you wanted to drink in stealth today! The feet of the brothers are washed every day from the other, muddy, well that you saw, because it is always warm. We have no idea where the loaves that you see are baked or who carries them to our larder. What we do know is that they are given to his servants from the great charity of God. …

After they had drunk three times, the abbot sounded a signal in the usual way. The brothers rose all together in great silence and gravity from the table, and preceded the holy fathers to the church. Behind them walked Saint Brendan and the father of the monastery. …

When they had finished the office of vespers Saint Brendan examined how the church was built. It was square, of the same length as breadth, and had seven lights — three before the altar, which was in the middle, and two each before the other two altars. The altars were made of crystal cut in a square, and likewise all the vessels were of crystal, namely patens, chalices and cruets. … There were twenty-four seats in a circle in the church. The abbot, however, sat between the two choirs. One group began from him and ended with him, and it was likewise with the other. No one on either side presumed to intone a verse but the abbot. No one in the monastery spoke or made any sound. …

While Saint Brendan was reflecting upon all these matters within himself, the abbot spoke to him:

'Father, it is now time to return to the refectory so that all that we

have to do will be done while there is light.'

This they did in the same way as before.

When they had completed the day's course in order, they all hurried with great eagerness to compline. When the abbot had intoned the versicle:

'God, come to my aid,' ...

When the order of psalms had been completed, all went out of the church, the brothers bringing their guests, each to his cell, ... But the abbot and Saint Brendan remained seated in the church to wait for the coming of the light. Saint Brendan questioned the holy father on their silence and their community life: 'how could human flesh endure such a life?'

The father replied with great reverence and humility:

'Abbot, I confess before my Christ. It is eighty years since we came to this island. We have heard no human voice except when singing praise to God. Among the twenty-four of us no voice is raised except by way of a signal given by a finger or the eyes, and that only by the elders. None of us has suffered ill in the flesh or from the spirits that infest the human race, since we came here.'
...

While they were thus conversing a fiery arrow sped through a window before their very eyes and lit all the lamps that were placed before the altars. Then the arrow immediately sped out again. But a bright light was left in the lamps. Saint Brendan again asked:

'Who will quench the lights in the morning?'

The holy father replied:

54

'Come and see the secret of it. You can see the tapers burning in the centre of the bowls. Nothing of them actually burns away so that they might get smaller or reduced in size, nor is there any deposit left in the morning. The light is spiritual.' …

They kept vigil the whole night until morning. Then, Brendan asked leave to set out on his journey. The elder said to him:

'No, father. You must celebrate Christmas with us until the octave of the Epiphany.'

The holy father, therefore, with his company stayed that time with the twenty-four fathers in the Island of the Community of Ailbe.

~ excerpted from The Voyage of Saint Brendan, translated by John J. O'Meara, pp. 25-32

"Living as Citizens of Heaven"

In the meeting between Ailbe and Brendan, we see two distinct visions of Celtic spirituality embracing one another. The monastic rule of the historical Ailbe explicitly forbade pilgrimage to its monks but, in this moment, the legendary abbot welcomes Brendan in a manner that transcends mere hospitality. It is a gesture of heartfelt fellowship, a recognition that these two Celtic saints share one faith and purpose despite their differences. Ailbe and his community offer hospitality to the travelers — both materially through nourishment and rest as well as spiritually through shared prayer — while Brendan and his companions remind Ailbe's monks of the earthly exile inherent to their own monastic vocation. Through their interaction, these two groups simultaneously give and receive spiritual blessings and graces that enrich both communities.

Monastic communities such as Ailbe's and Brendan's shaped the essential practices of Celtic spirituality but these monasteries varied greatly in size, membership, and spiritual practices. Under the leadership both of men or of women, with each leader creating their own particular rules and rituals, religious communities could range in size from small secluded groups in very desolate settings to large institutions that participated fully in local economic and civic life — with many monasteries becoming vital centers of learning and the arts. Some communities were exclusively for men while others included both men and women, even on occasion having both celibate and married members. Also, while all Celtic monasteries practiced rigorous forms of penance and self-denial, the particular ascetic practices of each group differed according to the rule of its founder.

Still, despite their differences, the Celtic monastic communities shared a common witness to the coming Kingdom of God — offering patterns of behavior that could be emulated by the world as a whole to foster God's desire for a redeemed human society. These monasteries were economically self-sufficient, so their members shared in the work experiences of the people living around them while maintaining their spiritual practices. Also, while striving to live in a principled manner consistent with the Gospel, the monks and nuns offered hospitality to anyone coming into their monastery and reached out to meet the needs of their neighbors. "Rooted in the world, serving it and intimately involved in its affairs, yet embodying radically other-worldly values," as Ian Bradley points out in *Celtic Christian Communities*, "the Celtic monasteries were, indeed 'colonies of heaven' planted on earth to point as a sign and harbinger of the Kingdom that was yet to come."[31]

---

[31]   Ian Bradley, *Celtic Christian Communities*, page 19.

In one of the central meditations of the Spiritual Exercises, *Ignatius directs the person to consider "how Christ calls and desires everybody to be under his standard" (#137) and to serve Christ by building his kingdom. So, as Michael Ivens states in* Keeping in Touch, *"Service can be considered a defining characteristic of Ignatian spirituality, and it is integral to the criteria proposed in the Exercises for every choice and orientation... For Ignatius this is a word which carries practical implications of action and labor, but which is inseparably linked with praise, reverence, and glory; and it is understood by Ignatius in a profound sense in which action and labor is a mode of union with Christ. For to serve Christ is to work, but not only to work for him, but with him — 'with' in the sense that the more wholeheartedly a person response to the call to serve, they become God's conjoined instrument. Through his servant, his 'instrument', Christ himself continues in the world the mission inaugurated in his mortal life." (pages 94-95)*

A few members of these communities became holy wanderers, either alone or in small groups. Rooted in the desert tradition of the early Church, this vocation was an essential aspect of Celtic monasticism from its very beginnings. But it was not about spiritual adventure. "The true object of pilgrimage had always been a loving attention to God," explains Philip Sheldrake in *Living Between Worlds*, "Even in the heyday of the wanderers there had been a deep suspicion of pilgrims who did not already carry with them the God whom they sought on their journey."[32] Since individuals following this path were no longer under the direct supervision of religious authorities, a monk or nun would be given permission to become a pilgrim or to live as a hermit only after years of faithful prayer, study and service within their monastery — ensuring that the men and women making these journeys already had a mature spiritual life and a profound knowledge of God, something they were meant to share with others during their travels.

These individuals called to live as pilgrims or hermits offered a very different testimony to Christian hope than the monks and nuns in the monasteries. "By leaving the religious settlement and home country, the ascetic also left his or her 'place in the world', that is, status. Beyond the normal boundaries of religious and social life there was no recognized position and therefore no protection," Philip Sheldrake asserts, "God alone became their country of origin and faithfulness to God was what gave them status."[33] Sacrificing the

---

[32]   Philip Sheldrake, *Living Between Worlds*, pages 68-69.

In Ignatian spirituality, the reverent desire fostered in the Spiritual Exercises *to offer everything he or she has (or is) as "one making a gift with heartfelt love" (#234) leads a person from contemplating the mysteries of God in history towards being able to fully participate in God's restorative action in our present world. Paul Coutinho describes this dynamic in An Ignatian Pathway: "Reverence, like service, is both the goal of our lives and the means to attain our salvation. Ignatius teaches us to pause before we begin our prayer, become aware of the presence of God, and fully enter the mystery we are contemplating with reverence. We allow ourselves to become an integral part of the mystery just as if we were present, with all possible devotion and reverence, until we find ourselves in the mystery we are contemplating. Ignatius wants this reverential involvement to transform us into the mystery we are contemplating." (pages 45-46)*

[33]   Philip Sheldrake, *Living Between Worlds*, page 66.

supportive community and structured life of the monastery, the holy wanderers willingly placed themselves at the mercy of the larger world in the hope of demonstrating God's care for each person regardless of their personal situation or social position.

Yet, despite their differences, these two spiritual visions complemented each other. Whether monks or nuns, pilgrims or hermits, the Celtic saints believed they lived in a world redeemed by Christ's victory over the cross and sustained by his continuing presence. Their penances and prayers reminded them of their own imperfections, and their generosity toward others gave witness to God's forgiving love. Offering hospitality and compassion to neighbors and strangers alike, those within the monastic enclosures manifested Christ's love while also honoring the presence of Christ in the people they served. Those leaving the monasteries as pilgrims or hermits became powerless strangers in order to bear witness to the protective presence of Christ in a world that often seemed cruel and indifferent. Through their different actions — whether communal or individual — the Celtic saints shared in a vocation to embody and share with others the love, hope and joy of living in Christ's redeemed kingdom and sharing those qualities with everyone they met.

This mission remains as significant today as it was centuries ago, so the spiritual lives of these ancient Celtic saints still offer us models of behavior we may emulate in our own times. Within their monastic enclosures, monks and nuns were expected to care for others — members of their community, their neighbors and strangers — while maintaining their own spiritual lives. The demands of traveling or surviving in solitude required that the pilgrims and hermits focus more on their material needs, but these holy wanderers also were expected to be as generous and open to others as their monastic counterparts. So, the example of the early Celtic Christians challenges us to maintain

---

Ignatian spirituality invites men and women to walk with Christ in paths of service that offer many challenges and few protections. Ignatius makes this clear in one of his letters, proclaiming, "For just as soon as you determined to bend every effort to procure the praise, honor, and service of God our Lord, you declared war against the world and raised your standard in its face, and got ready to reject what is lofty by embracing what is lowly, to accept indifferently honor and dishonor, riches and poverty, affection and hatred, welcome and repulse — in a word, the glory of the world or all the wrongs it could inflict upon you." (Letters of Saint Ignatius, page 11)

a balance between our contemplative habits of prayer and the active choices of social or pastoral engagement while addressing our own individual needs and those of the community around us.

The nature of community life in and beyond the Celtic monasteries may help us confront this challenge. The ancient Celts did not build walls around their religious communities, but they did regard the grounds of the monastery as a sacred space consecrated to God's kingdom — and their members as representatives of that holy domain. We should treat our modern churches with the same respect. Like the Celtic monasteries, most of our churches are now intentional communities of prayer marked off as enclaves of devotion. But, following the example of the Celtic saints, they also should manifest the love and confidence at the heart of the Gospel by fostering men and women of faith able to go out into the world as companions of Christ, whether locally with other members of their community or further abroad as solitary travelers.

When we live in this way, we announce that "our citizenship is in heaven, and it is from there that we are expecting a Savior, the Lord Jesus Christ."[34] As living signs of God's love, we participate in the miracles that Christ offers to our world when we open the eyes of those blinded by despair or hatred, feed those starving for bodily or spiritual nourishment, and heal those injured by social or economic injustice. Becoming the presence of Christ in our world, we announce the hopeful possibilities of God's kingdom as we proclaim the words of Psalm 103: "Bless the Lord, O my soul, and do not forget all his benefits — who forgives all your iniquity, who heals all your diseases, who redeems your life from the Pit, who crowns you with steadfast love and mercy, who satisfies you with good as long as you live."[35]

For prayer and reflection:
[1] Separately, meditate on Psalm 103: 1-22 and John 6: 1-27, 35-40. What are the signs of God's kingdom around you? How do you respond to them in the choices you make on a daily basis?
[2] Philip Sheldrake maintains in *Living Between Worlds*:

---

[34]   Philippians 3: 20.
[35]   Psalm 103: 2-5.

"The Colombanian tradition [following the Rule of Saint Columbanus]... believed that all people were called from birth to the experience of contemplation. So, 'monastic' enclosures were places of spiritual experience and of nonviolence and also places of education, wisdom and art. Within the enclosures there took place, ideally speaking, and integration of all elements of human life, as well as of all classes of human society. This approach contrasts favorably with the exclusive and impoverished understanding of enclosure as a means of protecting 'spiritual persons' from everyone else... [a view that] came, in due course, to dominate the rest of the western tradition of spirituality."[36]

Do you believe you are able to help build God's kingdom? If so, what actions and life-choices will help you in your efforts? If not, who might be able to help you understand how God's kingdom is built?

[3] Imagine life in a Celtic monastery. Form a mental picture of one day in this monastery — waking up in your cell, participating in communal prayers, eating meals and working on the grounds — and feel God's presence in each event. Then, take a sheet of paper and fold it in half (from top to bottom) and write a list of your activities during your imagined "monastic" life as well as the importance of each. Unfold the paper and write next to the items on your list the ways you might integrate these practices into the life you actually live. When you are finished, write a litany or long prayerful poem asking Christ to join you in each event of your imagined "monastic" daily order.

---

[36]   Philip Sheldrake, *Living Between Worlds*, pages 39-40.

This sense of enclosure is not found in the Ignatian tradition. Instead, a person's consideration of his or her life leads to a grateful love that allows him or her to experience God's presence in the world directly as a "contemplative in action". This requires the person to discern (on a moment-to-moment basis) the presence of Christ in the world — and his desires for the individual — while striving to avoid the traps hidden within worldly status and position. As Michael Ivens observes in Keeping in Touch, "As the enemy leads people into pride by way of worldly fame, so Christ leads to humility by way of whatever is antithetical to fame, broadly rather than narrowly understood: failure, experiences of diminishment, neglect or disparagement." (Page 70) In this regard, the Ignatian ideal is closer to the Celtic pilgrim, whose status emerged solely from his or her faithfulness to God, rather than to the monastic communities of the Celts which served as "colonies of heaven" here on earth.

VI • THE CRYSTAL PILLAR
& THE ISLAND OF SMITHS

After visiting the Community of Ailbe, holy Brendan and his brethren set sail once again and encounter two wondrous sights while upon the ocean — one awe-inspiring and the other terrifying.

(THE CRYSTAL PILLAR) One day when they had celebrated their Masses, a pillar in the sea appeared to them that seemed to be not far distant. Still it took them three days to come up to it. When the man of God approached it he tried to see the top of it — but he could not, it was so high. It was higher than the sky. Moreover a wide-meshed net was wrapped around it. The mesh was so wide that the boat could pass through its openings. They could not decide of what substance the net was made. It had the colour of silver, but they thought that it seemed harder than marble. The pillar was of bright crystal. Brendan spoke to his brothers:

'Ship the oars and take down the mast and sail. Let some of you at the same time take hold of the meshes of the net.'

There was a large space, roughly about a mile, at all points between the net and the pillar, and likewise the net went down a similar distance into the sea. When they had done what they had been ordered, the man of God said to them:

'Let the boat in through one of the meshes, so that we can have a close look at the wonders of our creator.'

When they had gone in and looked around here and there, the sea was as clear to them as glass, so that they could see everything that was underneath. They could examine the foundations of the pillar and also the edge of the net lying on the sea bed. The light of the sun was as bright below as above the water.

Then Saint Brendan measured the four sides of the opening of the net: it was about six to seven feet on every side.

They then sailed throughout the whole day near one side of the pillar and in its shadow they could still feel the heat of the sun. They stayed there until three o'clock. The man of God kept measuring the one side. The measurement of each of the four sides of that pillar was the same, namely about seven hundred yards. The venerable father was engaged for four days in this way around the four angles of the pillar.

On the fourth day, however, they found a chalice, of the same substance as the net, and a paten, of the same colour as the pillar, lying in a window in the side of the pillar facing the south. Saint Brendan took hold of these vessels immediately, saying:

'Our Lord Jesus Christ has shown us this wonder, and given me these two gifts, so that the wonder be manifested to many in order that they may believe.'

Then the man of God ordered his brothers to perform the divine office and then refresh their bodies, for they had had no slack time in which to take food or drink since they had seen the pillar.

When the night was over the brothers began to row towards the north. When they had passed through an opening in the net they raised the mast and sail, while some of the brothers still held the meshes of the net until all was made ready on the boat. When the sail had been spread, a favouring wind began to blow behind them so that they did not need to row but only to hold the ropes and rudder. So their boat was borne along for eight days towards the north.

(THE ISLAND OF SMITHS) After eight days they caught sight of an island not far away, very rough, rocky and full of slag, without trees or grass, full of smiths' forges. The venerable father said to his brothers:

'I am troubled about this island. I do not want to go on it or even come near it. But the wind is bringing us directly there.'

As they were sailing for a moment beside it, a stone's throw away, they heard the sound of bellows blowing, as if it were thunder, and the blows of hammers on iron and anvils. When he heard this the venerable father armed himself, making the sign of the Lord in all four directions, saying:

'Lord, Jesus Christ, deliver us from this island.'

When the man of God had finished speaking, one of the inhabitants of the island was seen to come out of doors apparently to do something or other. He was very shaggy and full at once of fire and darkness. When he saw the servants of Christ pass near the island, he went back into his forge. The man of God blessed himself again and said to his brothers:

'My sons, raise the sail higher still and row as fast as you can and let us flee from this island.'

Even before he had finished speaking, the same savage came to the shore near where they were, carrying a tongs in his hands that held a lump of burning slag of immense size and heat. He immediately threw the lump on top of the servants of Christ, but it did no hurt to them. It passed more than two hundred yards above them. Then the sea, where it fell, began to boil, as if a volcano were erupting there. The smoke rose from the sea as from a fiery furnace.

But when the man of God had got about a mile away from the spot where the lump fell, all the islanders came to the shore, each of them carrying a lump of his own. Some of them began to throw the lumps after the servants of Christ into the sea, the one throwing his lump over the other, all the while going back to the forges and setting the lumps on fire. It looked as if the whole island was ablaze, like one big furnace, and the sea boiled, just as a cooking pot full of meat boils when it is well plied with fire. All day long they could hear a great howling from the island. Even when they could no longer see it, the howling of its denizens still reached their ears, and the stench of the fire assailed their nostrils. The holy father comforted his monks, saying:

'Soldiers of Christ, be strengthened in faith unfeigned and in spiritual weapons, for we are in the confines of Hell. So, be on the watch and be brave.'

~ excerpted from The Voyage of Saint Brendan,
translated by John J. O'Meara, pp. 50-54

"Learning the Patterns of God's Presence"

Throughout his journey, Brendan recognizes more quickly than his companions the presence of God in the people and places they visit. He understands how some things we fear may become instruments of God's love while others that we find beautiful or pleasant may ensnare us and lead us away from God's care. For instance, the size of the crystal tower — and the fact that it is covered by a forbidding net-like structure — makes it appear dangerous but it offers Brendan and his companions important gifts when they have the courage to go below the webbing and to explore the mysteries underneath. In contrast to the tower's blessings, however, a favorable wind allows the monks to rest while guiding the travelers toward an island on which they certainly would have been killed. In both cases, Brendan's awareness of the spiritual forces shaping his material situation makes it possible for him and his companions either to receive blessings or to avoid danger.

Through this sensitivity to his surroundings, Brendan epitomized the spiritual vigilance toward which Celtic Christians aspired. The material world in which the Celts lived could be harsh — placing them at risk from disease, famine or war — and their spiritual world was similarly daunting since, as Ian Bradley notes in *Celtic Christian Communities*, "the many prayers for protection serve as a reminder that there was a very strong sense of the power of sin and of the almost tangible presence of dark and evil forces"[37] around them. This led the Celts to value the ability to discern the presence or desires of God — both in their day-to-day decisions as well as in their life choices. Knowing that God shared material and spiritual gifts without regard for social or religious position, the Celts also were comforted by the knowledge that this spiritual sensitivity was offered to everyone willing to seek it through prayer and reflection.

As the Celts confronted an often-challenging world, they knew that they could trust in God's help and that they would not face dangers alone — or undefended. "If one of the great themes of Celtic Christianity was an overwhelming sense of God's presence then another was a strong conviction of his role as protector," Ian Bradley explains in *The Celtic Way*, "The members of the Trinity and the whole glorious company of angels, archangels, disciples and saints who surrounded them in heaven were seen not simply as companions and friends but as defenders and protectors who could ward off evil forces."[38] The Celts experienced this protection in many different ways

---

[37]   Ian Bradley, *Celtic Christian Communities*, pages 68-69.

Both during the Spiritual Exercises *and in everyday life, Ignatius sees the person struggling against a personal force which would lead him or her away from God's love. In* Keeping in Touch, *Michael Ivens contends, "In our conflict with the 'enemy of human nature,' what is ultimately at issue is eternal salvation… but the phrase draws attention to the here-and-now and to the whole person, and evokes especially the inner turmoil and unfreedom of one led by the Evil One against the peace and integrity of lives given to Christ… In the* Exercises *he is essentially an omnipresent malign intelligence, which operates through plausibility and deceit: hence the importance of Lucifer, the fallen angel of light. To resist, and eventually overthrow, the 'enemy' it is therefore necessary to become aware of these deceits. This perspective gives the* Exercises *an essentially robust and practical attitude which must not degenerate on the one hand into anxiety or on the other into complacency."* (pages 75-76)

[38]   Ian Bradley, *The Celtic Way*, page 45.

During the consideration of human sinfulness in the Spiritual Exercises, *Ignatius presents an epiphany that should remain with each person as he or she struggles against sin: "An exclamation of wonder, with intense feeling, as I reflect on the whole range of created beings. How have they ever let me live and kept me alive? The Angels, who are the swords of divine justice,*

and in many different situations, making God's protective care a concrete aspect of their lives which could be examined. So, by gratefully acknowledging those moments in their lives when God protected them from external threats, the Celts learned the specific ways in which God cared for them.

Also, the Celts knew — through their understanding of the Incarnation — that the evils they faced were already defeated. For the Celtic saints, "Christ's mission was seen not in terms of confronting an intrinsically corrupt world but rather of liberating an essentially good world from its bondage to evil forces," Ian Bradley observes, saying that the Celts saw Christ "as the great liberator and emancipator, the one who draws us into the glorious liberty of the children of God."[39] Christ offered the world and its inhabitants a new life free from the tyranny of sin, allowing the Celts to profess — again, from personal experience — the words of Psalm 40: "He drew me up from the desolate pit, out of the miry bog, and set my feet upon a rock, making my steps secure. He put a new song in my mouth, a song of praise to our God."[40] While sin remained a part of their lives, the Celts experienced the renewed hope of redemption in each act of repentance — while also learning the concrete ways in which they had been tempted away from God's love.

So, from their experiences of prayer, the Celtic saints learned

------

how have they borne with me, and looked after me, and prayed for me? The Saints, too, how have they been able to intercede and pray for me? The heavens, the sun, the moon, the stars, and the elements, the fruits, the birds, the fishes and the animals, how have they kept me alive until now? As for the earth, how has it not opened up to engulf me, creating new hells where I might suffer for ever?" (#60)

[39] Ian Bradley, *The Celtic Way*, page 65.

Paul Coutinho maintains in An Ignatian Pathway, "Sin for Ignatius is forgetting who we are and thus losing our personal freedom. He confronts us with the insanity of our sinfulness, which causes us to break away from an ever-loving and generous God. Ignatius wants us to focus on the goodness of our relationship with the Divine and all that it means to us. This relationship helps us discover more and more that we are God's own children. Everything that God has given to us not just as our privilege, but as a right. This realization ought to give us more and more freedom in following our bliss every day for the rest of our lives." (page 60)

[40] Psalm 40: 2-3.

the patterns of God's care and gained confidence in their own ability to respond to that love. Through their breastplate and encircling prayers, the Celts looked outward to any threats they faced in their world and recognized the presence of God in the specific instances of protection they received. In a similar manner, the Celts' penitential practices both heightened their awareness of the moments when they succumbed to their own sinfulness and strengthened their desire to live in a manner worthy of God's love. Rather than being discouraged by the external forces buffeting them, or by their own failed attempts to live sinless lives, the Celts found hope through their efforts to remain faithful to God and learned from their human frailty — whether through temptations or sins — how to become more responsive to God's desires.

It remains important, however, to recognize — whether contemplating God's presence in the world around them or struggling in a moment of personal distress — that the Celts sought to recognize the patterns of God's presence and acknowledge the unflinching love permeating every aspect of their lives. "They had the imagination and the faith to find God in the ordinary and the commonplace as well as to invoke his aid in times of disruption and abnormality," Ian Bradley notes, asserting that, "The underlying note of Celtic spirituality is one of hope and joy not sorrow and despair."[41] In prayers praising God's presence in nature and in petitions asking for protection during times of trouble, the Celtic saints recognized the sustaining power of God in every moment of their lives and the tremendous love God showered on all the creatures of the earth.

Yet, the Celtic saints also understood that prayer teaches us the patterns of God's love in order to strengthen our desire to mirror that

---

[41]   Ian Bradley, *The Celtic Way*, page 49.

According to John English in Spiritual Freedom: From an Experience of the Ignatian Exercises to the Art of Spiritual Guidance *(Chicago: Loyola Press, 1995), "If we understand that life is a continual interchange with God, then it is important to appreciate the unique ways God relates to us. We can discover these ways through reflection on certain events in our lives. In human relationships of love we discovered the uniqueness of the relationship by pondering how long it has lasted. Similarly, praying over our life story from the perspective of God's continual love shows us the strength of our relationship with God." (page 270)*

presence in our own lives. "Consoling and comforting as they undoubtedly are, these prayers of presence and protection are also challenging and do not simply induce an introspective and cocooning sense of complacency. They are the outpourings of hearts which are not just full of thankfulness to God but also burn with love for all creation and they call those who say and hear them to lives of practical charity," Ian Bradley states, "In finding God's presence in everybody and everything, however high or however lowly, Celtic Christianity also found the most fundamental reason for loving and serving others."[42] Through their example, the ancient Celts challenge us to see the invitation that remains at the heart of our own prayer today — to discern in our own experiences the ways by which we may participate in the continuing expressions of God's love for the rest of humanity and for the world in which we live.

Accepting this challenge requires that we devote ourselves to discerning the patterns of God's presence in our own lives so we may respond to that loving concern and share it with others. From the example of the Celtic saints, we know that we should ask for God's help when we feel overwhelmed by the social and spiritual forces swirling around us — and that we will come to appreciate God's desires for us in the patterns of that protection. We also may learn to recognize God's hope for us when we are willing to acknowledge the ways in which we fail to respond to God's love and guidance. Yet, like the ancient Celts, we should never be discouraged by our weaknesses. Instead, we should recognize that we offer hope to others when we overcome — with God's help and grace — our own failings so we may reach out to others with love. In this way, we acknowledge that the world in which we live is being redeemed through Christ's Incarnation

---

[42]   Ian Bradley, *The Celtic Way*, page 50.

In Spiritual Freedom, *John English declares that Ignatian prayer "involves a dynamic of remembering, reflecting, and comparing. We begin by remembering persons, relationships, places and events in our graced history, and we proceed by considering the unique elements and quality contained in these memories... Remembering and appropriating concrete data from our history affirms our identity with God. It gives us a solid basis for judging our future consolations and we can discern our interior experiences in terms of Ignatius' words: 'For... in consolation the good spirit guides and counsels us (#318)'." (page 270-271)*

and that we are called to collaborate in that redemptive process.

For prayer and reflection:
[1] Separately, contemplate Psalm 40: 1-17 and John 11: 1-3, 17-46. What are the signs that God provides in your life that offer you a sense of purpose? Are the signs easy for you to recognize or obscured in some manner? Have you begun to discover patterns in the signs of purpose and guidance God provides for you in your life?
[2] Esther De Waal suggests in *The Celtic Way of Prayer*:
"The connection between suffering in creation is something that all early peoples knew as an essential part of their lives. In the seasonal cycle of the dying of the seed in the growth into new life, the farmer has to cut into the earth with his plow and has to harrow the soil — even the words themselves for sowing carry the connotation of pain. In the human lifecycle, pain is part of childbirth, as any mother can testify. Yet many people today, and trying to recover your Celtic roots, seem to be looking for some creation-centered spirituality that idealizes nature and present some romantic idyll of the past. The reality would have been far different and it is vitally important to realize this. Nature can be cruel, uncertain, menacing."[43]

---

[43]   Esther De Waal, The Celtic Way of Prayer, page 119.

Ignatius believed that individuals struggle with accepting the forgiveness of God, fostering suffering and sin — within the individual and in the larger world — through a battle between understanding and ignorance. Paul Coutinho elaborates on this conflict in An Ignatian Pathway, *declaring "Forgiveness comes from knowledge and understanding. True knowledge is that which touches our hearts and transforms our lives. True knowledge comes from experiencing through our nakedness the essence of who we are — the image and likeness of God and the Divine breath. True knowledge helps us understand and experience the interconnectedness of all of life — whatever happens to anyone affects all," whereas, "Lack of knowledge, or ignorance, comes from clinging to the transitory nature of things in this life and seeking our identity and the source of our happiness in them: material things of this world, what people say and think about us, and the power and authority we have in this life." (page 119)*

Have you ever found signs of joyful purpose amid the turbulence of pain or suffering in your life? Did this discovery change the way in which you saw the difficulties you were facing? If so, how did this change your understanding of God's desires for you? If not, who might be able to help you better understand your situation?

[3] Reflect on the suffering you have experienced in your own life. Allow your imagination to dwell on a particularly difficult or traumatic experience, and ask God to reveal the ways in which that event was healed. After taking a few moments to allow these ideas to coalesce, fold a piece of paper in half and write on one side the various ways that God has protected or healed you in the past. Then, on the other side of the paper, list the concerns that you have for the future. When you are finished, write a litany praising God's protection that begins with statements of gratitude for God's past actions and moves toward petitions asking God to help you in the future.

Often, this conflict is only resolved when the person feels the shame of seeing anew how Christ suffered and died for his or her sins — recognizing once again the tremendous love God has for each person and creature.

VII • UNHAPPY JUDAS

Continuing their journey on the ocean, holy Brendan and his companions meet Judas — buffeted by the waves as he sits precariously on a rock in the sea — and Saint Brendan defends him from the demons of hell.

(UNHAPPY JUDAS) When Saint Brendan had sailed towards the south for seven days, there appeared to them in the sea the outline as it were of a man sitting on a rock with a cloth suspended between two small iron fork-shaped supports about a cloak's length in front of him. The object was being tossed about by the waves just like a little boat in a whirlwind. Some of the brothers said that it was a bird, others a boat. When the man of God heard them discussing the matter among themselves, he said:

'Cease arguing. Steer the boat to the spot.'

When the man of God drew near, the waves, glued as it were in a circle, kept them at a distance. They found a man, shaggy and unsightly, sitting on a rock. As the waves flowed towards him from every side, they struck him even to the top of his head. When they receded, the bare rock where the unhappy man was sitting was exposed. The wind also sometimes drove the cloth hanging in front of him away from him, and sometimes blew it against his eyes and forehead.

Blessed Brendan questioned him as to who he was, or for what fault he was sent here, or what he deserved to justify the imposition of such penance? The man replied:

'I am unhappy Judas, the most evil trader ever. I am not here in accordance with my deserts but because of the ineffable mercy of Jesus Christ. This place is not reckoned as punishment but as an indulgence of the Saviour in honour of the Lord's Resurrection.'

That day was in fact the Lord's day.

'When I am sitting here I feel as if I were in a paradise of delights in contrast with my fear of the torments that lie before me this evening. For I burn, like a lump of molten lead in a pot, day and night, in the centre of the mountain that you have seen. ... But here I have a place of refreshment every Sunday from evening to evening, at Christmas until the Epiphany, at Easter until Pentecost, and on the feasts of the purification and assumption of the Mother of God. After and before these feasts I am tortured in the depth of Hell with Herod and Pilate and Annas and Caiphas. And so I beseech you through the Saviour of the world to be good enough to intercede with the Lord Jesus Christ that I be allowed to remain here until sunrise tomorrow, so that the demons may not torture me on your coming and bring me to the fate I have purchased with such an evil bargain.'

Saint Brendan said to him:

'May the Lord's will be done! Tonight until the morning you will not be eaten by the demons.'

The man of God questioned him again, saying:

'What is the meaning of this cloth?'

The other replied:

'I gave this cloth to a leper when I was procurator for the Lord. But it was not mine to give. It belonged to the Lord and the brothers. And so it gives me no relief but rather does me hurt. Likewise the iron forks, on which it hangs, I gave to the priests of the temple to hold up cooking-pots. With the rock on which I sit I filled a trench in the public road to support the feet of those passing by, before I was a disciple of the Lord.'

When the evening hour had darkened the sea, an innumerable number of demons covered its surface in a circle, shouting and saying:

'Go away, man of God, from us. We cannot come near our companion until you go away from him. Neither have we dared to look on the face of our chief until we return his friend to him. You have taken our mouthful away from us. Do not protect him this night.'

The man of God said to them:

'I do not protect him, but the Lord Jesus Christ allowed him to remain here this night until morning.'

The demons retorted:

'How can you invoke the Lord's name over him, when he is himself the betrayer of the Lord?'

The man of God said to them:

'I order you in the name of our Lord Jesus Christ that you do him no evil until morning.'

When, therefore, that night was passed, and when the man of God had begun to set out on his journey, an infinite number of demons was seen to cover the face of the ocean, emitting dire sounds and saying:

'Man of God, we curse your coming as well as your going, since our chief whipped us last night with terrible scourges because we did not bring to him that accursed prisoner.'

The man of God said to them:

'Your curse does not affect us, but rather yourselves. The man whom you curse is blessed; he whom you bless is cursed.'

The demons answered him:

'Unhappy Judas will suffer double punishment for the next six days because you protected him in the night that has passed.'

The venerable father said to them:

'You have no power over that, nor your chief: God will have the power.'

And he added:

'I order you and your chief in the name of our Lord Jesus Christ not to inflict on him more torments than before.'

They answered him:

'Are you the Lord of all, so that we obey your words?'

The man of God said to them:

'I am his servant, and whatever I order, I order in his name. My service lies in those matters which he has assigned to me.'

The demons followed him until Judas could no longer be seen. They then returned and lifted up the unhappy soul among them with great force and howling.

~ excerpted from The Voyage of Saint Brendan,
translated by John J. O'Meara, pp. 56-60

"Embracing the Standard of Christ"

In our world, where Christians are increasingly marginalized within their societies, it is easy to believe that we are powerless in the

74

face of evil and indifference. We may challenge disturbing policies or social attitudes on occasion but, for the vast majority of Christians, the *status quo* is something that is rigidly in place and unable to be changed. But this is not the understanding demonstrated by Brendan when he encounters Judas on an island in the middle of the ocean. Brendan responds to what he encounters with courage, both in showing compassion for Judas' suffering and in rebuking the demons sent to harass this notorious sinner. This sense of empowerment and confidence emerges from his knowledge that we share in the death and resurrection of Jesus — that we already live in the kingdom of God — and receive power from Christ to manifest his continuing presence in the world around us.

Certainly, as Esther De Waal notes in *Every Earthly Blessing*, Celtic spirituality "has a heroic character in which Jesus is the champion who delivers his people by means of a stupendous feat of physical prowess, the passion."[44] Yet, while they believed Christ defeated sin and death through his cross, the Celts also recognized the lingering presence of evil and darkness in their world and constantly prayed for protection from these forces. "These prayers are cries for help, an admission of human vulnerability, frailty and need, which start from a very honest acceptance of weakness and dependency upon God," Esther De Waal observes, while noting that the Celts believed,

---

[44]   Esther De Waal, *Every Earthly Blessing*, page 105.

Ignatian spirituality certainly regards Christ's Passion as a heroic achievement since, as John English declares in Spiritual Freedom, *"As sinners we are powerless, so we cannot save ourselves. But Christ can save us. Jesus Christ, therefore, is hanging not between us and God but between us and hell. God's love reaches out to us. The Only Begotten One was sent to join the human race and save it from hell." (page 69)*

But, while Ignatius uses heroic imagery in the Spiritual Exercises *contrasting Christ's eternal kingship with an earthly king (#91-100) and showing Christ calling his followers to his standard in the battle against evil (#136-147), the contemplation of the Passion focuses on the human suffering Christ endured through the self-emptying act of the Incarnation. As Paul Coutinho observes in* An Ignatian Pathway, *"Ignatius wrote in his* Spiritual Journal *that in the humanity of Jesus he experienced the whole being of God. In the* Spiritual Exercises *he sees the human Jesus as the Creator on the cross who became man in order to die for my sins." (page 79)*

"The passion of Christ promises victory for all who follow him."[45] By accepting their own human weakness and trusting in Christ's protection, the Celts mustered the courage to join Christ in an epic redemptive struggle that was begun on the cross.

In their efforts, the early Celtic Christians drew strength from those who preceded them. Stories of earlier Christian saints — whether in other parts of the world or in the Celtic lands — offered models of behavior as well as concrete manifestations of the spiritual courage needed in the struggle against evil. More important, the Celts felt a tangible connection to these earlier saints — they were now part of the heavenly host that could be called upon in times of weakness to offer strength and protection, something that was reinforced by placing images of saints from the early church on their monuments or venerating local places associated with their own saints. The Celts also drew hope in their own struggles by remembering, as Esther De Waal observes, "that for those who stand firm there is the promise of the faithfulness of God, the God who protects his followers today as he has done in the past."[46]

---

[45]   Esther De Waal, *Every Earthly Blessing*, pages 108-109.

For Ignatius, the humanity of Christ — especially during the Passion — becomes both an act of love and an invitation. As John English writes in Spiritual Freedom, "Jesus' human nature is like our own, without the self-inflicted wounds of sin. His nature became the instrument of the Trinity's redemptive act — the instrument by which sin and death are overcome. It was Jesus' personal relationship with God that enabled weak human nature to achieve the redemption of humanity. Jesus is inviting other individual humans to unite with him to bring about the salvation of the world... This is an extraordinary invitation. We are moved to another experience of grace, another expression of God's love. We are being called to be with Christ in his work to overcome the disorder that is in the universe and in ourselves." (page 96)

So, when Ignatius directs the person receiving the Spiritual Exercises to pray for "grief with Christ in grief, to be broken with Christ broken" (#203) when contemplating Christ's Passion, he both points to the loving action of God and asks the individual to embrace the redemptive aspects of their own humanity so he or she may share in the triumph of the resurrection.

[46]   Esther De Waal, *Every Earthly Blessing*, page 110.

The Celtic Saints also recognized that their surrender to God's protection allowed them to speak with power against the forces of evil in their world. God's loving presence offered guidance to the Celts in reforming their lives and shielding them from the attacks of others. But the Celts also believed they could invoke God's presence through blessings and curses to protect themselves and others, either by calling upon the persons of the Trinity directly or through the angels and saints. "With this understanding of the power of the spoken word, pronouncing a blessing or benediction was no mere pleasantry or routine greeting to pass the time of day," Ian Bradley writes in *Celtic Christian Communities*, "Rather it conveyed to the recipient in an almost physical sense a portion of God's goodness and grace."[47] This faith in their own safety — and their ability to offer protection to others — gave the Celtic saints the composure and courage that Brendan demonstrates when he confronts the demons in the name of Christ.

By recognizing their dependence upon God in their struggle

A central aspect of Ignatius' conversion — embedded in his Spiritual Exercises — *involved the recognition that he could share in God's continuing redemption of creation by joining in the work of earlier saints who served under Christ's standard. So, Christ's suffering and death on the cross is not solely personal. As John English explains in* Spiritual Freedom, *"Christ does not simply want to save our individual person — he invites us to join the struggle to save the world. The character of God's saving action is different from what we might expect. God not only forgives us, but wants to share life with us by including us in the [ongoing] work of the Trinity." (page 97)*

[47] Ian Bradley, *Celtic Christian Communities*, page 61.

Ignatian spirituality does not have a tradition of benedictions or blessings. Still, Ignatius does ask the person receiving the Spiritual Exercises *to pray for specific graces (which involve God becoming concretely present in the person's life) so that he or she may acquire the courage and freedom to participate in God's divine essence, leading John English to maintain in* Spiritual Freedom, *"We must view God as approving and affirming when we take a spiritual approach to all the events of our life story. Knowing that God regards us with unconditional love enables us to recall all the events of our lives, whether they are positive or negative. With reflection we recognize the unique way God relates to us… A series of events becomes graced history when it is approached and understood in terms of God's constant loving presence with each individual and the whole human race." (page 264)*

against sin and evil, the Celts also learned to empathize with their fellow sinners. The Celtic saints understood the traps of sin but they also knew the overwhelming forgiveness of God. So, their own personal experience echoed the words of Psalm 22: "You who fear the Lord, praise him! For he did not despise or abhor the affliction of the afflicted; he did not hide his face from me, but heard when I cried to him."[48] This gave the Celts, as Esther De Waal notes, a "sense of solidarity with all those, whoever they may be, who have experienced the battle, whether they are those known through the pages of the Bible, or the saints and martyrs of more recent times."[49] This sensitivity also extended to sinners who failed to remain faithful to God. So, while others might be tempted to gloat at the suffering that Judas endures for his sin of betraying Christ, Brendan shows him the compassion that comes from a love that genuinely forgives and puts an end to enmity.

Brendan's compassion also reflects the Celtic belief in "an ultimate and universal salvation in which all things would return to God through Christ."[50] The early Christian Celts understood that the redemptive mission of Christ involved returning all things — spiritual and material — to the sovereignty of God. This was a cosmic battle which began with the rebellion of the angels and Adam's sin and which would end with the full restoration of God's loving dominion over all of creation. Within this struggle, as Ian Bradley points out, "Humanity

---

[48]   Psalm 22: 23-24.

[49]   Esther De Waal, *Every Earthly Blessing*, page 109.

Through its use of imaginative prayer, Ignatian spirituality fosters a visceral connection to the men and women described in the Bible as well as to the saints and martyrs who embraced Christ's call to participate in God's redemption of creation.

[50]   Ian Bradley, *The Celtic Way*, page 60.

Like Celtic Christianity, Ignatian spirituality invites individuals to look at their own lives with gratitude and the struggles of others with compassion since, as Paul Coutinho writes in An Ignatian Pathway, *"We become aware of the many gifts of God with gratitude, and gratitude is a memory of the heart. Gratitude is that process where we allow the gifts we have received to touch our hearts and transform our lives. Our transformed lives help us feel more and more the interconnectedness of all of life. Therefore, the gifts that have transformed us now flow out of us because we realize that they belong to everyone." (page 140)*

was not so much fallen and hopelessly flawed by sin but rather immature and striving for completion and perfection."[51] With this in mind, the Celts developed rigorous penitential practices intended to develop habits of sinless behavior — displaying God's power by defeating evil or sinful forces within themselves and demonstrating God's ultimate authority over creation.

But, after receiving forgiveness for their own sins, the Celts also understood how God's love required them to mirror his compassion so that no sinner be left to suffer forever — no matter how heinous their sins or offenses. So, the early Celtic Christians also felt called to offer hope to their fellow sinners by sharing the liberating effects of striving to live in harmony with God's desires — the joy they experienced through God's forgiveness, the ways in which the remission of their sins changed their view of the world around them, or the courage God gave them when they faltered and needed to repent new sins. The Celtic saints also challenged the sinful practices of others — as well as broader social ills — so that their fellow men and women were liberated from their own sins as well as the sinful social snares that separated them from God's love. By living in a manner consistent with the demands of Christ's cross, whether through remarkable demonstrations of God's loving power or through humble acts of contrition, the Celtic saints presented a glimpse into a world redeemed by God's love.

So, as we are called in our own time to take up the standard of the cross, we need to struggle against the forces of sin and evil in our world with the same courage and humility as our Celtic forebears. Certainly, we can draw inspiration from their example by admitting to our own sins and striving to live lives worthy of God's love. But we also

---

[51]   Ian Bradley, *The Celtic Way*, page 61.

The recognition of human frailty as well as the infinite love shown by God requires constant self-examination and contrition to remain vital — requiring us to return humbly to the mystery of the cross so it may nourish and deepen our living faith. In An Ignatian Pathway, *Paul Coutinho maintains: "For Ignatius, faith is a relationship with the Divine. This loving relationship is also based on a personal experience. But our faith and our experience have to keep on growing deeper or else they will surely fade away and die. God is always bigger and greater than anything we might know about God, and deeper than any experience we might have of God. So if our faith and our relationship with God are not growing, then we might be slowly losing the gift." (page 150)*

need to demonstrate the same courage as the Celtic saints when we oppose the forces of violence, hatred and injustice that dominate much of our world or when we challenge the continuing destruction of the environment. Like the early Celtic Christians, we should offer blessings and prayers of protection for our world, but we also should remember that words spoken with love have a tremendous power — especially in the digital realm — to help calm voices raised in hatred and anger. In these ways, we will restore the positive presence and message of Christ's cross in a world that often dismisses it as a symbol of intolerance or ignorance.

For prayer and reflection:
[1] Separately, ponder Psalm 22: 1-11, 23-31 and John 18: 28 - John 19: 16. What are your feelings as you consider Christ's trial and crucifixion? How does his demeanor during the passion affect you? Why does Christ pray Psalm 22 on the cross?
[2] In *The Celtic Way of Prayer*, Esther De Waal claims:

"For our ancestors, trees were not merely natural objects, they were majestic signs of the connectedness of the heaven and the earth. They saw the pattern of the immense root system that bound the tree to the earth, and then above it that immense system of arms and handlike leaves stretching out into the sky above, and the trunk itself standing there so strongly, the axis that bound the underworld with the upper world, the human with the divine, the earthly with the spiritual, the world itself with God. So when Christ was lifted up from the earth and displayed spreadeagled on a dead tree set up on a hill, the ancient archetype of the tree of life suddenly blazed out in living historical actuality, fulfilled once and for all, and the primeval myth of the sacred tree-ladder connecting God with the world, the divine with the earthly, suddenly found real and historical expression — for there is an actual tree, the cross of the crucifixion, connecting us with God and God with us, once and for all, in the figure of Christ — Christ the axis of history."[52]

***

52   Esther De Waal, *The Celtic Way of Prayer*, pages 148-149.

Paul Coutinho points out in An Ignatian Pathway *that, "The cross is a symbol of what the Most Holy Trinity is all about. For Ignatius, God created the world by pouring all that is Divine into every creature. Redemption is the*

How did Christ's death on the cross change you and your history? What feelings and emotions do you feel when you consider Christ dying for you? How might you share these changes and feelings with others?

[3] In your imagination, see Christ crucified on an actual tree. Look at the leaf-covered branches spreading out above him and the roots below him. Take a moment to contemplate each part of this image. Then, watch as a crowd gathers around the base of the tree. As you watch them crying, imagine their tears falling into the soil before flowing into the roots of the tree and up the trunk through Christ to the branches where they flower into distinct leaves. Recognize that these are the saints who offered themselves to Christ, building the kingdom of God as their needs and desires are transformed by Christ's cross into graces for others. Now, approach the tree and allow your tears to nourish it and blossom into leaves. What do you see? Write a litany or prayerful poem to the crucified Christ offering yourself to his service, making each tear you shed a particular desire or need that blossoms into a specific action.

---

kenosis, *or the self-emptying, of the Son. It is through the outpouring of the Holy Spirit that we are sanctified." (page 63) For this reason, after asking the person to consider his or her sins and forgiveness by a loving God, Ignatius presents a meditation on the Trinity in the* Spiritual Exercises *before considering Christ's earthly life and death. Ignatius does not directly invoke the Trinity again until after the resurrection in the Contemplation to Attain the Love of God (#230-237), although he does direct the person receiving the Exercises to make a special colloquy (or conversation) involving both the Son and the Father while considering his or her invitation to share in Christ's redemptive mission.*

VIII • THE ISLAND OF PAUL THE HERMIT

After many months on the sea, Saint Brendan and his brothers come to another island where they are welcomed by a hermit named Paul. After recounting his own spiritual journey, Paul the Hermit tells holy Brendan the final things he and his companions must do to come to the Land of the Saints.

(THE ISLAND OF PAUL THE HERMIT) Saint Brendan and his comrades sailed towards the south, glorifying God in all. On the third day there appeared to them a small island far away. ... When his brothers had begun to row faster and they had come near the island. Saint Brendan said to them:

'Men, brothers, do not tire your bodies overmuch. You have enough toil. It is seven years to the coming Easter since we left our fatherland. You will now see Paul the spiritual Hermit, who has lived in this island for sixty years without any bodily food. For the previous thirty years he got food from an animal.'

When they had got to the shore they could not find a landing-place because of the height of the cliff. The island was small and circular — about two hundred yards in circumference. There was no earth on it, but it looked a naked rock like flint. It was as long as it was broad and as it was high. When they had rowed around the island they discovered a landing-place so narrow that it could scarcely take the prow of the boat and disembarkation was very difficult. Saint Brendan then said to his brothers:

'Wait here until I return to you. You may not go on land without permission from the man of God who lives in this spot.'

When the venerable father had come to the top of the island, he saw two caves, the entrance of one facing the entrance of the other, on the side of the island facing east. He also saw a minuscule spring, round like a plate, flowing from the rock before the entrance to the cave where the soldier of Christ lived. When the spring overflowed, the rock immediately absorbed the water. When Saint Brendan had come near the door of one of the caves, the elder came out to meet him from the other, saying:

'How good and joyful it is that brothers live together.'

When he said this he requested Saint Brendan to order all the brothers to come from the boat. As they embraced him and sat down he called each of them by his own name. When the brothers heard this, they greatly wondered not only at his power of divining, but also at his dress. For he was entirely covered by his hair from his head and beard and other hair down to his feet, and all the hair was white as snow on account of his great age. They could see only his face and eyes. He had no other clothing on him except the hair that grew from his body. When Saint Brendan saw this he was discouraged within himself and said:

'Alas for me who wear a monk's habit and have many owing allegiance to me by virtue of being monks: Here I see sitting before me a man already in the angelic state, untouched by the vices of the body, although he is still in human flesh.'

The man of God said to him:

'Venerable father, how great and marvellous are the wonders that God has shown you that he did not show to any of the holy fathers! You say in your heart that you are not worthy to carry the habit of a monk. But you are greater than a monk! A monk uses the labour of his hands with which to clothe himself. But God from his own secret supplies feeds and clothes both you and your companions for seven years. And I, unhappy, sit here like a bird on this rock, naked but for my hair.'

Saint Brendan then questioned him on his coming and where he came from and for how long he had endured such a life there. The other answered him.

'I was brought up in the monastery of Saint Patrick for fifty years where I looked after the cemetery of the brothers. One day, when my director had pointed out to me the place to bury one who had died, an unknown elder appeared to me and said: "Do not make a grave there, brother, for it is the burial place of another." I said to him: "Father, who are you?" He said: "Why do you not recognize me? Am I not your abbot?" I said to him: "Saint Patrick, my abbot?" He replied: "I am he. I died yesterday. That is the place of my burial. Make the grave of our brother here and tell no one what I have told you. But go tomorrow to the sea shore. There you will find a boat. Embark in it and it will bring you to the spot where you will await the day of your death."

'In the morning I went, in accordance with the holy father's command, to the shore and found exactly what he had told me I would find. When I had embarked, I sailed for three days and three nights. After that I let the boat go wherever the wind would drive it. Then on the seventh day this rock appeared to me. I got on to it immediately, letting the boat go and kicking it with my foot so that it would go back to where it came from. Straightaway I saw it ploughing waves like furrows through the plains of the sea so as to return to its home. But I stayed here. About three o'clock in the afternoon an otter brought me a meal from the sea, that is, one fish in his mouth. He also brought a small bundle of firewood to make a fire, carrying it between his front paws while walking on his two hind legs. When he had put the fish and kindling in front of me he returned where he came from. I took iron, struck flint, made a fire from the kindling and made a meal for myself on the fish. Thus it was for thirty years — always every third day the same servant brought the same food, that is one fish, to do for three days. … Then after thirty years I found these two caves and this well. For sixty years since, I have lived on this well without nourishment of any other food. I have been ninety years on this island, living on fish for thirty years and on the food afforded by the well for sixty. I lived for fifty years in my native land. The sum of the years of my life until now is one hundred and forty. Here I have but to await in the flesh, as I have been assured, the day of *my judgment. Go then to your native land, and bring with you vessels filled with water from this well. You must do this since you have a journey before you of forty days, which will take you till Holy Saturday. You will celebrate Holy Saturday and Easter Sunday and the holy days of Easter where you have celebrated them for the last six years. You will then, having received the blessing of your steward, set out for the Promised Land of the Saints. There you will stay for forty days and then the God of your fathers will bring you safe and sound to the land of your birth.'*

~ excerpted from The Voyage of Saint Brendan,
translated by John J. O'Meara, pp. 60-65

"Welcoming Others into the Resurrection"

In their journey, Brendan and his fellow monks encountered many wondrous things but none would have inspired as much awe as meeting Paul the Hermit. In addition to seeing God care for their own needs during their travels, the companions had seen the mysterious ways God provided for Ailbe's silent community. They also saw God's mercy demonstrated in their encounters with the angelic singing birds and with the suffering Judas. But in Paul the Hermit, Brendan and his companions met someone who relied entirely on the care and mercy of God as he lived in self-chosen exile on a barren island — first being brought food by an otter before God's grace allowed him to subsist on the periodic output of the island's single spring. An ethereal presence clothed only in his long white hair, nourished solely by the living water of God, Paul radiated the devotion of a life lived entirely in God's beneficence.

Dependent on God in every aspect of his life, Paul the Hermit epitomized the goal toward which Brendan and his companions aspired. "The ultimate point of spiritual wandering was to 'seek the place of one's resurrection,'" Philip Sheldrake explains in *Living Between Worlds*, "This involves seeking to enter the Kingdom of God more easily by means of living in the world as a stranger for Christ's sake. This 'place of resurrection' was the place appointed by God for the particular wanderer to settle and spend the remaining years of life doing penance and waiting for death."[53] Yet, there is no sorrow or reclusiveness in Paul's solitude. He joyfully welcomes the travelers — proclaiming simply, "How good and joyful it is that brothers live together." — before encouraging Brendan to persevere in his own pilgrimage and offering the companions water from his holy spring to nourish them in their journey. Having become a stranger to this earthly world, Paul happily shares the spiritual gifts he received by living solely in God's redeemed realm.

Yet, despite his kindness towards Brendan and his companions, Paul sought to live alone with Christ in his "place of resurrection". "The ascetic went freely away from [the]   protection [of a supportive community] and out into the wild to the place of demons to combat them and to the place of wild beasts to wrestle with sensual appetites," Philip Sheldrake writes, noting, "The real test of faith was to turn one's back on the security of kin. The abandonment of homeland, friends, original religious community, and above all family was looked upon as an outstanding sacrifice."[54] Alone, Paul the Hermit and other ascetics

---

[53]   Philip Sheldrake, *Living Between Worlds*, page 59.

In the final section of the Spiritual Exercises, *Ignatius asks the person to contemplate the resurrection — noting "how the divine nature, which in the Passion seemed to go into hiding, now in this holy resurrection appears and reveals itself so miraculously in its true and most holy effects" (#223) — and to consider the ways that God dwells and works in all of creation in The Contemplation to Attain the Love of God (#230-237). This recognition of redeemed creation — seen as both accomplished and continuing — invites a response of love and self-sacrifice that nurtures a desire to serve God in all things in whatever manner or place God desires, which Ignatius directs the person receiving the Exercises to express in the following prayer:*

"Take Lord and receive all my liberty, my memory, my understanding and my entire will, all that I have and possess. You gave it all to me; to you I return it. All is yours, dispose of it entirely according to your will. Give me only the love of you, together with your grace for that is enough for me." (#234)

[54]   Philip Sheldrake, *Living Between Worlds*, page 65.

In Spiritual Freedom, *John English explains that the person's desire to offer his or her complete self to God's service does not rely on knowledge — it flows naturally from the graces shaping the Ignatian Exercises, which lead a person from the awareness that they are a loved sinner to the liberation of living in the hope of Jesus' resurrection: "Our inability to know God's desire is*

like him continued the penitential journeys they began in their monasteries. But now, with Christ himself as their *anamchara* (or "soul friend"), they uprooted their deepest temptations, sins and failings in order to create a spiritual space — within themselves and in the world around them — where the presence of the living Christ might flourish.

So, like the Celtic monastery, the "place of resurrection" created an enclave of heaven in this world that gave witness to the loving presence of God. The ascetic pilgrims went out into the wilderness alone, assured of God's protection by the words of Psalm 91: "Because you have made the Lord your refuge, the Most High your dwelling place, no evil shall befall you, no scourge come near your tent. For he will command his angels concerning you to guard you in all your ways."[55] When their journey brought them to an appropriate place, something they would discern through their prayer, these holy wanderers settled into a new life of penance as they sought the presence of the resurrected Christ within themselves while also testifying to God's promise that, in the words of Psalm 91, "Those who love me, I will deliver; I will protect those who know my name. When they call to me, I will answer them; I will be with them in trouble, I will rescue them and honor them. With long life I will satisfy them, and show them my salvation."[56]

The testimony of the "place of resurrection" remains as important today as centuries ago, but it must be expressed in a way that speaks to our deepest aspirations — and those of our neighbors — while also confronting the forces of darkness and evil still threatening

---

not the most troubling problem. The hardest problem to overcome is our lack of freedom, indifference, and detachment. When I use the word indifference, *I do not mean that we should be indifferent to people; nor does the word* detachment *mean that we should be detached, unfeeling, unresponsive persons. Rather, I am speaking of freedom from everything that is not God — being solely oriented to Jesus Christ. This is the basic freedom we hope to obtain through the Exercises. In fact, it is an experience of grace. Once people have this kind of freedom, God's desire is very clear to them. Moreover, this freedom is often accompanied by the strength to do God's will. It is a difficult thing to accept from God, and this is the conquest of self that Ignatius outlines for us in the context of grace." (pages 20-21)*

[55]   Psalm 91: 9-11.

[56]   Psalm 91: 14-16.

our world. The early Celtic Christians admired the pilgrims who left their homes and families to be alone with God in the wilderness but, in our times, the call to live as hermits has become extremely rare and would be dismissed as eccentric in most modern societies. Still, our communities and cultures continue to admire individuals willing to risk ridicule and pain for the sake of seemingly impossible ideals. So, as we look at our own lives and at the world around us, Christians must have the faith and courage to heal the wounds of Christ we find there — in ourselves and in those around us — so we may to show others God's redemptive activity of renewing hope and reviving the possibility of a positive future. These are the "places of resurrection" in our world.

As we strive to find these situations of renewal, it is important to remember that each "place of resurrection" remains completely unique — an invitation to a new life particular to each person. For the Celtic saints, as David Adam reminds us in *A Desert in the Ocean*, the discovery of one's personal resurrection "was not somewhere after death but to be found in this world when they fulfilled their vocation. The place of their resurrection is the place where God's will is fulfilled."[57] So, just as the scriptural resurrection accounts show the risen Christ revealing himself in different ways to different disciples, Christ invites each of us into our own "place of resurrection" by unveiling something familiar within it — something that reflects the way in which he first touched and transformed our lives. Then, Christ gently leads us away from our previous identities through prayer to new

---

[57]   David Adam, *A Desert in the Ocean: God's Call to Adventurous Living* (London: Society for Promoting Christian Knowledge, 2000), page 99.

In Spiritual Freedom, *John English affirms, "Through the Holy Spirit dwelling in us, God's offering becomes the means to participate in the love of the Trinity — a love that can be expressed as an offering of one person to another. Thus, God our Creator offers us the Spirit in the Word and through the Word. Jesus, who is the Word made flesh, receives all and offers it back to God our Creator in the Word and in all creatures. This giving and receiving of persons is the very gift of the Spirit, the full expression of free-covenanted love. The Spirit is given interiorly to human beings and moves them to share in the love relationship of the Trinity." (page 238) By sharing in this mystery through an act of complete self-giving, men and women become hopeful signs of Christ's resurrection in a troubled world.*

lives that reveal the unique ways in which each of us is called to contribute to the building of God's kingdom.

This transformative encounter with the risen Christ awakens us to a new yet familiar sense of connection with other people and with the world at large. By learning how Christ bears our own wounds — healing them through his cross and resurrection — we also become aware of the ways in which Christ mends the wounds of others, inviting us to share in that redemptive process by reaching out to help our neighbors and erstwhile strangers. Our experience of the living Christ also opens us to a deeper affinity with the nonhuman realms of creation as we recognize our kinship with all of God's creatures. While remaining in the material world into which we were born, we increasingly come to see ourselves as "citizens of heaven" through our shared inheritance as children of God. As David Adam says, "When we come to the place of our resurrection we also know that we have come home, we have arisen and come to our Father."[58]

This does not mean, however, we have achieved perfection. We continue to be limited by our human frailties, and we occasionally will fall back into sin. But Christ remains with us when we falter, forgiving our failings and empowering us to move forward through his love. "This resurrection is not a one-off event but happens to us time and again," David Adam notes, counseling, "Time and again we will wander from God and from life, time and again we will fail to do his will and stand outside of his kingdom, and our God awaits our return. God waits to renew, refresh and restore us."[59] This gives us the courage

---

[58]   David Adam, *A Desert in the Ocean*, page 99.

In Stretched for Greater Glory, *George Aschenbrenner explains Ignatius' experience of "coming home" to God: "Ignatius found his way through the swirling waves and blustery winds of his heart. As he learned to read the signs properly, and overeager application of self became a wholehearted, watchful readiness for the greater glory revealed* de arriba *[from above] by the Divine Majesty. Once the greater glory was revealed, his humble freedom always found courage to follow anywhere in God's creation, because he knew he was never, never alone. This greater glory took him, and will continue to take Ignatian followers, to some very unlikely places." (page 202)*

[59]   David Adam, *A Desert in the Ocean*, page 99.

In Ignatian spirituality, the resurrection occurs with every recognition of God's renewing activity in creation. This recognition allows a person to pray

become instruments of God's redemptive love, welcoming friend and stranger alike into the "places of resurrection" through our acts of kindness and love — creating enclaves of heaven that contradict the violence and despair that surrounds us and offering hope to a wounded world.

For prayer and reflection:
[1] Separately, reflect on Psalm 91: 1-16 and John 20: 1-18. What are the concrete ways in which God protects you, in your personal choices and in your relationship to others? How does Christ's resurrection change your understanding of these divine protections? Does the resurrection change how you should behave in the world?
[2] David Adam points out in *The Cry of the Deer*:

> *"It is once we have learned to be at home with God that we are at home anywhere. The Celtic pilgrims were not restless, but restless until they found the place where he wanted them to be. Once they found his presence in the place, they sought to dwell there and let him be revealed there. In our turn, each person has to find his own place. Once found, we then are able to discover him in all places. There must be a starting place, but there is no end."*[60]

"Take and Receive" (from The Contemplation to Attain the Love of God) again and again, creating an ongoing cycle of renewal and oblation — a relationship of love between the human person and the Divine Majesty (a term Ignatius uses to refer both to Christ and to the Trinity). As John English suggests in Spiritual Freedom, *"The Contemplation to Attain the Love of God can be the basis of all prayer for contemplatives as they return to the scene of their daily activities. In spiritual direction, this meditation can become the pivotal point for self-awareness and self-realization — the covenant with God that underlies every choice, flows into every act, and finds God in all persons and in all things." (page 238)*

[60]   David Adam, *The Cry of the Deer*, pages 145-146.

In Stretched For Greater Glory, *George Aschenbrenner describes the Ignatian ideal of living as a companion of the Risen Christ: "A pilgrim mystic always on the road, aglow with thankfulness in the midst of all the gifts, serves in company with the risen Jesus. That great Faithful Witness is always present, with an intimacy and fidelity beyond imagining, until the final stretching of the*

Where do you find the presence of the resurrected Christ in your life and world? How does your recognition of this "place of resurrection" affect you, emotionally and spiritually? Do you feel called to any particular actions when you encounter this place?

[3] Remember a special time or place in which you strongly felt God's living presence. In your imagination, place yourself there and look around at the objects and people that you see. Allow yourself to remember this place or time and to relive your experiences there. Take a moment to consider what made this particular time or place unique, noting whether you felt God touch you through what you gave to others or from what you received. Then, see the resurrected Christ standing in front of you and speak to him in a casual and friendly manner about these experiences and your need to find a new place where you might encounter these feelings again. When you are finished, write a short prayerful poem asking God to help you find this new place of resurrection.

Holy Spirit for a greater glory, then dazzlingly ablaze in the eternity of God." *(page 202) In Ignatian spirituality, companionship with the risen Christ becomes a person's "place of resurrection" and opens him or her to whatever forms of loving service God desires — wherever that service is needed — in the hope of contributing to the ongoing redemption of creation.*

IX • THE PROMISED LAND OF THE SAINTS
& THE RETURN HOME

After leaving the island of Paul the Hermit, Saint Brendan and his companions sail to the south and return to some of the places they had visited before. After celebrating Easter and Pentecost, Saint Brendan and his brothers are guided to the Promised Land of the Saints — and then commanded to return home.

(THE ISLAND OF SHEEP, JASCONIUS AND THE PARADISE OF BIRDS AGAIN) Saint Brendan, … and his brothers, having received the blessing of the man of God, began to sail towards the south for the whole of Lent. Their boat was carried hither and thither, and their only food was the water which they had got on the island of the man of God. This they took every third day and, remaining untouched by hunger or thirst, all were joyful.

Then, as the man of God had foretold, they came to the island of the steward on Holy Saturday. As they arrived at the landing-place he came to meet them with great joy, and helped each of them out of the boat on his arm. When they had finished the divine office for the holy day, he spread supper before them. When evening came they embarked in their boat and the steward came with them.

When they had set sail they found the fish immediately in his usual place. There they sang praise to God all night and Masses in the morning. When Mass was over, however, Jasconius began to go his own way, and all the brothers who were with Saint Brendan began to call on the Lord, saying:

'Hear us, God, our Saviour, our hope throughout all the boundaries of the earth and in the distant sea.'

Saint Brendan comforted his brothers, saying:
'Do not be afraid. You will suffer no evil. Help for the journey is upon us.'

The fish went in a straight course to the shore of the island of the birds. There they stayed until the octave of Pentecost.

When the season of feast-days was over, the steward, who was with them, said to Saint Brendan:

'Embark in your boat and fill your water vessels from this well. This time I shall be the companion and guide of your journey. Without me you will not be able to find the Promised Land of the Saints.'

As they embarked in the boat, all the birds that were on the island began to say as it were with one voice:

'May God, the salvation of all of us, prosper your journey.'

(THE PROMISED LAND OF THE SAINTS) Saint Brendan and those who were with him sailed to the island of the steward, who was with them, and there they took on board provision for forty days. Their voyage was for forty days towards the east. The steward went to the front of the boat and showed them the way. When the forty days were up, as the evening drew on, a great fog enveloped them, so that one of them could hardly see another. The steward, however, said to Saint Brendan:

'Do you know what fog that is?'

Saint Brendan replied:

'What?'

Then the other said:

'That fog encircles the island for which you have been searching for seven years.'

After the space of an hour a mighty light shone all around them again and the boat rested on the shore.

On disembarking from the boat they saw a wide land full of trees bearing fruit as in autumn time. When they had gone in a circle around that land, night had still not come on them. They took what fruit they wanted and drank from the wells and so for the space of forty days they reconnoitred the whole land and could not find the end of it. But one day they came upon a great river flowing through the middle of the island. Then Saint Brendan said to his brothers:

'We cannot cross this river and we do not know the size of this land.'

They had been considering these thoughts within themselves when a youth met them and embraced them with great joy and, calling each by his name, said:

'Happy are they that live in your house. They shall praise you from generation to generation.'

When he said this, he spoke to Saint Brendan:

'There before you lies the land which you have sought for a long time. You could not find it immediately because God wanted to show you his varied secrets in the great ocean. Return, then, to the land of your birth, bringing with you some of the fruit of this land and as many of the precious stones as your boat can carry. The final day of your pilgrimage draws near so that you may sleep with your fathers. After the passage of many times this land will become known to your successors, when persecution of the Christians shall have come. The river that you see divides the island. Just as this land appears to you ripe with fruit, so shall it remain always without any shadow of night. For its light is Christ.'

Saint Brendan with his brothers, having taken samples of the fruits of the land and all of its varieties of precious stones, took his leave of the blessed steward and the youth. He then embarked in his boat and began to sail through the middle of the fog. When they had passed through it, they came to the island called the Island of Delights. They availed themselves of three days' hospitality there and then, receiving a blessing, Saint Brendan returned home directly.

(RETURN HOME AND DEATH OF SAINT BRENDAN) The brothers received him with thanksgiving, glorifying God who was unwilling that they should be deprived of seeing so lovable a father by whose absence they were for so long orphaned. Then the blessed man, commending them for their love, told them everything that he remembered happening on his journey and the great and marvellous wonders God deigned to show him.

Finally he mentioned also the speed of his approaching death — emphasizing its certainty — according to the prophecy of the youth in the Promised Land of the Saints. The outcome proved this to be correct. For when he had made all arrangements for after his death, and a short time had intervened, fortified by the divine sacraments, he migrated from among the hands of his disciples in glory to the Lord, to whom is honour and glory from generation to generation.

~ excerpted from The Voyage of Saint Brendan,
translated by John J. O'Meara, pp. 65-70

"Treasuring the Gifts of Pilgrimage"

As Brendan comes to the end of his journey, it is disconcerting that he does not remain in the place he sought for so long. Instead, he explores it with his companions until they reach a river they cannot cross. Then, when a messenger tells him that he has fulfilled his quest and should return to his monastery, Brendan gathers some fruit and precious gems from the island before going home with his companions. While the Celtic pilgrims most often were expected to take permanent refuge in the places prepared for them by God, Brendan carries his place of resurrection with him and finds his purpose in giving testimony to his experiences while on pilgrimage. This seems to repeat the experience of Barrind, who inspired Brendan's journey, until we recognize a key difference between the two saints — Barrind did not know how he reached the Island of Saints since he was taken there by his former student as a spiritual gift, while Brendan deliberately sought out that blessed land with God's guidance and could share the details of his journey with others.

Through this deliberate choice, Brendan's pilgrimage expressed a desire at the core of Celtic spirituality — "leaving one's country for God and forsaking a life of comfort and ease for one of austerity and virtue."[61] It also reflected the early Celtic Christian understanding that any spiritual journey needed to be undertaken for the correct reasons. In *The Celtic Way*, for example, Ian Bradley observes that the medieval Book of Lismore (a collection of saints' lives) praised the renunciation of home and family to follow God's leadings "as the highest [spiritual] calling of all."[62] It also praised individuals who desired to abandon the comforts of home and hearth to seek God on pilgrimage while being

---

[61]   Ian Bradley, *The Celtic Way*, page 80.

Like the Celtic saints, Ignatius advocates a radical following of Christ in the Spiritual Exercises, *saying "in order to imitate Christ our Lord and to be actually more like him, I want and choose poverty with Christ poor rather than wealth, and humiliations with Christ humiliated rather than fame, and I desire more to be thought worthless and a fool for Christ, who first was taken to be such, rather than to be esteemed as wise and prudent in this world." (#167)*

[62]   Ian Bradley, *The Celtic Way*, page 80.

While the acceptance of poverty and public humiliation was seen as a possible consequence of following Christ, Ignatius makes it clear that these possibilities are only to be accepted if they serve God's glory, suggesting that the person receiving the Spiritual Exercises *say in prayer, "My resolute wish and desire, and my considered determination — on the sole condition that this be for your greater service and praise —is to imitate you in enduring every kind of insult and abuse, and utter poverty both actual and spiritual, if your most holy majesty wishes to choose me and receive me into that life and state." (#98)*

unable fulfill this calling because of their other responsibilities. But it condemned those leaving country and kin without an inner conversion — from a simple desire for adventure — as "a waste of time and energy"[63] that would never lead to God.

The proper spiritual disposition toward pilgrimage was as important as the journey itself. As Ian Bradley notes, "To be a pilgrim was to live in imitation of Jesus, to take up his cross and to recognize that in this transitory world we have no abiding city."[64] So, Brendan's example encouraged and sanctified anyone willing to embrace the self-abandonment intrinsic to pilgrimage, whether they made an actual journey or not. By leaving Clonfert to find the Land of the Saints, Brendan consecrated the bold spiritual travelers buffeted on the open seas of pilgrimage. Yet, by returning home at the end of his travels, by making his ultimate "place of resurrection" the monastery that had been his home for many years, Brendan also blessed those men and women who traveled to their personal "place of resurrection" while honoring their obligations to service and hospitality at home.

Brendan's pilgrimage, therefore, also invites modern Christians to deepen in their love for — and dependence upon — God, to courageously go beyond the security of the familiar so that they may discover new possibilities in themselves and in their relationship to the world around them. After all, as David Adam declares in *The Cry of the Deer*, "We have a Creator who brings order out of chaos, a Savior who

---

63   Ian Bradley, The Celtic Way, page 80.

64   Ian Bradley, *The Celtic Way*, pages 80-81.

The graces of the Spiritual Exercises *sustain a person's desire and ability to live as a companion of the risen Christ by accepting his or her birthright as a "citizen of heaven," both separating the person from our transitory world through his or her liberation from the power of sin and calling him or her to share the hope of Christ's resurrection with others through a life of service. As George Aschenbrenner describes in* Stretched For Greater Glory, *"For Ignatius the extraordinary inner experience of divine love stretches the mystic to a pilgrimage for service in specific details of time and place. The incendiary power within the service is a gratitude — reverent, gracious, faithful — as in the risen Jesus, himself missioned to service from the heart of the Trinity. To love as God loves: it is the invitation of Ignatius because, first of all, it is the invitation of God in the risen Jesus. Therefore, the religious experience at the heart of Ignatian spirituality is a pilgrim mysticism of service." (page 135)*

offers life beyond the many deaths and hells of this world, a Spirit who breathes life into the inanimate; we should therefore be able to walk with a little more confidence."[65] For these reasons, he continues, "We should be the adventurers and explorers. We can live where people take the fullness of life seriously, and yet see that it is not a tragedy. We are able to face the full range and depth of human experience because we are not alone."[66] Through our shared experience of God's love, all Christians should have the faith to say boldly as pilgrims, "I walk before the Lord in the land of the living."[67]

Like the early Celtic Christians, our shared vocation to live an adventurous faith takes many different forms. Some leave their homes and families so they may offer bold public gestures of their faith in the broader world, while others serve Christ quietly within their families and local communities. Yet, at the heart of every Christian life, there should be a willingness to surrender personal desire or comfort in order to express the presence of the risen Christ through our lives and to build

---

[65]   David Adam, *The Cry of the Deer*, page 117.

[66]   David Adam, *The Cry of the Deer*, page 117.

For Ignatius, sharing in the cross and resurrection of Christ through the Spiritual Exercises *also empowers a person to confront a world marked by tragedy and suffering with new confidence and optimism. As Paul Coutinho explains in* An Ignatian Pathway, *"For Ignatius, the Resurrection is an experience that is known by its effects. Words cannot describe the experience, but our lives speak louder than our words. How can we describe the taste of sugar? Our responses to life's challenges are totally different. We become like a caterpillar that has woven its cocoon and then bursts forth into a beautiful butterfly. In this new existence, a butterfly can now sit unaffected on the thorns of life and make the thorns look more beautiful. The butterfly sits on the roses of life and is not affected by the thorns, but enhances the beauty of the roses… The Resurrection is the Divine presence and glory that is manifested in all of creation." (page 129)*

As companions of the risen Christ, men and women willingly share in the pain of others — and strive to alleviate that suffering — while also experiencing the liberating and healing power of Christ's resurrection that allows them to experience these things without being overwhelmed by despair, living as signs of hope as they radiate their changed nature to the world and people around them.

[67]   Psalm 116: 9.

enclaves of God's kingdom in the world around us. As we become strangers in the world for Christ's sake, as we deliberately embrace our diverse callings to holy wandering, we must have the courage to venture away from the comfortable and the familiar knowing that Christ walks with us as we seek our personal "place of resurrection," giving us the confidence to help the people we find there — whether family, neighbors or strangers — while God uses us as instruments of love and compassion in an all-too-often indifferent world.

As we strive to become signs of resurrection in our world, modern Christians should consider another spiritual gift we receive from the Celtic saints — their use of the imagination to illuminate the inner workings of God's presence in the world. The Celts "excelled at expressing their faith in symbols, metaphors and images, both visual and poetic," Ian Bradley observed in *The Celtic Way*, "They had the ability to invest the ordinary and the commonplace with sacramental significance, to find glimpses of God's glory throughout creation and to paint pictures in words, signs and music that acted as icons opening windows on heaven and pathways to eternity."[68] These creative gifts remain as important today as they were centuries ago, especially as suspicious and often hostile societies marginalize Christians by pointing to our past failings or relegating our religious beliefs to the realms of self-delusion and superstition.

---

[68]   Ian Bradley, *The Celtic Way*, page 84.

As in ancient Celtic Christianity, the Ignatian ideal of "finding God in all things" imbues the ordinary objects and events of daily life with profound spiritual significance since they allow men and women to discover — and respond to — the will of God. As George Aschenbrenner observes in Stretched for Greater Glory, *"The heart of mysticism is always an extraordinary gift from God, but the external expression of a mystical experience varies greatly. For Ignatius the external expression is as ordinary as hard work faithful to the task. The hidden motive of such work, of such service, is the extraordinary inner experience of a mystic: God's ravishing love vibrating in a zealous gratitude." (page 135)*

For practitioners of Ignatian spirituality, the joy of participating in God's redemption of creation often overflows into new and creative forms of expression that communicate a person's experience of God with others — whether through the arts or through forms of prayer and worship extending across cultural or religious boundaries.

Following the example of Brendan and the Celtic saints, especially the holy wanderers, we learn to embrace the uncertainty of traveling into an unknown future while trusting that Christ will never abandon us. But this also challenges us to speak with the same creativity and courage that the early Celtic Christians demonstrated in their spiritual testimonies. As Ian Bradley points out, "Again and again in Celtic Christianity we find the imagination of the artist and the poet being harnessed, not to explain and pin down the mysteries of the faith or open them up on the dissecting table but to suggest and marvel at their infinite depths and subtleties."[69] Like Brendan and the other Celtic saints, we must have the humility to share the struggles that often shape our prayer while confidently presenting the glimpses of heaven we experience in our "places of resurrection" — showing how our faith emerges in response to our redemptive encounters with a loving God who reaches out to transform our lives and communities, not adherence to rigid dogmas protecting us from an uncomfortable world.

For prayer and reflection:
[1] Separately, consider Psalm 116: 1-19 and John 21: 1-14. How do you express your gratitude for God's love for you? Where in your life do you feel God's continuing presence, especially the redemptive power of the resurrection? How do you celebrate these experiences, either with God or with others?
[2] In *The Celtic Way*, Ian Bradley states:
"Celtic Christians took seriously Christ's strictures about laying up treasures on earth where moth and rust will corrupt them. They had a very clear sense of the transience and impermanence of this life and

---

[69]   Ian Bradley, *The Celtic Way*, page 98.

In *An Ignatian Pathway, Paul Coutinho notes, "Ignatian reverence is not a static, distant respect for God but one that comes from an ever-growing intimacy with God. Reverence for Ignatius is one of warm affection and surging emotion that draws a person into union and communion with God at the deepest possible level." (page 45)* Imagination plays a central role in Ignatian prayer – opening individuals to this reverent wonder at God's goodness and generosity – and it has often served as a creative outlet for sharing the fruits of that prayer with others, especially through poetry and music.

of our status in this world being that of pilgrims and strangers. But we should not forget too their clear feel for the essential goodness of the world, their enjoyment of the beauties of creation and their positive and affirmative view of nature, including human nature. They were not people who hated the world and denied its power to lift the human spirit and raise it to God.[70]

Do you celebrate change in the world as an expression of God's continuing renewal or mourn the loss of what has passed away? Are you able to welcome the changes God asks of you on a daily basis? What did these feelings tell you about your relationship with God?

[3] Take a moment to consider a normal day in your life, whether the last day or a day in the last week. Think about the people that you met and the activities which occupied your time. Allow yourself to feel pleasure or sorrow as you bring these memories to mind. Then, imagining that God is with you, slowly remember that day again and

---

[70]   Ian Bradley, *The Celtic Way*, pages 81-82.

Ignatius maintains in one of his letters, "It is to misuse the light of the understanding to keep it busy with things of little account and never apply it to those which are of supreme importance for our happiness. One can thus spend an entire lifetime seeking to pass these few days of our pilgrimage in the midst of honors, wealth, and self-satisfactions, without a thought of that which must be the cause of inestimable and unending riches, honor, prosperity, and satisfaction in our heavenly fatherland." (Letters of St. Ignatius of Loyola, *pages 332-333)*

But, in a letter to priests and seminarians in one of his religious communities, Ignatius also asserts that our earthly pilgrimage should be seen as an opportunity to share in God's redemptive mission as companions of the risen Christ, recommending that the pursuit of spiritual growth be "joined with that virtue which is a compendium of all the others and which Jesus Christ so earnestly recommends when he calls it his especial commandment: 'This is my commandment, that you love one another'," continuing, *"I wish that you preserve this union and lasting love, not only among yourselves, but that you extend it to all, and endeavor to enkindle in your souls the lively desire for the salvation of your neighbor, gauging the value of each soul from the price our Lord paid out of his life's blood."* (Letters of St. Ignatius of Loyola, *page 128)*

Like ancient Celtic Christians, Ignatius believed that we are "citizens of heaven" on a pilgrimage of service as we give witness to the universal hope and transformative power of Christ's resurrection.

take time after each event or meeting to stop the flow of time so you may look at it carefully. As you look at each part of the day, speak with God in a casual manner about the pleasures, concerns or hopes evoked in that particular moment. When you are finished, write a litany or long prayerful poem praising God's activity in the people or events you experienced during your recollected day.

Adam, David. *A Desert in the Ocean: God's Call to Adventurous Living*. London: Society for Promoting Christian Knowledge, 2000.

———. *The Cry of the Deer: Meditations on the Hymn of Saint Patrick*. London: Society for Promoting Christian Knowledge, 1987.

Bradley, Ian. *Celtic Christian Communities: Live the Tradition*. Kelowna, British Columbia: Northstone Publishing, 2000

———. *The Celtic Way*. London: Darton, Longman & Todd Ltd, 1993

Davies, Oliver (ed.), with the collaboration of Thomas O'Loughlin. *Celtic Spirituality*. New York: Paulist Press, 1999.

De Waal, Esther. *The Celtic Way of Prayer: the Recovery of the Religious Tradition*. New York: Image Books, 1997

———. *Every Earthly Blessing: Rediscovering the Celtic Tradition*. Harrisburg, PA: Morehouse Publishing, 1999.

O'Meara, John J. (trans.). *The Voyage of Saint Brendan: Journey to the Promised Land*. Gerrards Cross, Buckinghamshire, UK: Colin Smythe Limited, 1991.

Sheldrake, Philip. *Living Between Worlds: Place and Journey in Celtic Spirituality*. Boston, MA: Cowley Publications, 1995.

A Journey to the Land of the Saints

a Sequence of Prayer Services
adapted from traditional Gaelic prayers
collected in Alexander Carmichael's *Carmina Gadelica*

Considerations

preparing these prayer services for your community

Instructions on downloading the digital files designed to accompany this section may be found in the resources section at the end of this book. These include audio recordings of the selections from *The Voyage of Saint Brendan* and their companion meditations from the previous section (that are presented during these prayer services) as well as a variety of pre-formatted programs for the prayer services (with and without the Eucharistic Prayer).

This sequence of prayer services has been designed to offer a wide range of options to the different communities conducting them. Depending on the various elements you choose to include in them (e.g., Eucharist, silence, music, etc.), these services may range from thirty minutes to an hour in length. So, as you prepare to present these services, you should consider the following concerns:

Selecting Songs for Worship

Before conducting the prayer services, you should discern the various ways in which music might contribute to your experience of them. If your group is large enough to support singing, there are two or three optional hymns included in the services (depending on whether you use the Eucharistic Prayer). There also are periods of silence where you might want to present instrumental music. "Sing and Make Melody to the Lord" (part of the resources section at the end of this book) suggests Celtic hymnals and song collections that you might find useful as well as offers guidelines for coordinating songs to the themes and topics of the prayer services.

Approaching Silence during the Services

These services are intended to be contemplative in nature and contain a number of invitations to silent prayer: short intervals after various readings, reflections and prayers as well as a period of silence around the reading from *The Voyage of Saint Brendan* before the services. You should gauge the comfort level of your community before choosing either to maintain silence during these moments or to present instrumental music during them.

If you decide to use music during these interludes, and you have the necessary resources, it is highly recommended that you use tunes from the songs you choose to sing during earlier prayer services. While there are many different collections of Celtic instrumental music available, this choice will help deepen the participants' experience of prayer by linking the music with the spiritual undercurrents of this sequence of prayer services.

Presenting the Reflective Readings

The two reflective readings used during the service — the selection from *The Voyage of Saint Brendan* (presented prior to the beginning of the service) and the companion meditation (presented during the Word of God, with the possible exception of the final service in the sequence) — may be read by members of your community or presented using the audio files that accompany this book. You should decide which format is best suited to the prayerful rhythms of your community. However, it is highly recommended that these readings be presented in a manner that allows the members of your community to listen reflectively to the readings without being distracted by their presentation.

Adapting the Scriptural Readings and the Lord's Prayer

In deference to the conversational tone of surviving prayers and religious poetry from the early Celtic Christian communities, the Gospel readings and psalms used in these prayer services (as well as the biblical citations embedded in the Eucharistic Prayer and the final Prayers and Blessings) come from the New Revised Standard Version Bible. But, if your community is more comfortable with a more traditional translation, you may choose to use the Authorized Version for the Gospel readings and the Scottish Metrical Psalter for the psalms (which also will preserve the Gaelic quality of the services).

Note: Depending on the practice of your community, you may want to simplify the announcement of the Gospel (by deleting the specific verses to be read) or remove the declaration of the psalm before its recitation. Also, you should consider whether you want to say aloud the biblical references in the Eucharistic Prayer and after the Lord's Prayer.

Also, you may want to substitute another version of the Lord's Prayer (in the "Prayers and Blessings" section of the services) if you believe the biblical rendering presented in this book is too unfamiliar and would present difficulties for your community.

Offering the Scriptural Readings to the Congregation

Depending on the size of the group participating in the prayer services, you may want to offer members of the congregation copies of the scriptural readings. This will allow individuals to prayerfully consider these readings before the services and possibly deepen their participation in them. In smaller groups, if your group chooses to elicit reflections and prayers from the community, this would also help the members of the congregation to clarify any thoughts they might wish to share after the Gospel or during the personal petitions at the end of the prayer services.

Providing Reflective Readings to Participants

Some individuals may decide to complete the cycle of spiritual readings described earlier in this book or conduct the retreat presented in *A Pilgrimage to the Land of the Saints* while participating in the prayer services. It is recommended that they purchase the appropriate guidebook since these provide instructions and follow-up suggestions designed to enrich the different spiritual journeys that parallel the prayer services.

However, for various reasons, you may want to provide copies of the readings from *The Voyage of Saint Brendan* and their companion meditations to these individuals. If so, the permission agreements for this book require that you offer these materials without charging a fee of any sort.

Including the Eucharistic Prayer

You should decide whether you plan to use the Eucharistic Prayer during these prayer services. If you do, you will need a member of the clergy to consecrate the elements — either during the service or prior to it — and decide how to preserve them in a respectful manner during the course of each service. So, you may need to find a small tabernacle in which to place the Eucharistic elements or (depending on your spiritual tradition) place them near the focal point of your chapel or prayer room until they are needed during communion.

I • BARRIND'S STORY

The members of the community enter and pray in silence. After the community is fully assembled, the prelude should be presented.

Prelude   "Barrind's Story"
                    (*from* The Voyage of Saint Brendan, *translated by John J. O'Meara*)

> The legendary journey of Saint Brendan, who came to be known as 'The Navigator', begins with an amazing story told one evening by a visitor to the saint's abbey.

A period of silent meditation follows the reading before the leader begins the penitential prayers.

Penitential Prayers

A bell rings and the members of the community kneel. If anyone cannot kneel, they should remain seated with their head bowed.

Leader   We bend our knees
All   *(making the sign of the cross)*
                in the eye of the Father who created us,
                in the eye of the Son who purchased us,
                in the eye of the Spirit who cleansed us.
                Amen.

All stand.

Leader   Lord Jesus Christ,
                give us the grace of repentance;
                give us the grace of earnestness;
                give us the grace of submission.
Community   **Give us the strength and courage to confess our guilt**
                as earnestly as were this the moment of our death.
Leader   Lord Jesus,
                you are shade to those in the heat;
                you are shelter to those in the cold;
                you are a well to those in the desert.

	Lord Jesus, have mercy on us.
Community	**Lord Jesus, have mercy on us.**
Leader	Christ Jesus,
	you are eyes to those who are blind;
	you are ears to those who are deaf;
	you are health to those who are ailing.
	Christ Jesus, have mercy on us.
Community	**Christ Jesus, have mercy on us.**
Leader	Lord Jesus,
	you are the joy of all joyous things;
	you are the beam of the sun in the day;
	you are the guiding star in the night.
	Lord Jesus, have mercy on us.
Community	**Lord Jesus, have mercy on us.**
Leader	Lord Jesus Christ,
	with the Father who created us and the Spirit that cleansed us,
	Purify our hearts, make holy our souls and confirm our faith,
	keep safe our minds and compass our bodies all about.
	Enfold us…
Community	**… and surround us.**
Leader	Guide our speech…
Community	**… and our thoughts.**
Leader	Guard us in our sleeping…
Community	**… and in our waking.**
Leader	Nurture us in our watching…
Community	**… and in our hoping.**
Leader	Shield us in our lives…
Community	**… and grant us peace in eternity.**
Leader	Holy God,
	Father, Son and Spirit,
	pour down upon us from heaven
	the rich blessing of your forgiveness.
	Be patient with us and grant to us
	the fear of God, the love of God, and your affection
	so we may do your will on earth at all times …
Community	**… as the angels and saints do in heaven.**
Leader	Holy God,
	Father, Son and Spirit,

	pour down upon us from heaven
	the rich blessing of your peace.
	Peace between nations …
Community	**… peace between neighbors.**
Leader	Peace between kindred …
Community	**… peace between lovers.**
Leader	Peace between persons injured …
Community	**… peace between foes.**
Leader	Holy God,
	Father, Son and Spirit,
	help us to love and bless your creation,
	all that we see, all that we hear, all that we touch.
	Let us share your peace with our fellow creatures at all times,
	living as signs of forgiveness and reconciliation on the earth …
All	**… as the angels and saints do in heaven:**
	without malice, without jealousy, without envy,
	without fear, without terror of anyone under the sun.
	And may the Father, the Son and the Spirit
	kindle in our hearts the flame of love to our neighbors,
	to our foes, to our friends, to our kindred all,
	to the brave, to the knave, to the thrall.
Leader	The peace of the Father of Joy,
	the peace of Christ the Lamb,
	the peace of the Spirit of Grace, be with you.
Community	**The peace of the Father of Joy,**
	of Christ the Lamb, and of the Spirit of Grace,
	be with us all.
Leader	Let us share a sign of peace with those present here
	as a testimony to the peace God offers to the world.

The members of the community share a sign of peace before sitting down. A brief period of silence follows before the reader begins the Word of God.

The Word of God

Reader	I set the teachings of Christ before you;
	I set the guarding of God about you.

Community   **May it possess us and protect us all.**

Reader   A reading from the Gospel according to Saint John.

Jesus left Judea and started back to Galilee. But he had to go through Samaria. So he came to a Samaritan city called Sychar, near the plot of ground that Jacob had given to his son Joseph. Jacob's well was there, and Jesus, tired out by his journey, was sitting by the well. It was about noon.

A Samaritan woman came to draw water, and Jesus said to her, "Give me a drink." (His disciples had gone to the city to buy food.) The Samaritan woman said to him, "How is it that you, a Jew, ask a drink of me, a woman of Samaria?" (Jews do not share things in common with Samaritans.) Jesus answered her, "If you knew the gift of God, and who it is that is saying to you, 'Give me a drink,' you would have asked him, and he would have given you living water." The woman said to him, "Sir, you have no bucket, and the well is deep. Where do you get that living water? Are you greater than our ancestor Jacob, who gave us the well, and with his sons and his flocks drank from it?" Jesus said to her, "Everyone who drinks of this water will be thirsty again, but those who drink of the water that I will give them will never be thirsty. The water that I will give will become in them a spring of water gushing up to eternal life." The woman said to him, "Sir, give me this water, so that I may never be thirsty or have to keep coming here to draw water."

Jesus said to her, "Go, call your husband, and come back." The woman answered him, "I have no husband." Jesus said to her, "You are right in saying, 'I have no husband'; for you have had five husbands, and the one you have now is not your husband. What you have said is true!" The woman said to him, "Sir, I see that you are a prophet. Our ancestors worshiped on this mountain, but you say that the place where people must worship is in Jerusalem." Jesus said to her, "Woman, believe me, the hour is coming when you will worship

112

the Father neither on this mountain nor in Jerusalem. You worship what you do not know; we worship what we know, for salvation is from the Jews. But the hour is coming, and is now here, when the true worshipers will worship the Father in spirit and truth, for the Father seeks such as these to worship him. God is spirit, and those who worship him must worship in spirit and truth." The woman said to him, "I know that Messiah is coming" (who is called Christ). "When he comes, he will proclaim all things to us." Jesus said to her, "I am he, the one who is speaking to you."

The gospel of Jesus Christ, source of strength,
Source of salvation, source of healing grace.

Community **May it be a mantle to our bodies.**

A brief silence follows the reading, until the leader begins the psalm.

Leader Psalm 19, Verses 1 through 14.

The heavens are telling the glory of God;
and the firmament proclaims his handiwork.

Community **Day to day pours forth speech,**
and night to night declares knowledge.

Leader There is no speech, nor are there words;
their voice is not heard;

Community **yet their voice goes out through all the earth,**
and their words to the end of the world.

Leader In the heavens he has set a tent for the sun,
which comes out like a bridegroom from his wedding canopy,

Community **and like a strong man runs its course with joy.**

Leader Its rising is from the end of the heavens,
and its circuit to the end of them;

Community **and nothing is hid from its heat.**

Leader The law of the Lord is perfect,
reviving the soul;

Community **the decrees of the Lord are sure,**
making wise the simple.

Leader The precepts of the Lord are right,

	rejoicing the heart;
Community	**the commandment of the Lord is clear,**
	enlightening the eyes.
Leader	The fear of the Lord is pure,
	enduring forever;
Community	**the ordinances of the Lord are true**
	righteous altogether.
Leader	More to be desired are they than gold,
	even much fine gold;
Community	**sweeter also than honey,**
	and drippings of the honeycomb.
Leader	Moreover by them is your servant warned;
	in keeping them there is great reward.
Community	**But who can detect their errors?**
	Clear me from hidden faults.
Leader	Keep back your servant also from the insolent;
	do not let them have dominion over me.
Community	**Then I shall be blameless,**
	and innocent of great transgression.
Leader	Let the words of my mouth and the meditation of my heart
	be acceptable to you,
Community	**O Lord, my rock and my redeemer.**

There is a brief silence after the psalm before reading or presenting the audio version of the following reflection.

Reflection   "Walking with the Celtic Saints"
                                by Timothy J. Ray

A period of silence is observed after the reflection for private meditation, with or without music. Afterward, the leader continues the service — proceeding either to the Eucharistic Prayer or to the Prayers and Blessings after the optional hymn.

Hymn (optional)

Eucharistic Prayer

If the community wishes to share the Eucharist, the table is prepared during the hymn. If there is no hymn, the table should be prepared in silence — slowly and deliberately. Then, the leader begins the Eucharistic Prayer.

Leader	Thanks be to you, Holy Father of Glory, father-kind, ever-loving, ever-powerful, because of all the abundance, favor and deliverance you bestow on us in our need.
Community	**May your name be praised forever, in the heavens above and here on earth.**
Leader	Whatever Providence befalls us as your children, in our portion, in our lot, in our path, give to us with it the riches of your hand and the joyous blessing of your mouth.
Community	**May your kingdom be seen to flourish through the joy of your people, always grateful.**
Leader	In the steep common path of our calling, be it easy or uneasy to our flesh, be it bright or dark for us to follow, your perfect guidance will be upon us.
Community	**Provide for us in all our needs, material and spiritual, this day and every day.**
Leader	Be a shield to us from the wiles of the deceiver, from the arch-destroyer with his arrows pursuing us, and in each secret thought our minds get to weave, guide and protect us.
Community	**Do not allow us to be tossed about by temptations and protect us from all evils that would do us harm.**
Leader	O Loving Christ, who was hanged upon a tree, each day and each night we remember your covenant; in our lying down and rising up, we yield ourselves to your cross, in our lives and our deaths, we seek in you our peace. Each day, may we remember the source of the mercies bestowed on us, gently and generously; each day, may we become fuller in love with you. My brothers and sisters, with St. Paul, I say to you: "I received from the Lord what I also handed on to you, that the Lord Jesus on the night when he was betrayed

took a loaf of bread, and when he had given thanks, he broke it and said, 'This is my body that is for you. Do this in remembrance of me.' In the same way he took the cup also, after supper, saying, 'This cup is the new covenant in my blood. Do this, as often you drink it, in remembrance of me.' For as often as you eat this bread and drink the cup, you proclaim the Lord's death until he comes." (1 Corinthians 11: 23-26)

O Gracious God, *(making the sign of the cross)* your Spirit come upon us, and upon this bread and wine,
so that it might illumine our understanding, kindle our will, incite our love, strengthen our weakness, and enfold our desires.

Community **O Generous Lord,**
cleanse our hearts, make holy our souls,
confirm our faith,
keep safe our minds, encompass our bodies about
so that in our own hearts, we may feel your presence.

Leader O Holy Spirit, of greatest power,
come down upon us and subdue us;
from your glorious mansion in the heavens.
The knee that is stiff, O healer, make pliant,
the heart that is cold, make warm beneath your wing;
guide the soul that is wandering from your path
and it shall not die.
Each thing that is foul, may you cleanse,
each thing that is hard, may you soften with your grace,
each wound that is causing us pain, may you make whole.
Now to the Father who created each creature,
now to the Son who paid ransom for his people,
now to the Holy Spirit, comforter of might:
shield and protect us from every wound.

Community **Encompass the beginning and the end of our race,**
give us courage to sing in glory,
in peace, in rest, in reconciliation.

Leader Come share in the table of the Lord,
source of love for those who cherish his kindness,
source of solace for those who need his forgiveness,

source of hope for those who fear his judgement.
Come share in the table of the Lord.

Community **Where no tear shall be shed,
where death comes no more. Amen.**

The community shares the Eucharist in silence. Afterward, the table is cleared during the hymn. If there is no hymn, the members of the community use this time for private prayer.

Hymn (optional)

Then, the leader continues the service.

Prayers and Blessings

Leader   Praise to the Father,
            praise to the Son,
            praise to the Spirit.
Community   **The three in one.**

All stand.

Leader   Let us pray for the coming of the Kingdom,
            in the words our Lord taught us:
All   **"Our Father in heaven,
            hallowed be your name.
            Your kingdom come.
            Your will be done,
            on earth as it is in heaven.
            Give us this day our daily bread.
            And forgive us our debts,
            as we also have forgiven our debtors.
            And do not bring us to the time of trial,
            but rescue us from the evil one."**
            (Matthew 6: 9-13)
Leader   Thanks be to you, Eternal Father,
            for you have enwrapped our bodies and our souls,
            safeguarding us in the sanctuary of your love ...
Community   **... and sheltering us under the mantle of your care.**
Leader   O God, bless our homesteads and care for all therein.

	Help us to remember those without home or refuge, especially those displaced by war and poverty.
Community	**May we all find refuge in the fellowship of Christ.**
Leader	O God, bless our kindred and protect those who are close to us. Help us also to remember those who are alone, without family or friends.
Community	**May we all find companionship in the fellowship of Christ.**
Leader	O God, bless our words and help them bring joy and comfort to others. Help us also to remember those who are harmed by unkind words and verbal abuse.
Community	**May we all hear the gentle voice welcoming us into the fellowship of Christ.**
Leader	O God, bless us in our errands and protect us in our travels. Help us also to remember those who are lost, walking through life without direction or hope.
Community	**May we all be guided into the fellowship of Christ.**
Leader	O God, lessen our sins and increase our trust in you. Help us also to remember those burdened by guilt and shame, especially those deep in despair.
Community	**May we all find forgiveness in the fellowship of Christ.**
Leader	O God, guard us from distress and protect us from misfortune. Help us also to remember those feeling battered by the turbulence of their lives, whether through their own choices or the actions of others.
Community	**May we all find consolation in the fellowship of Christ.**
Leader	O God, shelter us from harm and aid us in life's struggles, protect us under your shield and guard us from harm, guide us in your ways and clear the paths before us. Be by our knees, by our backs and by our sides in every step we take in this stormy world.
Community	**Amen.**
Leader	In the silence of your heart, bring your special needs or concerns before God. If you wish us to join in your prayers for these needs, speak them aloud, saying when you are finished, "For this I pray."

Members of the community offer their particular prayers. The community's response to these individual petitions is:

**May God's blessing be yours,
and well may it befall you.**

When these personal prayers are finished, the leader offers the final blessing.

Leader   May God our Father
be with you lying down,
be with you rising up.
May Christ our Brother
be with you sleeping,
be with you waking.
May the Spirit our Guide
be with you resting,
be with you acting.
May God the Father be with you, protecting;
may Christ our Lord be with you, directing;
may the Spirit of Grace be with you, strengthening.

Community   **For ever and for ever more. Amen.**

Leader   Praise to the Father,
praise to the Son,
praise to the Spirit.

Community   **The three in one.**

Leader   *(making the sign of the cross)*
The guarding of the God of life be on you,
the guarding of the loving Christ be on you,
the guarding of the Holy Spirit be on you,
aiding and enfolding you
each day and night of your lives.

Community   **May God, the three in one, encompass us all,
shielding us on sea and on land, in day and in night,
guarding each step and each path we travel. Amen.**

Hymn (optional)

The members of the community sit or kneel after the service concludes, as they prefer. Silence is observed to allow private prayer or meditation. Individuals should leave quietly as the Spirit moves them.

II • THE BROTHERS VISIT HOLY ENDA
& AN UNINHABITED HOUSE

The members of the community enter and pray in silence. After the community is fully assembled, the prelude should be presented.

Prelude   "The Brothers Visit Holy Enda & An Uninhabited House"
(*from* The Voyage of Saint Brendan, *translated by John J. O'Meara*)

Inspired by Barrind's story, Saint Brendan decides to make his own pilgrimage to the Land of the Saints. So, he gathers some of his brother monks and begins his journey.

A period of silent meditation follows the reading before the leader begins the penitential prayers.

Penitential Prayers

A bell rings and the members of the community kneel. If anyone cannot kneel, they should remain seated with their head bowed.

Leader   We bend our knees
All   *(making the sign of the cross)*
      in the eye of the Father who created us,
      in the eye of the Son who purchased us,
      in the eye of the Spirit who cleansed us.
      Amen.

All stand.

Leader   Lord Jesus Christ,
      give us the grace of repentance;
      give us the grace of earnestness;
      give us the grace of submission.
Community   **Give us the strength and courage to confess our guilt**
      as earnestly as were this the moment of our death.
Leader   Lord Jesus,
      you are shade to those in the heat;

	you are shelter to those in the cold;
	you are a well to those in the desert.
	Lord Jesus, have mercy on us.
Community	**Lord Jesus, have mercy on us.**
Leader	Christ Jesus,
	you are eyes to those who are blind;
	you are ears to those who are deaf;
	you are health to those who are ailing.
	Christ Jesus, have mercy on us.
Community	**Christ Jesus, have mercy on us.**
Leader	Lord Jesus,
	you are the joy of all joyous things;
	you are the beam of the sun in the day;
	you are the guiding star in the night.
	Lord Jesus, have mercy on us.
Community	**Lord Jesus, have mercy on us.**
Leader	Lord Jesus Christ,
	with the Father who created us and the Spirit that cleansed us,
	Purify our hearts, make holy our souls and confirm our faith,
	keep safe our minds and compass our bodies all about.
	Enfold us…
Community	**… and surround us.**
Leader	Guide our speech…
Community	**… and our thoughts.**
Leader	Guard us in our sleeping…
Community	**… and in our waking.**
Leader	Nurture us in our watching…
Community	**… and in our hoping.**
Leader	Shield us in our lives…
Community	**… and grant us peace in eternity.**
Leader	Holy God,
	Father, Son and Spirit,
	pour down upon us from heaven
	the rich blessing of your forgiveness.
	Be patient with us and grant to us
	the fear of God, the love of God, and your affection
	so we may do your will on earth at all times …
Community	**… as the angels and saints do in heaven.**

Leader	Holy God,
	Father, Son and Spirit,
	pour down upon us from heaven
	the rich blessing of your peace.
	Peace between nations …
Community	**… peace between neighbors.**
Leader	Peace between kindred …
Community	**… peace between lovers.**
Leader	Peace between persons injured …
Community	**… peace between foes.**
Leader	Holy God,
	Father, Son and Spirit,
	help us to love and bless your creation,
	all that we see, all that we hear, all that we touch.
	Let us share your peace with our fellow creatures at all times,
	living as signs of forgiveness and reconciliation on the earth …
All	**… as the angels and saints do in heaven:**
	without malice, without jealousy, without envy,
	without fear, without terror of anyone under the sun.
	And may the Father, the Son and the Spirit
	kindle in our hearts the flame of love to our neighbors,
	to our foes, to our friends, to our kindred all,
	to the brave, to the knave, to the thrall.
Leader	The peace of the Father of Joy,
	the peace of Christ the Lamb,
	the peace of the Spirit of Grace, be with you.
Community	**The peace of the Father of Joy,**
	of Christ the Lamb, and of the Spirit of Grace,
	be with us all.
Leader	Let us share a sign of peace with those present here
	as a testimony to the peace God offers to the world.

The members of the community share a sign of peace before sitting down. A brief period of silence follows before the reader begins the Word of God.

The Word of God

Reader	I set the teachings of Christ before you;
	I set the guarding of God about you.
Community	**May it possess us and protect us all.**
Reader	A reading from the Gospel according to Saint John.

John (called the Baptist) was standing with two of his disciples, and as he watched Jesus walk by, he exclaimed, "Look, here is the Lamb of God!" The two disciples heard him say this, and they followed Jesus. When Jesus turned and saw them following, he said to them, "What are you looking for?" They said to him, "Rabbi, where are you staying?" He said to them, "Come and see." They came and saw where he was staying, and they remained with him that day. It was about four o'clock in the afternoon. One of the two who heard John speak and followed him was Andrew, Simon Peter's brother. He first found his brother Simon and said to him, "We have found the Messiah" (which is translated Anointed). He brought Simon to Jesus, who looked at him and said, "You are Simon son of John. You are to be called Cephas" (which is translated Peter).

The next day Jesus decided to go to Galilee. He found Philip and said to him, "Follow me." Now Philip was from Bethsaida, the city of Andrew and Peter. Philip found Nathanael and said to him, "We have found him about whom Moses in the law and also the prophets wrote, Jesus son of Joseph from Nazareth." Nathanael said to him, "Can anything good come out of Nazareth?" Philip said to him, "Come and see." When Jesus saw Nathanael coming toward him, he said of him, "Here is truly an Israelite in whom there is no deceit!" Nathanael asked him, "Where did you get to know me?" Jesus answered, "I saw you under the fig tree before Philip called you." Nathanael replied, "Rabbi, you are the Son of God! You are the King of Israel!" Jesus answered, "Do you believe because I told you that I saw you under the fig tree? You will see greater things than these." And he said to him, "Very truly, I tell you, you will see heaven opened and the angels of God ascending and descending upon the Son of Man."

The gospel of Jesus Christ, source of strength,
Source of salvation, source of healing grace.

Community   **May it be a mantle to our bodies.**

A brief silence follows the reading, until the leader begins the psalm.

Leader   Psalm 139, Verses 1 through 17 and 23 through 24.

O Lord, you have searched me and known me.

Community   **You know when I sit down and when I rise up;**
              you discern my thoughts from far away.

Leader   You search out my path and my lying down,
              and are acquainted with all my ways.

Community   **Even before a word is on my tongue,**
              O Lord, you know it completely.

Leader   You hem me in, behind and before,
              and lay your hand upon me.

Community   **Such knowledge is too wonderful for me;**
              it is so high that I cannot attain it.

Leader   Where can I go from your spirit?
              Or where can I flee from your presence?

Community   **If I ascend to heaven, you are there;**
              if I make my bed in Sheol, you are there.

Leader   If I take the wings of the morning
              and settle at the farthest limits of the sea,

Community   **even there your hand shall lead me,**
              and your right hand shall hold me fast.

Leader   If I say, "Surely the darkness shall cover me,
              and the light around me become night,"

Community   **even the darkness is not dark to you;**
              the night is as bright as the day,
              for darkness is as light to you.

Leader   For it was you who formed my inward parts;
Community   **you knit me together in my mother's womb.**
Leader   I praise you, for I am fearfully and wonderfully made.
Community   **Wonderful are your works;**
              that I know very well.
Leader   My frame was not hidden from you,

	when I was being made in secret,
	intricately woven in the depths of the earth.
Community	**Your eyes beheld my unformed substance.**
Leader	In your book were written
	all the days that were formed for me,
	when none of them as yet existed.
Community	**How weighty to me are your thoughts, O God!**
	How vast is the sum of them!
Leader	Search me, O God, and know my heart;
	test me and know my thoughts.
Community	**See if there is any wicked way in me,**
	and lead me in the way everlasting.

There is a brief silence after the psalm before reading or presenting the audio version of the following reflection.

Reflection   "Finding Christ in All Things"
                           by Timothy J. Ray

A period of silence is observed after the reflection for private meditation, with or without music. Afterward, the leader continues the service — proceeding either to the Eucharistic Prayer or to the Prayers and Blessings after the optional hymn.

Hymn (optional)

Eucharistic Prayer

If the community wishes to share the Eucharist, the table is prepared during the hymn. If there is no hymn, the table should be prepared in silence — slowly and deliberately. Then, the leader begins the Eucharistic Prayer.

Leader	Thanks be to you, Holy Father of Glory,
	father-kind, ever-loving, ever-powerful,
	because of all the abundance, favor and deliverance
	you bestow on us in our need.
Community	**May your name be praised forever,**
	in the heavens above and here on earth.
Leader	Whatever Providence befalls us as your children,

	in our portion, in our lot, in our path,

in our portion, in our lot, in our path,
give to us with it the riches of your hand
and the joyous blessing of your mouth.

Community **May your kingdom be seen to flourish**
through the joy of your people, always grateful.

Leader In the steep common path of our calling,
be it easy or uneasy to our flesh,
be it bright or dark for us to follow,
your perfect guidance will be upon us.

Community **Provide for us in all our needs,**
material and spiritual, this day and every day.

Leader Be a shield to us from the wiles of the deceiver,
from the arch-destroyer with his arrows pursuing us,
and in each secret thought our minds get to weave,
guide and protect us.

Community **Do not allow us to be tossed about by temptations**
and protect us from all evils that would do us harm.

Leader O Loving Christ, who was hanged upon a tree,
each day and each night we remember your covenant;
in our lying down and rising up, we yield ourselves to
your cross,
in our lives and our deaths, we seek in you our peace.
Each day, may we remember the source of the mercies
bestowed on us, gently and generously;
each day, may we become fuller in love with you.

My brothers and sisters, with St. Paul, I say to
you:
"I received from the Lord what I also handed on to you,
that the Lord Jesus on the night when he was betrayed
took a loaf of bread, and when he had given thanks, he
broke it and said, 'This is my body that is for you. Do
this in remembrance of me.' In the same way he took
the cup also, after supper, saying, 'This cup is the new
covenant in my blood. Do this, as often you drink it, in
remembrance of me.' For as often as you eat this bread
and drink the cup, you proclaim the Lord's death until
he comes." (1 Corinthians 11: 23-26)

O Gracious God, *(making the sign of the cross)*
your Spirit come upon us, and upon this bread and
wine,

	so that it might illumine our understanding, kindle our will, incite our love, strengthen our weakness, and enfold our desires.
Community	**O Generous Lord,** **cleanse our hearts, make holy our souls,** **confirm our faith,** **keep safe our minds, encompass our bodies about** **so that in our own hearts, we may feel your presence.**
Leader	O Holy Spirit, of greatest power, come down upon us and subdue us; from your glorious mansion in the heavens. The knee that is stiff, O healer, make pliant, the heart that is cold, make warm beneath your wing; guide the soul that is wandering from your path and it shall not die. Each thing that is foul, may you cleanse, each thing that is hard, may you soften with your grace, each wound that is causing us pain, may you make whole. Now to the Father who created each creature, now to the Son who paid ransom for his people, now to the Holy Spirit, comforter of might: shield and protect us from every wound.
Community	**Encompass the beginning and the end of our race,** **give us courage to sing in glory,** **in peace, in rest, in reconciliation.**
Leader	Come share in the table of the Lord, source of love for those who cherish his kindness, source of solace for those who need his forgiveness, source of hope for those who fear his judgement. Come share in the table of the Lord.
Community	**Where no tear shall be shed,** **where death comes no more. Amen.**

The community shares the Eucharist in silence. Afterward, the table is cleared during the hymn. If there is no hymn, the members of the community use this time for private prayer.

Hymn (optional)

Then, the leader continues the service.

Prayers and Blessings

Leader   Praise to the Father,
                  praise to the Son,
                  praise to the Spirit.
Community **The three in one.**

All stand.

Leader   Let us pray for the coming of the Kingdom,
                  in the words our Lord taught us:
All   **"Our Father in heaven,**
                  hallowed be your name.
                  Your kingdom come.
                  Your will be done,
                  on earth as it is in heaven.
                  Give us this day our daily bread.
                  And forgive us our debts,
                  as we also have forgiven our debtors.
                  And do not bring us to the time of trial,
                  but rescue us from the evil one."
                  (Matthew 6: 9-13)
Leader   Thanks be to you, Eternal Father,
                  for you have enwrapped our bodies and our souls,
                  safeguarding us in the sanctuary of your love …
Community **… and sheltering us under the mantle of your care.**
Leader   O God, bless our homesteads and care for all therein.
                  Help us to remember those without home or refuge,
                  especially those displaced by war and poverty.
Community **May we all find refuge in the fellowship of Christ.**
Leader   O God, bless our kindred and protect those who are
                  close to us. Help us also to remember those who are
                  alone, without family or friends.
Community **May we all find companionship in the fellowship of**
                  Christ.
Leader   O God, bless our words and help them bring joy and
                  comfort to others. Help us also to remember those who
                  are harmed by unkind words and verbal abuse.

Community	**May we all hear the gentle voice welcoming us into the fellowship of Christ.**
Leader	O God, bless us in our errands and protect us in our travels. Help us also to remember those who are lost, walking through life without direction or hope.
Community	**May we all be guided into the fellowship of Christ.**
Leader	O God, lessen our sins and increase our trust in you. Help us also to remember those burdened by guilt and shame, especially those deep in despair.
Community	**May we all find forgiveness in the fellowship of Christ.**
Leader	O God, guard us from distress and protect us from misfortune. Help us also to remember those feeling battered by the turbulence of their lives, whether through their own choices or the actions of others.
Community	**May we all find consolation in the fellowship of Christ.**
Leader	O God, shelter us from harm and aid us in life's struggles, protect us under your shield and guard us from harm, guide us in your ways and clear the paths before us. Be by our knees, by our backs and by our sides in every step we take in this stormy world.
Community	**Amen.**
Leader	In the silence of your heart, bring your special needs or concerns before God. If you wish us to join in your prayers for these needs, speak them aloud, saying when you are finished, "For this I pray."

Members of the community offer their particular prayers. The community's response to these individual petitions is:

**May God's blessing be yours,
and well may it befall you.**

When these personal prayers are finished, the leader offers the final blessing.

Leader	May God our Father be with you lying down, be with you rising up. May Christ our Brother be with you sleeping,

129

	be with you waking.
	May the Spirit our Guide
	be with you resting,
	be with you acting.
	May God the Father be with you, protecting;
	may Christ our Lord be with you, directing;
	may the Spirit of Grace be with you, strengthening.
Community	**For ever and for ever more. Amen.**
Leader	Praise to the Father,
	praise to the Son,
	praise to the Spirit.
Community	**The three in one.**
Leader	*(making the sign of the cross)*
	The guarding of the God of life be on you,
	the guarding of the loving Christ be on you,
	the guarding of the Holy Spirit be on you,
	aiding and enfolding you
	each day and night of your lives.
Community	**May God, the three in one, encompass us all,**
	shielding us on sea and on land, in day and in night,
	guarding each step and each path we travel. Amen.

Hymn (optional)

The members of the community sit or kneel after the service concludes, as they prefer. Silence is observed to allow private prayer or meditation. Individuals should leave quietly as the Spirit moves them.

III • THE ISLAND OF SHEEP
& THE LEVIATHAN JASCONIUS

The members of the community enter and pray in silence. After the community is fully assembled, the prelude should be presented.

Prelude   "The Island of Sheep & The Leviathan Jasconius"
                   (*from* The Voyage of Saint Brendan, *translated by John J. O'Meara*)

                   Saint Brendan and his companions set sail again after refreshing themselves on the island with the uninhabited house. Their travels take them to two other islands filled with wonders and surprises.

A period of silent meditation follows the reading before the leader begins the penitential prayers.

Penitential Prayers

A bell rings and the members of the community kneel. If anyone cannot kneel, they should remain seated with their head bowed.

Leader   We bend our knees
All   *(making the sign of the cross)*
              in the eye of the Father who created us,
              in the eye of the Son who purchased us,
              in the eye of the Spirit who cleansed us.
              Amen.

All stand.

Leader   Lord Jesus Christ,
              give us the grace of repentance;
              give us the grace of earnestness;
              give us the grace of submission.
Community   **Give us the strength and courage to confess our guilt**
              as earnestly as were this the moment of our death.
Leader   Lord Jesus,
              you are shade to those in the heat;

	you are shelter to those in the cold;
	you are a well to those in the desert.
	Lord Jesus, have mercy on us.
Community	**Lord Jesus, have mercy on us.**
Leader	Christ Jesus,
	you are eyes to those who are blind;
	you are ears to those who are deaf;
	you are health to those who are ailing.
	Christ Jesus, have mercy on us.
Community	**Christ Jesus, have mercy on us.**
Leader	Lord Jesus,
	you are the joy of all joyous things;
	you are the beam of the sun in the day;
	you are the guiding star in the night.
	Lord Jesus, have mercy on us.
Community	**Lord Jesus, have mercy on us.**
Leader	Lord Jesus Christ,
	with the Father who created us and the Spirit that cleansed us,
	Purify our hearts, make holy our souls and confirm our faith,
	keep safe our minds and compass our bodies all about.
	Enfold us…
Community	**… and surround us.**
Leader	Guide our speech…
Community	**… and our thoughts.**
Leader	Guard us in our sleeping…
Community	**… and in our waking.**
Leader	Nurture us in our watching…
Community	**… and in our hoping.**
Leader	Shield us in our lives…
Community	**… and grant us peace in eternity.**
Leader	Holy God,
	Father, Son and Spirit,
	pour down upon us from heaven
	the rich blessing of your forgiveness.
	Be patient with us and grant to us
	the fear of God, the love of God, and your affection
	so we may do your will on earth at all times …
Community	**… as the angels and saints do in heaven.**

Leader	Holy God,
	Father, Son and Spirit,
	pour down upon us from heaven
	the rich blessing of your peace.
	Peace between nations …
Community	**… peace between neighbors.**
Leader	Peace between kindred …
Community	**… peace between lovers.**
Leader	Peace between persons injured …
Community	**… peace between foes.**
Leader	Holy God,
	Father, Son and Spirit,
	help us to love and bless your creation,
	all that we see, all that we hear, all that we touch.
	Let us share your peace with our fellow creatures at all times,
	living as signs of forgiveness and reconciliation on the earth …
All	**… as the angels and saints do in heaven:**
	without malice, without jealousy, without envy,
	without fear, without terror of anyone under the sun.
	And may the Father, the Son and the Spirit
	kindle in our hearts the flame of love to our neighbors,
	to our foes, to our friends, to our kindred all,
	to the brave, to the knave, to the thrall.
Leader	The peace of the Father of Joy,
	the peace of Christ the Lamb,
	the peace of the Spirit of Grace, be with you.
Community	**The peace of the Father of Joy,**
	of Christ the Lamb, and of the Spirit of Grace,
	be with us all.
Leader	Let us share a sign of peace with those present here
	as a testimony to the peace God offers to the world.

The members of the community share a sign of peace before sitting down. A brief period of silence follows before the reader begins the Word of God.

The Word of God

Reader	I set the teachings of Christ before you;
	I set the guarding of God about you.
Community	**May it possess us and protect us all.**

Reader	A reading from the Gospel according to Saint John.

There was a wedding in Cana of Galilee, and the mother of Jesus was there. Jesus and his disciples had also been invited to the wedding. When the wine gave out, the mother of Jesus said to him, "They have no wine." And Jesus said to her, "Woman, what concern is that to you and to me? My hour has not yet come." His mother said to the servants, "Do whatever he tells you." Now standing there were six stone water jars for the Jewish rites of purification, each holding twenty or thirty gallons. Jesus said to them, "Fill the jars with water." And they filled them up to the brim. He said to them, "Now draw some out, and take it to the chief steward." So they took it. When the steward tasted the water that had become wine, and did not know where it came from (though the servants who had drawn the water knew), the steward called the bridegroom and said to him, "Everyone serves the good wine first, and then the inferior wine after the guests have become drunk. But you have kept the good wine until now." Jesus did this, the first of his signs, in Cana of Galilee, and revealed his glory; and his disciples believed in him.

The gospel of Jesus Christ, source of strength,
Source of salvation, source of healing grace.

Community	**May it be a mantle to our bodies.**

A brief silence follows the reading, until the leader begins the psalm.

Leader	Psalm 27, Verses 1 through 14.

The Lord is my light and my salvation;
whom shall I fear?

Community	**The Lord is the stronghold of my life;**

	of whom shall I be afraid?
Leader	When evildoers assail me
	to devour my flesh —
Community	**my adversaries and foes —**
	they shall stumble and fall.
Leader	Though an army encamp against me,
	my heart shall not fear;
Community	**though war rise up against me,**
	yet I will be confident.
Leader	One thing I asked of the Lord,
	that will I seek after:
	to live in the house of the Lord
Community	**all the days of my life,**
	to behold the beauty of the Lord,
	and to inquire in his temple.
Leader	For he will hide me in his shelter
	in the day of trouble;
Community	**he will conceal me under the cover of his tent;**
	he will set me high on a rock.
Leader	Now my head is lifted up
	my enemies all around me,
Community	**and I will offer in his tent**
	sacrifices with shouts of joy;
	I will sing and make melody to the Lord.
Leader	Hear, O Lord, when I cry aloud,
Community	**be gracious to me and answer me!**
Leader	"Come," my heart says, "seek his face!"
	Your face, Lord, do I seek.
Community	**Do not hide your face from me.**
	Do not turn your servant away in anger,
	you who have been my help.
Leader	Do not cast me off, do not forsake me,
	O God of my salvation!
Community	**If my father and mother forsake me,**
	the Lord will take me up.
Leader	Teach me your way, O Lord,
	and lead me on a level path
	because of my enemies.
Community	**Do not give me up to the will of my adversaries,**
	for false witnesses have risen against me,

	and they are breathing out violence.
Leader	I believe that I shall see the goodness of the Lord in the land of the living.
Community	**Wait for the Lord;** **be strong, and let your heart take courage,** **wait for the Lord!**

There is a brief silence after the psalm before reading or presenting the audio version of the following reflection.

Reflection	"Sharing in the Love of the Trinity" by Timothy J. Ray

A period of silence is observed after the reflection for private meditation, with or without music. Afterward, the leader continues the service — proceeding either to the Eucharistic Prayer or to the Prayers and Blessings after the optional hymn.

Hymn (optional)

Eucharistic Prayer

If the community wishes to share the Eucharist, the table is prepared during the hymn. If there is no hymn, the table should be prepared in silence — slowly and deliberately. Then, the leader begins the Eucharistic Prayer.

Leader	Thanks be to you, Holy Father of Glory, father-kind, ever-loving, ever-powerful, because of all the abundance, favor and deliverance you bestow on us in our need.
Community	**May your name be praised forever,** **in the heavens above and here on earth.**
Leader	Whatever Providence befalls us as your children, in our portion, in our lot, in our path, give to us with it the riches of your hand and the joyous blessing of your mouth.
Community	**May your kingdom be seen to flourish** **through the joy of your people, always grateful.**
Leader	In the steep common path of our calling,

	be it easy or uneasy to our flesh,
	be it bright or dark for us to follow,
	your perfect guidance will be upon us.
Community	**Provide for us in all our needs,** **material and spiritual, this day and every day.**
Leader	Be a shield to us from the wiles of the deceiver, from the arch-destroyer with his arrows pursuing us, and in each secret thought our minds get to weave, guide and protect us.
Community	**Do not allow us to be tossed about by temptations** **and protect us from all evils that would do us harm.**
Leader	O Loving Christ, who was hanged upon a tree, each day and each night we remember your covenant; in our lying down and rising up, we yield ourselves to your cross, in our lives and our deaths, we seek in you our peace. Each day, may we remember the source of the mercies bestowed on us, gently and generously; each day, may we become fuller in love with you.

My brothers and sisters, with St. Paul, I say to you:

"I received from the Lord what I also handed on to you, that the Lord Jesus on the night when he was betrayed took a loaf of bread, and when he had given thanks, he broke it and said, 'This is my body that is for you. Do this in remembrance of me.' In the same way he took the cup also, after supper, saying, 'This cup is the new covenant in my blood. Do this, as often you drink it, in remembrance of me.' For as often as you eat this bread and drink the cup, you proclaim the Lord's death until he comes." (1 Corinthians 11: 23-26)

O Gracious God, *(making the sign of the cross)* your Spirit come upon us, and upon this bread and wine,

so that it might illumine our understanding, kindle our will, incite our love, strengthen our weakness, and enfold our desires.

Community	**O Generous Lord,** **cleanse our hearts, make holy our souls,** **confirm our faith,**

	keep safe our minds, encompass our bodies about
	so that in our own hearts, we may feel your presence.
Leader	O Holy Spirit, of greatest power,
	come down upon us and subdue us;
	from your glorious mansion in the heavens.
	The knee that is stiff, O healer, make pliant,
	the heart that is cold, make warm beneath your wing;
	guide the soul that is wandering from your path
	and it shall not die.
	Each thing that is foul, may you cleanse,
	each thing that is hard, may you soften with your grace,
	each wound that is causing us pain, may you make whole.
	Now to the Father who created each creature,
	now to the Son who paid ransom for his people,
	now to the Holy Spirit, comforter of might:
	shield and protect us from every wound.

Community	**Encompass the beginning and the end of our race,**
	give us courage to sing in glory,
	in peace, in rest, in reconciliation.
Leader	Come share in the table of the Lord,
	source of love for those who cherish his kindness,
	source of solace for those who need his forgiveness,
	source of hope for those who fear his judgement.
	Come share in the table of the Lord.
Community	**Where no tear shall be shed,**
	where death comes no more. Amen.

The community shares the Eucharist in silence. Afterward, the table is cleared during the hymn. If there is no hymn, the members of the community use this time for private prayer.

Hymn (optional)

Then, the leader continues the service.

Prayers and Blessings

Leader	Praise to the Father,
	praise to the Son,

praise to the Spirit.

Community **The three in one.**

All stand.

Leader Let us pray for the coming of the Kingdom,
in the words our Lord taught us:
All **"Our Father in heaven,**
hallowed be your name.
Your kingdom come.
Your will be done,
on earth as it is in heaven.
Give us this day our daily bread.
And forgive us our debts,
as we also have forgiven our debtors.
And do not bring us to the time of trial,
but rescue us from the evil one."
(Matthew 6: 9-13)
Leader Thanks be to you, Eternal Father,
for you have enwrapped our bodies and our souls,
safeguarding us in the sanctuary of your love …
Community **… and sheltering us under the mantle of your care.**
Leader O God, bless our homesteads and care for all therein.
Help us to remember those without home or refuge,
especially those displaced by war and poverty.
Community **May we all find refuge in the fellowship of Christ.**
Leader O God, bless our kindred and protect those who are
close to us. Help us also to remember those who are
alone, without family or friends.
Community **May we all find companionship in the fellowship of**
Christ.
Leader O God, bless our words and help them bring joy and
comfort to others. Help us also to remember those who
are harmed by unkind words and verbal abuse.
Community **May we all hear the gentle voice welcoming us into the**
fellowship of Christ.
Leader O God, bless us in our errands and protect us in our
travels. Help us also to remember those who are lost,
walking through life without direction or hope.
Community **May we all be guided into the fellowship of Christ.**

Leader	O God, lessen our sins and increase our trust in you. Help us also to remember those burdened by guilt and shame, especially those deep in despair.
Community	**May we all find forgiveness in the fellowship of Christ.**
Leader	O God, guard us from distress and protect us from misfortune. Help us also to remember those feeling battered by the turbulence of their lives, whether through their own choices or the actions of others.
Community	**May we all find consolation in the fellowship of Christ.**
Leader	O God, shelter us from harm and aid us in life's struggles, protect us under your shield and guard us from harm, guide us in your ways and clear the paths before us. Be by our knees, by our backs and by our sides in every step we take in this stormy world.
Community	**Amen.**
Leader	In the silence of your heart, bring your special needs or concerns before God. If you wish us to join in your prayers for these needs, speak them aloud, saying when you are finished, "For this I pray."

Members of the community offer their particular prayers. The community's response to these individual petitions is:

> **May God's blessing be yours,**
> **and well may it befall you.**

When these personal prayers are finished, the leader offers the final blessing.

Leader	May God our Father be with you lying down, be with you rising up. May Christ our Brother be with you sleeping, be with you waking. May the Spirit our Guide be with you resting, be with you acting. May God the Father be with you, protecting; may Christ our Lord be with you, directing;

	may the Spirit of Grace be with you, strengthening.
Community	**For ever and for ever more. Amen.**
Leader	Praise to the Father,
	praise to the Son,
	praise to the Spirit.
Community	**The three in one.**
Leader	*(making the sign of the cross)*
	The guarding of the God of life be on you,
	the guarding of the loving Christ be on you,
	the guarding of the Holy Spirit be on you,
	aiding and enfolding you
	each day and night of your lives.
Community	**May God, the three in one, encompass us all,**
	shielding us on sea and on land, in day and in night,
	guarding each step and each path we travel. Amen.

Hymn (optional)

*The members of the community sit or kneel after the service concludes,
as they prefer. Silence is observed to allow private prayer or meditation.
Individuals should leave quietly as the Spirit moves them.*

IV • THE PARADISE OF BIRDS

The members of the community enter and pray in silence. After the community is fully assembled, the prelude should be presented.

Prelude   "The Paradise of Birds"
                   (*from* The Voyage of Saint Brendan, *translated by John J. O'Meara*)

                   Stopping to rest on Easter, Saint Brendan and his companions come ashore on an island called The Paradise of Birds and join its unique community of prayer and praise until Pentecost.

A period of silent meditation follows the reading before the leader begins the penitential prayers.

Penitential Prayers

A bell rings and the members of the community kneel. If anyone cannot kneel, they should remain seated with their head bowed.

Leader   We bend our knees
All   (*making the sign of the cross*)
                in the eye of the Father who created us,
                in the eye of the Son who purchased us,
                in the eye of the Spirit who cleansed us.
                Amen.

All stand.

Leader   Lord Jesus Christ,
                give us the grace of repentance;
                give us the grace of earnestness;
                give us the grace of submission.
Community   **Give us the strength and courage to confess our guilt**
                as earnestly as were this the moment of our death.
Leader   Lord Jesus,
                keep the eye of God between us and every other eye;
                keep the purpose of God between us and every other

142

purpose;
keep the desire of God between us and every other desire;
and no mouth can curse us.
Lord Jesus, have mercy on us.

Community	**Lord Jesus, have mercy on us.**
Leader	Christ Jesus,

keep your pain between us and every other pain;
keep your love between us and every other love;
keep your dearness between us and every other dearness;
and no venom can wound us.
Christ Jesus, have mercy on us.

Community	**Christ Jesus, have mercy on us.**
Leader	Lord Jesus,

keep the desire of God between us and every other desire;
keep the might of God between us and every other might;
keep the right of God between us and every other right;
and no ill thing can touch us.
Lord Jesus, have mercy on us.

Community	**Lord Jesus, have mercy on us.**
Leader	Lord Jesus Christ,

with the Father who created us and the Spirit that cleansed us,
Purify our hearts, make holy our souls and confirm our faith,
keep safe our minds and compass our bodies all about.
Enfold us…

Community	**… and surround us.**
Leader	Guide our speech…
Community	**… and our thoughts.**
Leader	Guard us in our sleeping…
Community	**… and in our waking.**
Leader	Nurture us in our watching…
Community	**… and in our hoping.**
Leader	Shield us in our lives…
Community	**… and grant us peace in eternity.**
Leader	Holy God,

	Father, Son and Spirit,
	pour down upon us from heaven
	the rich blessing of your forgiveness.
	Be patient with us and grant to us
	the fear of God, the love of God, and your affection
	so we may do your will on earth at all times …
Community	**… as the angels and saints do in heaven.**
Leader	Holy God,
	Father, Son and Spirit,
	pour down upon us from heaven
	the rich blessing of your peace.
	Peace between nations …
Community	**… peace between neighbors.**
Leader	Peace between kindred …
Community	**… peace between lovers.**
Leader	Peace between persons injured …
Community	**… peace between foes.**
Leader	Holy God,
	Father, Son and Spirit,
	help us to love and bless your creation,
	all that we see, all that we hear, all that we touch.
	Let us share your peace with our fellow creatures at all times,
	living as signs of forgiveness and reconciliation on the earth …
All	**… as the angels and saints do in heaven:**
	without malice, without jealousy, without envy,
	without fear, without terror of anyone under the sun.
	And may the Father, the Son and the Spirit
	kindle in our hearts the flame of love to our neighbors,
	to our foes, to our friends, to our kindred all,
	to the brave, to the knave, to the thrall.
Leader	The peace of the Father of Joy,
	the peace of Christ the Lamb,
	the peace of the Spirit of Grace, be with you.
Community	**The peace of the Father of Joy,**
	of Christ the Lamb, and of the Spirit of Grace,
	be with us all.
Leader	Let us share a sign of peace with those present here
	as a testimony to the peace God offers to the world.

The members of the community share a sign of peace before sitting down. A brief period of silence follows before the reader begins the Word of God.

The Word of God

Reader   I set the teachings of Christ before you;
            I set the guarding of God about you.
Community   **May it possess us and protect us all.**

Reader   A reading from the Gospel according to Saint John.

As [Jesus] walked along, he saw a man blind from birth. His disciples asked him, "Rabbi, who sinned, this man or his parents, that he was born blind?" Jesus answered, "Neither this man nor his parents sinned; he was born blind so that God's works might be revealed in him. We must work the works of him who sent me while it is day; night is coming when no one can work. As long as I am in the world, I am the light of the world." When he had said this, he spat on the ground and made mud with the saliva and spread the mud on the man's eyes, saying to him, "Go, wash in the pool of Siloam". Then he went and washed and came back able to see. The neighbors and those who had seen him before as a beggar began to ask, "Is this not the man who used to sit and beg?" Some were saying, "It is he." Others were saying, "No, but it is someone like him." He kept saying, "I am the man." But they kept asking him, "Then how were your eyes opened?" He answered, "The man called Jesus made mud, spread it on my eyes, and said to me, 'Go to Siloam and wash.' Then I went and washed and received my sight." They said to him, "Where is he?" He said, "I do not know."

They brought to the Pharisees the man who had formerly been blind. Now it was a sabbath day when Jesus made the mud and opened his eyes. Then the Pharisees also began to ask him how he had received his sight. He said to them, "He put mud on my eyes. Then I washed, and now I see." Some of the Pharisees said, "This man is not from God, for he does not observe the sabbath." But others said, "How can a man who is a sinner perform such signs?" And they were divided. So they said again to the blind man, "What do you say about him? It was your eyes he opened." He said, "He is a prophet."

The Jews did not believe that he had been blind and had received his sight until they called the parents of the man who had received his sight and asked them, "Is this your son, who you say was born blind? How then does he now see?" His parents answered, "We know that this is our son, and that he was born blind; but we do not know how it is that now he sees, nor do we know who opened his eyes. Ask him; he is of age. He will speak for himself." His parents said this because they were afraid of the Jews; for the Jews had already agreed that anyone who confessed Jesus to be the Messiah would be put out of the synagogue.

The gospel of Jesus Christ, source of strength,
Source of salvation, source of healing grace.

Community　**May it be a mantle to our bodies.**

A brief silence follows the reading, until the leader begins the psalm.

Leader　Psalm 33, Verses 1 through 22.

Rejoice in the Lord, O you righteous.
Praise befits the upright.

Community　**Praise the Lord with the lyre;**
make melody to him with the harp of ten strings.

Leader　Sing to him a new song;
play skillfully on the strings, with loud shouts.

Community　**For the word of the Lord is upright,**
and all his work is done in faithfulness.

Leader　He loves righteousness and justice;

Community　**the earth is full of the steadfast love of the Lord.**

Leader　By the word of the Lord the heavens were made,

Community	**and all their host by the breath of his mouth.**
Leader	He gathered the waters of the sea as in a bottle;
Community	**he put the deeps in storehouses.**
Leader	Let all the earth fear the Lord;
Community	**let all the inhabitants of the world stand in awe of him.**
Leader	For he spoke, and it came to be;
Community	**he commanded, and it stood firm.**
Leader	The Lord brings the counsel of the nations to nothing;
Community	**he frustrates the plans of the peoples.**
Leader	The counsel of the Lord stands forever,
Community	**the thoughts of his heart to all generations.**
Leader	Happy is the nation whose God is the Lord,
Community	**people whom he has chosen as his heritage.**
Leader	The Lord looks down from heaven; he sees all humankind.
Community	**From where he sits enthroned he watches all the inhabitants of the earth —**
Leader	he who fashions the hearts of them all,
Community	**and observes all their deeds.**
Leader	A king is not saved by his great army;
Community	**a warrior is not delivered by his great strength.**
Leader	The war horse is a vain hope for victory,
Community	**and by its great might it cannot save.**
Leader	Truly the eye of the Lord is on those who fear him, on those who hope in his steadfast love,
Community	**to deliver their soul from death, and to keep them alive in famine.**
Leader	Our soul waits for the Lord;
Community	**he is our help and shield.**
Leader	Our heart is glad in him,
Community	**because we trust in his holy name.**
Leader	Let your steadfast love, O Lord, be upon us,
Community	**even as we hope in you.**

There is a brief silence after the psalm before reading or presenting the audio version of the following reflection.

Reflection	"Accepting Forgiveness as a Loved Sinner" by Timothy J. Ray

147

A period of silence is observed after the reflection for private meditation, with or without music. Afterward, the leader continues the service — proceeding either to the Eucharistic Prayer or to the Prayers and Blessings after the optional hymn.

Hymn (optional)

Eucharistic Prayer

If the community wishes to share the Eucharist, the table is prepared during the hymn. If there is no hymn, the table should be prepared in silence — slowly and deliberately. Then, the leader begins the Eucharistic Prayer.

Leader	Thanks be to you, Holy Father of Glory, father-kind, ever-loving, ever-powerful, because of all the abundance, favor and deliverance you bestow on us in our need.
Community	**May your name be praised forever, in the heavens above and here on earth.**
Leader	Whatever Providence befalls us as your children, in our portion, in our lot, in our path, give to us with it the riches of your hand and the joyous blessing of your mouth.
Community	**May your kingdom be seen to flourish through the joy of your people, always grateful.**
Leader	In the steep common path of our calling, be it easy or uneasy to our flesh, be it bright or dark for us to follow, your perfect guidance will be upon us.
Community	**Provide for us in all our needs, material and spiritual, this day and every day.**
Leader	Be a shield to us from the wiles of the deceiver, from the arch-destroyer with his arrows pursuing us, and in each secret thought our minds get to weave, guide and protect us.
Community	**Do not allow us to be tossed about by temptations and protect us from all evils that would do us harm.**
Leader	O Loving Christ, who was hanged upon a tree, each day and each night we remember your covenant;

in our lying down and rising up, we yield ourselves to your cross,
in our lives and our deaths, we seek in you our peace.
Each day, may we remember the source of the mercies bestowed on us, gently and generously;
each day, may we become fuller in love with you.

My brothers and sisters, with St. Paul, I say to you:
"I received from the Lord what I also handed on to you, that the Lord Jesus on the night when he was betrayed took a loaf of bread, and when he had given thanks, he broke it and said, 'This is my body that is for you. Do this in remembrance of me.' In the same way he took the cup also, after supper, saying, 'This cup is the new covenant in my blood. Do this, as often you drink it, in remembrance of me.' For as often as you eat this bread and drink the cup, you proclaim the Lord's death until he comes." (1 Corinthians 11: 23-26)

O Gracious God, *(making the sign of the cross)* your Spirit come upon us, and upon this bread and wine,
so that it might illumine our understanding, kindle our will, incite our love, strengthen our weakness, and enfold our desires.

Community	**O Generous Lord,** **cleanse our hearts, make holy our souls,** **confirm our faith,** **keep safe our minds, encompass our bodies about** **so that in our own hearts, we may feel your presence.**
Leader	O Holy Spirit, of greatest power, come down upon us and subdue us; from your glorious mansion in the heavens. The knee that is stiff, O healer, make pliant, the heart that is cold, make warm beneath your wing; guide the soul that is wandering from your path and it shall not die. Each thing that is foul, may you cleanse, each thing that is hard, may you soften with your grace, each wound that is causing us pain, may you make whole.

	Now to the Father who created each creature, now to the Son who paid ransom for his people, now to the Holy Spirit, comforter of might: shield and protect us from every wound.
Community	**Encompass the beginning and the end of our race,** **give us courage to sing in glory,** **in peace, in rest, in reconciliation.**
Leader	Come share in the table of the Lord, source of love for those who cherish his kindness, source of solace for those who need his forgiveness, source of hope for those who fear his judgement. Come share in the table of the Lord.
Community	**Where no tear shall be shed,** **where death comes no more. Amen.**

The community shares the Eucharist in silence. Afterward, the table is cleared during the hymn. If there is no hymn, the members of the community use this time for private prayer.

Hymn (optional)

Then, the leader continues the service.

Prayers and Blessings

| Leader | Praise to the Father,
praise to the Son,
praise to the Spirit. |
| Community | **The three in one.** |

All stand.

| Leader | Let us pray for the coming of the Kingdom,
in the words our Lord taught us: |
| All | **"Our Father in heaven,**
hallowed be your name.
Your kingdom come.
Your will be done,
on earth as it is in heaven.
Give us this day our daily bread. |

And forgive us our debts,
as we also have forgiven our debtors.
And do not bring us to the time of trial,
but rescue us from the evil one."
(Matthew 6: 9-13)

Leader   Thanks be to you, Eternal Father,
for you have enwrapped our bodies and our souls,
safeguarding us in the sanctuary of your love …

Community   **… and sheltering us under the mantle of your care.**

Leader   O holy God, be a smooth path before us,
a guiding star above us, a keen eye behind us,
this day, this night, forever.
We are weary and forlorn, O God,
lead us to your house, to the peace of heaven.

Community   **Lead us to your house, to the peace of heaven.**

Leader   Help us do your will…

Community   **… and bridle our own.**

Leader   Help us give you your due…

Community   **… and put aside our entitlement.**

Leader   Help us travel your path…

Community   **… and leave behind our own.**

Leader   Help us ponder Christ's death…

Community   **… and find hope in our own.**

Leader   Help us meditate on Christ agony…

Community   **… and strengthen our love for you.**

Leader   Help us carry Christ's cross…

Community   **… and forget our own burdens.**

Leader   Help us embrace repentance…

Community   **… and accept your forgiveness.**

Leader   O holy God,
help us to control our tongues and our thoughts,
so we may trust your wisdom,
embrace Christ's redemptive love,
and accept the Spirit's gentle graces.
For we are weary and forlorn …

Community   **… and ask you lead us to your house, to the peace of**
heaven. Amen.

Leader   In the silence of your heart,
bring your special needs or concerns before God.
If you wish us to join in your prayers for these needs,

speak them aloud, saying when you are finished,
"For this I pray."

*Members of the community offer their particular prayers. The
community's response to these individual petitions is:*
**May God's blessing be yours,
and well may it befall you.**
*When these personal prayers are finished, the leader offers the final
blessing.*

Leader   May the God of life encompass you,
            protecting your form and your frame.
            May the Christ of love encompass you,
            shielding you from hatred and from harm.
            May the spirit of grace encompass you,
            guiding you towards goodness and away from ill.
            The blessings of the Triune God surround you …
Community   **… abiding in us forever and eternally. Amen.**
Leader   Praise to the Father,
            praise to the Son,
            praise to the Spirit.
Community   **The three in one.**
Leader   *(making the sign of the cross)*
            The guarding of the God of life be on you,
            the guarding of the loving Christ be on you,
            the guarding of the Holy Spirit be on you,
            aiding and enfolding you
            each day and night of your lives.
Community   **May God, the three in one, encompass us all,
            shielding us on sea and on land, in day and in night,
            guarding each step and each path we travel. Amen.**

Hymn (optional)

*The members of the community sit or kneel after the service concludes,
as they prefer. Silence is observed to allow private prayer or meditation.
Individuals should leave quietly as the Spirit moves them.*

V • THE COMMUNITY OF AILBE

The members of the community enter and pray in silence. After the community is fully assembled, the prelude should be presented.

Prelude   "The Community of Ailbe"
           (*from* The Voyage of Saint Brendan, *translated by John J. O'Meara*)

           Leaving the Paradise of Birds, Saint Brendan and his companions wander on the ocean for many months before landing on another island where they are welcomed by the Community of Saint Ailbe.

A period of silent meditation follows the reading before the leader begins the penitential prayers.

Penitential Prayers

A bell rings and the members of the community kneel. If anyone cannot kneel, they should remain seated with their head bowed.

Leader   We bend our knees
All   *(making the sign of the cross)*
           in the eye of the Father who created us,
           in the eye of the Son who purchased us,
           in the eye of the Spirit who cleansed us.
           Amen.

All stand.

Leader   Lord Jesus Christ,
           give us the grace of repentance;
           give us the grace of earnestness;
           give us the grace of submission.
Community   **Give us the strength and courage to confess our guilt**
           as earnestly as were this the moment of our death.
Leader   Lord Jesus,
           keep the eye of God between us and every other eye;
           keep the purpose of God between us and every other

153

purpose;

keep the desire of God between us and every other desire;

and no mouth can curse us.

Lord Jesus, have mercy on us.

| Community | **Lord Jesus, have mercy on us.** |
| Leader | Christ Jesus, |

keep your pain between us and every other pain;

keep your love between us and every other love;

keep your dearness between us and every other dearness;

and no venom can wound us.

Christ Jesus, have mercy on us.

| Community | **Christ Jesus, have mercy on us.** |
| Leader | Lord Jesus, |

keep the desire of God between us and every other desire;

keep the might of God between us and every other might;

keep the right of God between us and every other right;

and no ill thing can touch us.

Lord Jesus, have mercy on us.

| Community | **Lord Jesus, have mercy on us.** |
| Leader | Lord Jesus Christ, |

with the Father who created us and the Spirit that cleansed us,

Purify our hearts, make holy our souls and confirm our faith,

keep safe our minds and compass our bodies all about.

Enfold us…

Community	**… and surround us.**
Leader	Guide our speech…
Community	**… and our thoughts.**
Leader	Guard us in our sleeping…
Community	**… and in our waking.**
Leader	Nurture us in our watching…
Community	**… and in our hoping.**
Leader	Shield us in our lives…
Community	**… and grant us peace in eternity.**
Leader	Holy God,

	Father, Son and Spirit,
	pour down upon us from heaven
	the rich blessing of your forgiveness.
	Be patient with us and grant to us
	the fear of God, the love of God, and your affection
	so we may do your will on earth at all times …
Community	**… as the angels and saints do in heaven.**
Leader	Holy God,
	Father, Son and Spirit,
	pour down upon us from heaven
	the rich blessing of your peace.
	Peace between nations …
Community	**… peace between neighbors.**
Leader	Peace between kindred …
Community	**… peace between lovers.**
Leader	Peace between persons injured …
Community	**… peace between foes.**
Leader	Holy God,
	Father, Son and Spirit,
	help us to love and bless your creation,
	all that we see, all that we hear, all that we touch.
	Let us share your peace with our fellow creatures at all times,
	living as signs of forgiveness and reconciliation on the earth …
All	**… as the angels and saints do in heaven:**
	without malice, without jealousy, without envy,
	without fear, without terror of anyone under the sun.
	And may the Father, the Son and the Spirit
	kindle in our hearts the flame of love to our neighbors,
	to our foes, to our friends, to our kindred all,
	to the brave, to the knave, to the thrall.
Leader	The peace of the Father of Joy,
	the peace of Christ the Lamb,
	the peace of the Spirit of Grace, be with you.
Community	**The peace of the Father of Joy,**
	of Christ the Lamb, and of the Spirit of Grace,
	be with us all.
Leader	Let us share a sign of peace with those present here
	as a testimony to the peace God offers to the world.

The members of the community share a sign of peace before sitting down. A brief period of silence follows before the reader begins the Word of God.

The Word of God

Reader   I set the teachings of Christ before you;
                I set the guarding of God about you.
Community   **May it possess us and protect us all.**

Reader   A reading from the Gospel according to Saint John.

Jesus went to the other side of the Sea of Galilee, also called the Sea of Tiberias. A large crowd kept following him, because they saw the signs that he was doing for the sick. Jesus went up the mountain and sat down there with his disciples. When he looked up and saw a large crowd coming toward him, Jesus said to Philip, "Where are we to buy bread for these people to eat?" He said this to test him, for he himself knew what he was going to do. Philip answered him, "Six months' wages would not buy enough bread for each of them to get a little." One of his disciples, Andrew, Simon Peter's brother, said to him, "There is a boy here who has five barley loaves and two fish. But what are they among so many people?" Jesus said, "Make the people sit down." Now there was a great deal of grass in the place; so they sat down, about five thousand in all. Then Jesus took the loaves, and when he had given thanks, he distributed them to those who were seated; so also the fish, as much as they wanted. When they were satisfied, he told his disciples, "Gather up the fragments left over, so that nothing may be lost." so they gathered them up, and from the fragments of the five barley loaves, left by those who had eaten, they filled twelve baskets. When the people saw the sign that he had done, they began to say, "This is indeed the prophet who is to come into the world."

When Jesus realized that they were about to come and take him by force to make him king, he withdrew again to the mountain by himself.

When evening came, his disciples went down to the sea, got into a boat, and started across the sea to Capernaum. It was now dark, and Jesus had not yet come to them. The sea became rough because a strong wind was blowing. When they had rowed about three or four miles, they saw Jesus walking on the sea and coming near the boat, and they were terrified. But he said to them, "It is I; do not be afraid." Then they wanted to take him into the boat, and immediately the boat reached the land toward which they were going.
The next day the crowd that had stayed on the other side of the sea went to Capernaum looking for Jesus.

When they found him on the other side of the sea, they said to him, "Rabbi, when did you come here?" Jesus answered them, "Very truly, I tell you, you are looking for me, not because you saw signs, but because you ate your fill of the loaves. Do not work for the food that perishes, but for the food that endures for eternal life, which the Son of Man will give you. For it is on him that God the Father has set his seal."

Jesus [then] said to them, "I am the bread of life. Whoever comes to me will never be hungry, and whoever believes in me will never be thirsty."

The gospel of Jesus Christ, source of strength,
Source of salvation, source of healing grace.

Community **May it be a mantle to our bodies.**

A brief silence follows the reading, until the leader begins the psalm.

Leader Psalm 103, Verses 1 through 22.

Bless the Lord, O my soul,
and all that is within me, bless his holy name.

Community **Bless the Lord, O my soul,**
and do not forget all his benefits —

Leader who forgives all your iniquity,

	who heals all your diseases,
Community	**who redeems your life from the Pit,**
	who crowns you with steadfast love and mercy,
Leader	who satisfies you with good as long as you live
Community	**so that your youth is renewed like the eagle's.**
Leader	The Lord works vindication
Community	**and justice for all who are oppressed.**
Leader	He made known his ways to Moses,
Community	**his acts to the people of Israel.**
Leader	The Lord is merciful and gracious,
Community	**slow to anger and abounding in steadfast love.**
Leader	He will not always accuse,
Community	**nor will he keep his anger forever.**
Leader	He does not deal with us according to our sins,
Community	**nor repay us according to our iniquities.**
Leader	For as the heavens are high above the earth,
	so great is his steadfast love toward those who fear him;
Community	**as far as the east is from the west,**
	so far he removes our transgressions from us.
Leader	As a father has compassion for his children,
	so the Lord has compassion for those who fear him.
Community	**For he knows how we were made;**
	he remembers that we are dust.
Leader	As for mortals, their days are like grass;
	they flourish like a flower of the field;
Community	**for the wind passes over it, and it is gone,**
	and its place knows it no more.
Leader	But the steadfast love of the Lord is from
	everlasting to everlasting on those who fear him,
Community	**and his righteousness to children's children,**
	to those who keep his covenant
	and remember to do his commandments.
Leader	The Lord has established his throne in the heavens,
Community	**and his kingdom rules over all.**
Leader	Bless the Lord, O you his angels,
Community	**you mighty ones who do his bidding,**
	obedient to his spoken word.
Leader	Bless the Lord, all his hosts,
Community	**his ministers that do his will.**
Leader	Bless the Lord, all his works,

in all places of his dominion.

Community **Bless the Lord, O my soul.**

There is a brief silence after the psalm before reading or presenting the audio version of the following reflection.

Reflection "Living as Citizens of Heaven"
by Timothy J. Ray

A period of silence is observed after the reflection for private meditation, with or without music. Afterward, the leader continues the service — proceeding either to the Eucharistic Prayer or to the Prayers and Blessings after the optional hymn.

Hymn (optional)

Eucharistic Prayer

If the community wishes to share the Eucharist, the table is prepared during the hymn. If there is no hymn, the table should be prepared in silence — slowly and deliberately. Then, the leader begins the Eucharistic Prayer.

Leader Thanks be to you, Holy Father of Glory,
father-kind, ever-loving, ever-powerful,
because of all the abundance, favor and deliverance
you bestow on us in our need.

Community **May your name be praised forever,**
in the heavens above and here on earth.

Leader Whatever Providence befalls us as your children,
in our portion, in our lot, in our path,
give to us with it the riches of your hand
and the joyous blessing of your mouth.

Community **May your kingdom be seen to flourish**
through the joy of your people, always grateful.

Leader In the steep common path of our calling,
be it easy or uneasy to our flesh,
be it bright or dark for us to follow,
your perfect guidance will be upon us.

Community **Provide for us in all our needs,**

	material and spiritual, this day and every day.
Leader	Be a shield to us from the wiles of the deceiver,
	from the arch-destroyer with his arrows pursuing us,
	and in each secret thought our minds get to weave,
	guide and protect us.
Community	**Do not allow us to be tossed about by temptations**
	and protect us from all evils that would do us harm.

Leader   O Loving Christ, who was hanged upon a tree,
each day and each night we remember your covenant;
in our lying down and rising up, we yield ourselves to
your cross,
in our lives and our deaths, we seek in you our peace.
Each day, may we remember the source of the mercies
bestowed on us, gently and generously;
each day, may we become fuller in love with you.

My brothers and sisters, with St. Paul, I say to
you:
"I received from the Lord what I also handed on to you,
that the Lord Jesus on the night when he was betrayed
took a loaf of bread, and when he had given thanks, he
broke it and said, 'This is my body that is for you. Do
this in remembrance of me.' In the same way he took
the cup also, after supper, saying, 'This cup is the new
covenant in my blood. Do this, as often you drink it, in
remembrance of me.' For as often as you eat this bread
and drink the cup, you proclaim the Lord's death until
he comes." (1 Corinthians 11: 23-26)

O Gracious God, *(making the sign of the cross)*
your Spirit come upon us, and upon this bread and
wine,
so that it might illumine our understanding, kindle our
will, incite our love, strengthen our weakness, and
enfold our desires.

Community   **O Generous Lord,**
cleanse our hearts, make holy our souls,
confirm our faith,
keep safe our minds, encompass our bodies about
so that in our own hearts, we may feel your presence.

Leader   O Holy Spirit, of greatest power,
come down upon us and subdue us;

160

from your glorious mansion in the heavens.
The knee that is stiff, O healer, make pliant,
the heart that is cold, make warm beneath your wing;
guide the soul that is wandering from your path
and it shall not die.
Each thing that is foul, may you cleanse,
each thing that is hard, may you soften with your grace,
each wound that is causing us pain, may you make whole.
Now to the Father who created each creature,
now to the Son who paid ransom for his people,
now to the Holy Spirit, comforter of might:
shield and protect us from every wound.

Community **Encompass the beginning and the end of our race,**
give us courage to sing in glory,
in peace, in rest, in reconciliation.

Leader Come share in the table of the Lord,
source of love for those who cherish his kindness,
source of solace for those who need his forgiveness,
source of hope for those who fear his judgement.
Come share in the table of the Lord.

Community **Where no tear shall be shed,**
where death comes no more. Amen.

The community shares the Eucharist in silence. Afterward, the table is cleared during the hymn. If there is no hymn, the members of the community use this time for private prayer.

Hymn (optional)

Then, the leader continues the service.

Prayers and Blessings

Leader Praise to the Father,
praise to the Son,
praise to the Spirit.

Community **The three in one.**

All stand.

161

Leader	Let us pray for the coming of the Kingdom, in the words our Lord taught us:
All	**"Our Father in heaven,** **hallowed be your name.** **Your kingdom come.** **Your will be done,** **on earth as it is in heaven.** **Give us this day our daily bread.** **And forgive us our debts,** **as we also have forgiven our debtors.** **And do not bring us to the time of trial,** **but rescue us from the evil one."** (Matthew 6: 9-13)
Leader	Thanks be to you, Eternal Father, for you have enwrapped our bodies and our souls, safeguarding us in the sanctuary of your love …
Community	**… and sheltering us under the mantle of your care.**
Leader	O holy God, be a smooth path before us, a guiding star above us, a keen eye behind us, this day, this night, forever. We are weary and forlorn, O God, lead us to your house, to the peace of heaven.
Community	**Lead us to your house, to the peace of heaven.**
Leader	Help us do your will…
Community	**… and bridle our own.**
Leader	Help us give you your due…
Community	**… and put aside our entitlement.**
Leader	Help us travel your path…
Community	**… and leave behind our own.**
Leader	Help us ponder Christ's death…
Community	**… and find hope in our own.**
Leader	Help us meditate on Christ agony…
Community	**… and strengthen our love for you.**
Leader	Help us carry Christ's cross…
Community	**… and forget our own burdens.**
Leader	Help us embrace repentance…
Community	**… and accept your forgiveness.**
Leader	O holy God, help us to control our tongues and our thoughts,

	so we may trust your wisdom,
	embrace Christ's redemptive love,
	and accept the Spirit's gentle graces.
	For we are weary and forlorn …
Community	**… and ask you lead us to your house, to the peace of heaven. Amen.**
Leader	In the silence of your heart,
	bring your special needs or concerns before God.
	If you wish us to join in your prayers for these needs,
	speak them aloud, saying when you are finished,
	"For this I pray."

Members of the community offer their particular prayers. The community's response to these individual petitions is:

**May God's blessing be yours,
and well may it befall you.**

When these personal prayers are finished, the leader offers the final blessing.

Leader	May the God of life encompass you,
	protecting your form and your frame.
	May the Christ of love encompass you,
	shielding you from hatred and from harm.
	May the spirit of grace encompass you,
	guiding you towards goodness and away from ill.
	The blessings of the Triune God surround you …
Community	**… abiding in us forever and eternally. Amen.**
Leader	Praise to the Father,
	praise to the Son,
	praise to the Spirit.
Community	**The three in one.**
Leader	*(making the sign of the cross)*
	The guarding of the God of life be on you,
	the guarding of the loving Christ be on you,
	the guarding of the Holy Spirit be on you,
	aiding and enfolding you
	each day and night of your lives.
Community	**May God, the three in one, encompass us all, shielding us on sea and on land, in day and in night, guarding each step and each path we travel. Amen.**

Hymn (optional)

The members of the community sit or kneel after the service concludes, as they prefer. Silence is observed to allow private prayer or meditation. Individuals should leave quietly as the Spirit moves them.

VI • THE CRYSTAL PILLAR
& THE ISLAND OF SMITHS

The members of the community enter and pray in silence. After the community is fully assembled, the prelude should be presented.

Prelude   "The Crystal Pillar & The Island of Smiths"
(*from* The Voyage of Saint Brendan, *translated by John J. O'Meara*)

After visiting the Community of Ailbe, holy Brendan and his brethren set sail once again and encounter two wondrous sights while upon the ocean — one awe-inspiring and the other terrifying.

A period of silent meditation follows the reading before the leader begins the penitential prayers.

Penitential Prayers

A bell rings and the members of the community kneel. If anyone cannot kneel, they should remain seated with their head bowed.

Leader   We bend our knees
All   *(making the sign of the cross)*
            in the eye of the Father who created us,
            in the eye of the Son who purchased us,
            in the eye of the Spirit who cleansed us.
            Amen.

All stand.

Leader   Lord Jesus Christ,
            give us the grace of repentance;
            give us the grace of earnestness;
            give us the grace of submission.
Community   **Give us the strength and courage to confess our guilt**
            as earnestly as were this the moment of our death.
Leader   Lord Jesus,
            keep the eye of God between us and every other eye;

keep the purpose of God between us and every other purpose;

keep the desire of God between us and every other desire;

and no mouth can curse us.

Lord Jesus, have mercy on us.

Community **Lord Jesus, have mercy on us.**

Leader Christ Jesus,

keep your pain between us and every other pain;

keep your love between us and every other love;

keep your dearness between us and every other dearness;

and no venom can wound us.

Christ Jesus, have mercy on us.

Community **Christ Jesus, have mercy on us.**

Leader Lord Jesus,

keep the desire of God between us and every other desire;

keep the might of God between us and every other might;

keep the right of God between us and every other right;

and no ill thing can touch us.

Lord Jesus, have mercy on us.

Community **Lord Jesus, have mercy on us.**

Leader Lord Jesus Christ,

with the Father who created us and the Spirit that cleansed us,

Purify our hearts, make holy our souls and confirm our faith,

keep safe our minds and compass our bodies all about.

Enfold us…

Community **… and surround us.**

Leader Guide our speech…

Community **… and our thoughts.**

Leader Guard us in our sleeping…

Community **… and in our waking.**

Leader Nurture us in our watching…

Community **… and in our hoping.**

Leader Shield us in our lives…

Community **… and grant us peace in eternity.**

Leader	Holy God, Father, Son and Spirit, pour down upon us from heaven the rich blessing of your forgiveness. Be patient with us and grant to us the fear of God, the love of God, and your affection so we may do your will on earth at all times …
Community	**… as the angels and saints do in heaven.**
Leader	Holy God, Father, Son and Spirit, pour down upon us from heaven the rich blessing of your peace. Peace between nations …
Community	**… peace between neighbors.**
Leader	Peace between kindred …
Community	**… peace between lovers.**
Leader	Peace between persons injured …
Community	**… peace between foes.**
Leader	Holy God, Father, Son and Spirit, help us to love and bless your creation, all that we see, all that we hear, all that we touch. Let us share your peace with our fellow creatures at all times, living as signs of forgiveness and reconciliation on the earth …
All	**… as the angels and saints do in heaven: without malice, without jealousy, without envy, without fear, without terror of anyone under the sun. And may the Father, the Son and the Spirit kindle in our hearts the flame of love to our neighbors, to our foes, to our friends, to our kindred all, to the brave, to the knave, to the thrall.**
Leader	The peace of the Father of Joy, the peace of Christ the Lamb, the peace of the Spirit of Grace, be with you.
Community	**The peace of the Father of Joy, of Christ the Lamb, and of the Spirit of Grace, be with us all.**
Leader	Let us share a sign of peace with those present here

167

as a testimony to the peace God offers to the world.

The members of the community share a sign of peace before sitting down. A brief period of silence follows before the reader begins the Word of God.

The Word of God

Reader	I set the teachings of Christ before you; I set the guarding of God about you.
Community	**May it possess us and protect us all.**

Reader	A reading from the Gospel according to Saint John.

Now a certain man was ill, Lazarus of Bethany, the village of Mary and her sister Martha. Mary was the one who anointed the Lord with perfume and wiped his feet with her hair; her brother Lazarus was ill. So the sisters sent a message to Jesus, "Lord, he whom you love is ill."

But when Jesus arrived, he found that Lazarus had already been in the tomb four days. Now Bethany was near Jerusalem, some two miles away, and many of the Jews had come to Martha and Mary to console them about their brother. When Martha heard that Jesus was coming, she went and met him, while Mary stayed at home.

When Mary came where Jesus was and saw him, she knelt at his feet and said to him, "Lord, if you had been here, my brother would not have died." When Jesus saw her weeping, and the Jews who came with her also weeping, he was greatly disturbed in spirit and deeply moved. He said, "Where have you laid him?" They said to him, "Lord, come and see." Jesus began to weep. So the Jews said, "See how he loved him!" But some of them said, "Could not he who opened the eyes of the blind man have kept this man from dying?"

Then Jesus, again greatly disturbed, came to the tomb. It was a cave, and a stone was lying against it.

Jesus said, "Take away the stone." Martha, the sister of the dead man, said to him, "Lord, already there is a stench because he has been dead four days." Jesus said to her, "Did I not tell you that if you believed, you would see the glory of God?" So they took away the stone. And Jesus looked upward and said, "Father, I thank you for having heard me. I knew that you always hear me, but I have said this for the sake of the crowd standing here, so that they may believe that you sent me." When he had said this, he cried with a loud voice, "Lazarus, come out!" The dead man came out, his hands and feet bound with strips of cloth, and his face wrapped in a cloth. Jesus said to them, "Unbind him, and let him go."

Many of the Jews therefore, who had come with Mary and had seen what Jesus did, believed in him. But some of them went to the Pharisees and told them what he had done.

The gospel of Jesus Christ, source of strength,
Source of salvation, source of healing grace.

Community	**May it be a mantle to our bodies.**

A brief silence follows the reading, until the leader begins the psalm.

Leader	Psalm 40, Verses 1 through 17.

	I waited patiently for the Lord;
Community	**he inclined to me and heard my cry.**
Leader	He drew me up from the desolate pit, out of the miry bog,
Community	**and set my feet upon a rock, making my steps secure.**
Leader	He put a new song in my mouth, a song of praise to our God.
Community	**Many will see and fear, and put their trust in the Lord.**
Leader	Happy are those who make the Lord their trust,
Community	**who do not turn to the proud,**

	to those who go astray after false gods.
Leader	You have multiplied, O Lord my God,
	your wondrous deeds and your thoughts toward us;
Community	**none can compare with you.**
	Were I to proclaim and tell of them,
	they would be more than can be counted.
Leader	Sacrifice and offering you do not desire,
	but you have given me an open ear.
Community	**Burnt offering and sin offering you have not required.**
Leader	Then I said, "Here I am;
	in the scroll of the book it is written of me.
Community	**I delight to do your will, O my God;**
	your law is within my heart."
Leader	I have told the glad news of deliverance
	in the great congregation;
Community	**see, I have not restrained my lips,**
	as you know, O Lord.
Leader	I have not hidden your saving help within my heart,
	I have spoken of your faithfulness and your salvation;
Community	**I have not concealed your steadfast love and your faithfulness**
	from the great congregation.
Leader	Do not, O Lord,
	withhold your mercy from me;
Community	**let your steadfast love and your faithfulness**
	keep me safe forever.
Leader	For evils have encompassed me
	without number;
Community	**my iniquities have overtaken me,**
	until I cannot see;
	they are more than the hairs of my head,
	and my heart fails me.
Leader	Be pleased, O Lord, to deliver me;
	O Lord, make haste to help me.
Community	**Let all those be put to shame and confusion**
	who seek to snatch away my life;
Leader	let those be turned back and brought to dishonor
	who desire my hurt.
Community	**Let those be appalled because of their shame**
	who say to me, "Aha, Aha!"

Leader	But may all who seek you
	rejoice and be glad in you;
Community	**may those who love your salvation**
	say continually, "Great is the Lord!"
Leader	As for me, I am poor and needy,
	but the Lord takes thought for me.
Community	**You are my help and my deliverer;**
	do not delay, O my God.

There is a brief silence after the psalm before reading or presenting the audio version of the following reflection.

Reflection   "Learning the Patterns of God's Presence"
                        by Timothy J. Ray

A period of silence is observed after the reflection for private meditation, with or without music. Afterward, the leader continues the service — proceeding either to the Eucharistic Prayer or to the Prayers and Blessings after the optional hymn.

Hymn (optional)

Eucharistic Prayer

If the community wishes to share the Eucharist, the table is prepared during the hymn. If there is no hymn, the table should be prepared in silence — slowly and deliberately. Then, the leader begins the Eucharistic Prayer.

Leader	Thanks be to you, Holy Father of Glory,
	father-kind, ever-loving, ever-powerful,
	because of all the abundance, favor and deliverance
	you bestow on us in our need.
Community	**May your name be praised forever,**
	in the heavens above and here on earth.
Leader	Whatever Providence befalls us as your children,
	in our portion, in our lot, in our path,
	give to us with it the riches of your hand
	and the joyous blessing of your mouth.
Community	**May your kingdom be seen to flourish**

	through the joy of your people, always grateful.
Leader	In the steep common path of our calling,
	be it easy or uneasy to our flesh,
	be it bright or dark for us to follow,
	your perfect guidance will be upon us.
Community	**Provide for us in all our needs,**
	material and spiritual, this day and every day.
Leader	Be a shield to us from the wiles of the deceiver,
	from the arch-destroyer with his arrows pursuing us,
	and in each secret thought our minds get to weave,
	guide and protect us.
Community	**Do not allow us to be tossed about by temptations**
	and protect us from all evils that would do us harm.
Leader	O Loving Christ, who was hanged upon a tree,

each day and each night we remember your covenant;
in our lying down and rising up, we yield ourselves to
your cross,
in our lives and our deaths, we seek in you our peace.
Each day, may we remember the source of the mercies
bestowed on us, gently and generously;
each day, may we become fuller in love with you.

My brothers and sisters, with St. Paul, I say to
you:
"I received from the Lord what I also handed on to you,
that the Lord Jesus on the night when he was betrayed
took a loaf of bread, and when he had given thanks, he
broke it and said, 'This is my body that is for you. Do
this in remembrance of me.' In the same way he took
the cup also, after supper, saying, 'This cup is the new
covenant in my blood. Do this, as often you drink it, in
remembrance of me.' For as often as you eat this bread
and drink the cup, you proclaim the Lord's death until
he comes." (1 Corinthians 11: 23-26)

O Gracious God, *(making the sign of the cross)*
your Spirit come upon us, and upon this bread and
wine,
so that it might illumine our understanding, kindle our
will, incite our love, strengthen our weakness, and
enfold our desires.

Community	**O Generous Lord,**

	cleanse our hearts, make holy our souls, confirm our faith,
	keep safe our minds, encompass our bodies about
	so that in our own hearts, we may feel your presence.
Leader	O Holy Spirit, of greatest power,
	come down upon us and subdue us;
	from your glorious mansion in the heavens.
	The knee that is stiff, O healer, make pliant,
	the heart that is cold, make warm beneath your wing;
	guide the soul that is wandering from your path
	and it shall not die.
	Each thing that is foul, may you cleanse,
	each thing that is hard, may you soften with your grace,
	each wound that is causing us pain, may you make whole.
	Now to the Father who created each creature,
	now to the Son who paid ransom for his people,
	now to the Holy Spirit, comforter of might:
	shield and protect us from every wound.
Community	**Encompass the beginning and the end of our race,**
	give us courage to sing in glory,
	in peace, in rest, in reconciliation.
Leader	Come share in the table of the Lord,
	source of love for those who cherish his kindness,
	source of solace for those who need his forgiveness,
	source of hope for those who fear his judgement.
	Come share in the table of the Lord.
Community	**Where no tear shall be shed,**
	where death comes no more. Amen.

The community shares the Eucharist in silence. Afterward, the table is cleared during the hymn. If there is no hymn, the members of the community use this time for private prayer.

Hymn (optional)

Then, the leader continues the service.

Prayers and Blessings

Leader	Praise to the Father,
	praise to the Son,
	praise to the Spirit.
Community	**The three in one.**

All stand.

Leader	Let us pray for the coming of the Kingdom,
	in the words our Lord taught us:
All	**"Our Father in heaven,**
	hallowed be your name.
	Your kingdom come.
	Your will be done,
	on earth as it is in heaven.
	Give us this day our daily bread.
	And forgive us our debts,
	as we also have forgiven our debtors.
	And do not bring us to the time of trial,
	but rescue us from the evil one."
	(Matthew 6: 9-13)
Leader	Thanks be to you, Eternal Father,
	for you have enwrapped our bodies and our souls,
	safeguarding us in the sanctuary of your love …
Community	**… and sheltering us under the mantle of your care.**
Leader	O holy God, be a smooth path before us,
	a guiding star above us, a keen eye behind us,
	this day, this night, forever.
	We are weary and forlorn, O God,
	lead us to your house, to the peace of heaven.
Community	**Lead us to your house, to the peace of heaven.**
Leader	Help us do your will…
Community	**… and bridle our own.**
Leader	Help us give you your due…
Community	**… and put aside our entitlement.**
Leader	Help us travel your path…
Community	**… and leave behind our own.**
Leader	Help us ponder Christ's death…
Community	**… and find hope in our own.**
Leader	Help us meditate on Christ agony…
Community	**… and strengthen our love for you.**

Leader	Help us carry Christ's cross…
Community	**… and forget our own burdens.**
Leader	Help us embrace repentance…
Community	**… and accept your forgiveness.**
Leader	O holy God, help us to control our tongues and our thoughts, so we may trust your wisdom, embrace Christ's redemptive love, and accept the Spirit's gentle graces. For we are weary and forlorn …
Community	**… and ask you lead us to your house, to the peace of heaven. Amen.**
Leader	In the silence of your heart, bring your special needs or concerns before God. If you wish us to join in your prayers for these needs, speak them aloud, saying when you are finished, "For this I pray."

Members of the community offer their particular prayers. The community's response to these individual petitions is:

May God's blessing be yours,
and well may it befall you.

When these personal prayers are finished, the leader offers the final blessing.

Leader	May the God of life encompass you, protecting your form and your frame. May the Christ of love encompass you, shielding you from hatred and from harm. May the spirit of grace encompass you, guiding you towards goodness and away from ill. The blessings of the Triune God surround you …
Community	**… abiding in us forever and eternally. Amen.**
Leader	Praise to the Father, praise to the Son, praise to the Spirit.
Community	**The three in one.**
Leader	*(making the sign of the cross)* The guarding of the God of life be on you, the guarding of the loving Christ be on you,

175

the guarding of the Holy Spirit be on you,
aiding and enfolding you
each day and night of your lives.

Community   **May God, the three in one, encompass us all,
shielding us on sea and on land, in day and in night,
guarding each step and each path we travel. Amen.**

Hymn (optional)

*The members of the community sit or kneel after the service concludes,
as they prefer. Silence is observed to allow private prayer or meditation.
Individuals should leave quietly as the Spirit moves them.*

VII • UNHAPPY JUDAS

The members of the community enter and pray in silence. After the community is fully assembled, the prelude should be presented.

Prelude   "Unhappy Judas"
                      (from The Voyage of Saint Brendan, *translated by John J. O'Meara)*

                      Continuing their journey on the ocean, holy Brendan and his companions meet Judas — buffeted by the waves as he sits precariously on a rock in the sea — and Saint Brendan defends him from the demons of hell.

A period of silent meditation follows the reading before the leader begins the penitential prayers.

Penitential Prayers

A bell rings and the members of the community kneel. If anyone cannot kneel, they should remain seated with their head bowed.

Leader	We bend our knees
All	*(making the sign of the cross)*
	in the eye of the Father who created us,
	in the eye of the Son who purchased us,
	in the eye of the Spirit who cleansed us.
	Amen.

All stand.

Leader	Lord Jesus Christ,
	give us the grace of repentance;
	give us the grace of earnestness;
	give us the grace of submission.
Community	**Give us the strength and courage to confess our guilt**
	as earnestly as were this the moment of our death.
Leader	Lord Jesus,
	Bless and protect us beneath your glorious mantle.
	There is no plant in the ground, nor form in the strand,

that is not full of your virtue.
Lord Jesus, have mercy on us.

Community   **Lord Jesus, have mercy on us.**

Leader   Christ Jesus,
Guard and secure us behind the strength of your shield,
There is no life, in the sea or river, in air or on land,
that does not proclaim your goodness.
Christ Jesus, have mercy on us.

Community   **Christ Jesus, have mercy on us.**

Leader   Lord Jesus,
Help and teach us to trust in your constant care.
There is nothing in the firmament,
nor beneath sun and moon,
that is not full of your blessing.
Lord Jesus, have mercy on us.

Community   **Lord Jesus, have mercy on us.**

Leader   Lord Jesus Christ,
with the Father who created us and the Spirit that cleansed us,
Purify our hearts, make holy our souls and confirm our faith,
keep safe our minds and compass our bodies all about.
Enfold us…

Community   **… and surround us.**

Leader   Guide our speech…

Community   **… and our thoughts.**

Leader   Guard us in our sleeping…

Community   **… and in our waking.**

Leader   Nurture us in our watching…

Community   **… and in our hoping.**

Leader   Shield us in our lives…

Community   **… and grant us peace in eternity.**

Leader   Holy God,
Father, Son and Spirit,
pour down upon us from heaven
the rich blessing of your forgiveness.
Be patient with us and grant to us
the fear of God, the love of God, and your affection
so we may do your will on earth at all times …

Community   **… as the angels and saints do in heaven.**

Leader	Holy God, Father, Son and Spirit, pour down upon us from heaven the rich blessing of your peace. Peace between nations …
Community	**… peace between neighbors.**
Leader	Peace between kindred …
Community	**… peace between lovers.**
Leader	Peace between persons injured …
Community	**… peace between foes.**
Leader	Holy God, Father, Son and Spirit, help us to love and bless your creation, all that we see, all that we hear, all that we touch. Let us share your peace with our fellow creatures at all times, living as signs of forgiveness and reconciliation on the earth …
All	**… as the angels and saints do in heaven: without malice, without jealousy, without envy, without fear, without terror of anyone under the sun. And may the Father, the Son and the Spirit kindle in our hearts the flame of love to our neighbors, to our foes, to our friends, to our kindred all, to the brave, to the knave, to the thrall.**
Leader	The peace of the Father of Joy, the peace of Christ the Lamb, the peace of the Spirit of Grace, be with you.
Community	**The peace of the Father of Joy, of Christ the Lamb, and of the Spirit of Grace, be with us all.**
Leader	Let us share a sign of peace with those present here as a testimony to the peace God offers to the world.

The members of the community share a sign of peace before sitting down. A brief period of silence follows before the reader begins the Word of God.

The Word of God

Reader   I set the teachings of Christ before you;
              I set the guarding of God about you.
Community   **May it possess us and protect us all.**

Reader   A reading from the Gospel according to Saint John.

[After questioning Jesus in private], Pilate went out to the Jews and told them, "I find no case against him. But you have a custom that I release someone for you at the Passover. Do you want me to release for you the King of the Jews?" They shouted in reply, "Not this man, but Barabbas!" Now Barabbas was a bandit.

Then Pilate took Jesus and had him flogged. And the soldiers wove a crown of thorns and put it on his head, and they dressed him in a purple robe. They kept coming up to him, saying, "Hail, King of the Jews!" and striking him on the face. Pilate went out again and said to them, "Look, I am bringing him out to you to let you know that I find no case against him." So Jesus came out, wearing the crown of thorns and the purple robe. Pilate said to them, "Here is the man!" When the chief priests and the police saw him, they shouted, "Crucify him! Crucify him!" Pilate said to them, "Take him yourselves and crucify him; I find no case against him." The Jews answered him, "We have a law, and according to that law he ought to die because he has claimed to be the Son of God."

Now when Pilate heard this, he was more afraid than ever. He entered his headquarters again and asked Jesus, "Where are you from?" But Jesus gave him no answer. Pilate therefore said to him, "Do you refuse to speak to me? Do you not know that I have power to release you, and power to crucify you?" Jesus answered him, "You would have no power over me unless it had been given you from above; therefore the one who handed me over to you is guilty of a greater sin." From then on Pilate tried to release him, but the Jews cried out, "If you release this man, you are no friend of the emperor. Everyone who claims to be a king sets himself against the emperor."

When Pilate heard these words, he brought Jesus outside and sat on the judge's bench at a place called The Stone Pavement, or in Hebrew Gabbatha. Now it was the day of Preparation for the Passover; and it was about noon. He said to the Jews, "Here is your King!" They cried out, "Away with him! Away with him! Crucify him!" Pilate asked them, "Shall I crucify your King?" The chief priests answered, "We have no king but the emperor." Then he handed Jesus over to them to be crucified.

The gospel of Jesus Christ, source of strength,
Source of salvation, source of healing grace.

Community   **May it be a mantle to our bodies.**

A brief silence follows the reading, until the leader begins the psalm.

Leader   Psalm 22, Verses 1 through 11 and 23 through 31.

My God, my God, why have you forsaken me?
Why are you so far from helping me, from the words of my groaning?

Community   **O my God, I cry by day, but you do not answer;**
and by night, but find no rest.

Leader   Yet you are holy,
enthroned on the praises of Israel.

Community   **In you our ancestors trusted;**
they trusted, and you delivered them.

Leader   To you they cried, and were saved;

Community   **in you they trusted, and were not put to shame.**

Leader   But I am a worm, and not human;
scorned by others, and despised by the people.

Community   **All who see me mock at me;**
they make mouths at me, they shake their heads;

Leader   "Commit your cause to the Lord; let him deliver —

Community   **let him rescue the one in whom he delights!"**

Leader   Yet it was you who took me from the womb;
you kept me safe on my mother's breast.

Community   **On you I was cast from my birth,**

	and since my mother bore me you have been my God.
Leader	Do not be far from me,
Community	**for trouble is near and there is no one to help.**
Leader	You who fear the Lord, praise him! All you offspring of Jacob, glorify him;
Community	**stand in awe of him, all you offspring of Israel!**
Leader	For he did not despise or abhor the affliction of the afflicted;
Community	**he did not hide his face from me,** **but heard when I cried to him.**
Leader	From you comes my praise in the great congregation; my vows I will pay before those who fear him.
Community	**The poor shall eat and be satisfied;** **those who seek him shall praise the Lord.** **May your hearts live forever!**
Leader	All the ends of the earth shall remember and turn to the Lord;
Community	**and all the families of the nations** **shall worship before him.**
Leader	For dominion belongs to the Lord,
Community	**and he rules over the nations.**
Leader	To him, indeed, shall all who sleep in the earth bow down;
Community	**before him shall bow all who go down to the dust,** **and I shall live for him.**
Leader	Posterity will serve him; future generations will be told about the Lord,
Community	**and proclaim his deliverance to a people yet unborn,** **saying that he has done it.**

There is a brief silence after the psalm before reading or presenting the audio version of the following reflection.

Reflection	"Embracing the Standard of Christ" by Timothy J. Ray

A period of silence is observed after the reflection for private meditation, with or without music. Afterward, the leader continues the service — proceeding either to the Eucharistic Prayer or to the Prayers and Blessings after the optional hymn.

Hymn (optional)

Eucharistic Prayer

If the community wishes to share the Eucharist, the table is prepared during the hymn. If there is no hymn, the table should be prepared in silence — slowly and deliberately. Then, the leader begins the Eucharistic Prayer.

Leader	Thanks be to you, Holy Father of Glory, father-kind, ever-loving, ever-powerful, because of all the abundance, favor and deliverance you bestow on us in our need.
Community	**May your name be praised forever, in the heavens above and here on earth.**
Leader	Whatever Providence befalls us as your children, in our portion, in our lot, in our path, give to us with it the riches of your hand and the joyous blessing of your mouth.
Community	**May your kingdom be seen to flourish through the joy of your people, always grateful.**
Leader	In the steep common path of our calling, be it easy or uneasy to our flesh, be it bright or dark for us to follow, your perfect guidance will be upon us.
Community	**Provide for us in all our needs, material and spiritual, this day and every day.**
Leader	Be a shield to us from the wiles of the deceiver, from the arch-destroyer with his arrows pursuing us, and in each secret thought our minds get to weave, guide and protect us.
Community	**Do not allow us to be tossed about by temptations and protect us from all evils that would do us harm.**
Leader	O Loving Christ, who was hanged upon a tree, each day and each night we remember your covenant; in our lying down and rising up, we yield ourselves to your cross, in our lives and our deaths, we seek in you our peace. Each day, may we remember the source of the mercies

bestowed on us, gently and generously;
each day, may we become fuller in love with you.

My brothers and sisters, with St. Paul, I say to
you:
"I received from the Lord what I also handed on to you,
that the Lord Jesus on the night when he was betrayed
took a loaf of bread, and when he had given thanks, he
broke it and said, 'This is my body that is for you. Do
this in remembrance of me.' In the same way he took
the cup also, after supper, saying, 'This cup is the new
covenant in my blood. Do this, as often you drink it, in
remembrance of me.' For as often as you eat this bread
and drink the cup, you proclaim the Lord's death until
he comes." (1 Corinthians 11: 23-26)

O Gracious God, *(making the sign of the cross)*
your Spirit come upon us, and upon this bread and
wine,
so that it might illumine our understanding, kindle our
will, incite our love, strengthen our weakness, and
enfold our desires.

Community | **O Generous Lord,**
cleanse our hearts, make holy our souls,
confirm our faith,
keep safe our minds, encompass our bodies about
so that in our own hearts, we may feel your presence.

Leader | O Holy Spirit, of greatest power,
come down upon us and subdue us;
from your glorious mansion in the heavens.
The knee that is stiff, O healer, make pliant,
the heart that is cold, make warm beneath your wing;
guide the soul that is wandering from your path
and it shall not die.
Each thing that is foul, may you cleanse,
each thing that is hard, may you soften with your grace,
each wound that is causing us pain, may you make
whole.
Now to the Father who created each creature,
now to the Son who paid ransom for his people,
now to the Holy Spirit, comforter of might:
shield and protect us from every wound.

184

Community	**Encompass the beginning and the end of our race,**
	give us courage to sing in glory,
	in peace, in rest, in reconciliation.
Leader	Come share in the table of the Lord,
	source of love for those who cherish his kindness,
	source of solace for those who need his forgiveness,
	source of hope for those who fear his judgement.
	Come share in the table of the Lord.
Community	**Where no tear shall be shed,**
	where death comes no more. Amen.

The community shares the Eucharist in silence. Afterward, the table is cleared during the hymn. If there is no hymn, the members of the community use this time for private prayer.

Hymn (optional)

Then, the leader continues the service.

Prayers and Blessings

Leader	Praise to the Father,
	praise to the Son,
	praise to the Spirit.
Community	**The three in one.**

All stand.

Leader	Let us pray for the coming of the Kingdom,
	in the words our Lord taught us:
All	**"Our Father in heaven,**
	hallowed be your name.
	Your kingdom come.
	Your will be done,
	on earth as it is in heaven.
	Give us this day our daily bread.
	And forgive us our debts,
	as we also have forgiven our debtors.
	And do not bring us to the time of trial,
	but rescue us from the evil one."

(Matthew 6: 9-13)

Leader	Thanks be to you, Eternal Father,
	for you have enwrapped our bodies and our souls,
	safeguarding us in the sanctuary of your love …
Community	**… and sheltering us under the mantle of your care.**
Leader	O Holy God,
	guide us with your wisdom,
	chastise us with your justice,
	help us with your mercy,
	protect us with your strength.
	In our dreams…
Community	**… arouse holy ambitions.**
Leader	In our repose…
Community	**… strengthen us for your service.**
Leader	In our hearts…
Community	**… nurture love for all your creatures.**
Leader	In our minds…
Community	**… implant saintly thoughts.**
Leader	In our deeds…
Community	**… may others see your kindness.**
Leader	In our words…
Community	**… may others hear your mercy.**
Leader	In our wishes…
Community	**… may others feel your compassion.**
Leader	In our reason…
Community	**… may others discern your wisdom.**
Leader	Divine Majesty,
	fill us with your goodness,
	shield us with your shade,
	and change us with your grace.
Community	**Amen.**
Leader	In the silence of your heart,
	bring your special needs or concerns before God.
	If you wish us to join in your prayers for these needs,
	speak them aloud, saying when you are finished,
	"For this I pray."

Members of the community offer their particular prayers. The community's response to these individual petitions is:
May God's blessing be yours,

and well may it befall you.

When these personal prayers are finished, the leader offers the final blessing.

Leader	May God our Creator
	guard you from hurt and
	protect you from harm
	in the nearness of his love.
	May Christ our Savior
	shield you from mischance and
	shelter you from grief
	in the nearness of his love.
	May the Guiding Spirit
	keep you from ill and
	bring you to the land of peace
	in the nearness of his love.
	Praise to the Father,
	praise to the Son,
	praise to the Spirit.
Community	**May the three in one bring us to the peace of eternity. Amen.**
Leader	Praise to the Father,
	praise to the Son,
	praise to the Spirit.
Community	**The three in one.**
Leader	*(making the sign of the cross)*
	The guarding of the God of life be on you,
	the guarding of the loving Christ be on you,
	the guarding of the Holy Spirit be on you,
	aiding and enfolding you
	each day and night of your lives.
Community	**May God, the three in one, encompass us all,**
	shielding us on sea and on land, in day and in night,
	guarding each step and each path we travel. Amen.

Hymn (optional)

The members of the community sit or kneel after the service concludes, as they prefer. Silence is observed to allow private prayer or meditation. Individuals should leave quietly as the Spirit moves them.

VIII • THE ISLAND OF PAUL THE HERMIT

The members of the community enter and pray in silence. After the community is fully assembled, the prelude should be presented.

Prelude   "The Island of Paul the Hermit"
                    (*from* The Voyage of Saint Brendan, *translated by John J. O'Meara*)

                    After many months on the sea, Saint Brendan and his brothers come to an island where they are welcomed by a hermit named Paul. After recounting his own spiritual journey, Paul the Hermit tells holy Brendan the final things he and his companions must do to come to the Land of the Saints.

A period of silent meditation follows the reading before the leader begins the penitential prayers.

Penitential Prayers

A bell rings and the members of the community kneel. If anyone cannot kneel, they should remain seated with their head bowed.

Leader   We bend our knees
All   *(making the sign of the cross)*
                in the eye of the Father who created us,
                in the eye of the Son who purchased us,
                in the eye of the Spirit who cleansed us.
                Amen.

All stand.

Leader   Lord Jesus Christ,
                give us the grace of repentance;
                give us the grace of earnestness;
                give us the grace of submission.
Community   **Give us the strength and courage to confess our guilt**
                as earnestly as were this the moment of our death.
Leader   Lord Jesus,

	Bless and protect us beneath your glorious mantle.
	There is no plant in the ground, nor form in the strand,
	that is not full of your virtue.
	Lord Jesus, have mercy on us.
Community	**Lord Jesus, have mercy on us.**
Leader	Christ Jesus,
	Guard and secure us behind the strength of your shield,
	There is no life, in the sea or river, in air or on land,
	that does not proclaim your goodness.
	Christ Jesus, have mercy on us.
Community	**Christ Jesus, have mercy on us.**
Leader	Lord Jesus,
	Help and teach us to trust in your constant care.
	There is nothing in the firmament,
	nor beneath sun and moon,
	that is not full of your blessing.
	Lord Jesus, have mercy on us.
Community	**Lord Jesus, have mercy on us.**
Leader	Lord Jesus Christ,
	with the Father who created us and the Spirit that cleansed us,
	Purify our hearts, make holy our souls and confirm our faith,
	keep safe our minds and compass our bodies all about.
	Enfold us…
Community	**… and surround us.**
Leader	Guide our speech…
Community	**… and our thoughts.**
Leader	Guard us in our sleeping…
Community	**… and in our waking.**
Leader	Nurture us in our watching…
Community	**… and in our hoping.**
Leader	Shield us in our lives…
Community	**… and grant us peace in eternity.**
Leader	Holy God,
	Father, Son and Spirit,
	pour down upon us from heaven
	the rich blessing of your forgiveness.
	Be patient with us and grant to us
	the fear of God, the love of God, and your affection

	so we may do your will on earth at all times …
Community	**… as the angels and saints do in heaven.**
Leader	Holy God,
	Father, Son and Spirit,
	pour down upon us from heaven
	the rich blessing of your peace.
	Peace between nations …
Community	**… peace between neighbors.**
Leader	Peace between kindred …
Community	**… peace between lovers.**
Leader	Peace between persons injured …
Community	**… peace between foes.**
Leader	Holy God,
	Father, Son and Spirit,
	help us to love and bless your creation,
	all that we see, all that we hear, all that we touch.
	Let us share your peace with our fellow creatures at all times,
	living as signs of forgiveness and reconciliation on the earth …
All	**… as the angels and saints do in heaven:**
	without malice, without jealousy, without envy,
	without fear, without terror of anyone under the sun.
	And may the Father, the Son and the Spirit
	kindle in our hearts the flame of love to our neighbors,
	to our foes, to our friends, to our kindred all,
	to the brave, to the knave, to the thrall.
Leader	The peace of the Father of Joy,
	the peace of Christ the Lamb,
	the peace of the Spirit of Grace, be with you.
Community	**The peace of the Father of Joy,**
	of Christ the Lamb, and of the Spirit of Grace,
	be with us all.
Leader	Let us share a sign of peace with those present here
	as a testimony to the peace God offers to the world.

The members of the community share a sign of peace before sitting down. A brief period of silence follows before the reader begins the Word of God.

The Word of God

Reader   I set the teachings of Christ before you;
                    I set the guarding of God about you.

Community   **May it possess us and protect us all.**

Reader   A reading from the Gospel according to Saint John.

Early on the first day of the week, while it was still dark, Mary Magdalene came to the tomb and saw that the stone had been removed from the tomb. So she ran and went to Simon Peter and the other disciple, the one whom Jesus loved, and said to them, "They have taken the Lord out of the tomb, and we do not know where they have laid him." Then Peter and the other disciple set out and went toward the tomb. The two were running together, but the other disciple outran Peter and reached the tomb first. He bent down to look in and saw the linen wrappings lying there, but he did not go in. Then Simon Peter came, following him, and went into the tomb. He saw the linen wrappings lying there, and the cloth that had been on Jesus' head, not lying with the linen wrappings but rolled up in a place by itself. Then the other disciple, who reached the tomb first, also went in, and he saw and believed; for as yet they did not understand the scripture, that he must rise from the dead. Then the disciples returned to their homes

But Mary stood weeping outside the tomb. As she wept, she bent over to look into the tomb; and she saw two angels in white, sitting where the body of Jesus had been lying, one at the head and the other at the feet. They said to her, "Woman, why are you weeping?" She said to them, "They have taken away my Lord, and I do not know where they have laid him." When she had said this, she turned around and saw Jesus standing there, but she did not know that it was Jesus. Jesus said to her, "Woman, why are you weeping? Whom are you looking for?" Supposing him to be the gardener, she said to him, "Sir, if you have carried him away, tell me where you have laid him, and I will take him away." Jesus said to her, "Mary!" She turned and said to him in Hebrew, "Rabbouni!" (which means Teacher). Jesus said to her, "Do not hold on to me, because I have not yet ascended to the Father. But go to my brothers and say to them, 'I am ascending to my Father and your Father, to my God and your God.'" Mary Magdalene went and announced to the disciples, "I have seen the Lord"; and she told them that he had said these things to her.

The gospel of Jesus Christ, source of strength,
Source of salvation, source of healing grace.

Community **May it be a mantle to our bodies.**

A brief silence follows the reading, until the leader begins the psalm.

Leader   Psalm 91, Verses 1 through 16.

You who live in the shelter of the Most High,
who abide in the shadow of the Almighty,

Community   **will say to the Lord, "My refuge and my fortress;**
my God, in whom I trust."

Leader   For he will deliver you from the snare of the fowler
and from the deadly pestilence;

Community   **he will cover you with his pinions,**
and under his wings you will find refuge;
his faithfulness is a shield and buckler.

Leader   You will not fear the terror of the night,
or the arrow that flies by day,

Community   **or the pestilence that stalks in darkness,**
or the destruction that wastes at noonday.

Leader   A thousand may fall at your side,
ten thousand at your right hand,
but it will not come near you.

Community   **You will only look with your eyes**
and see the punishment of the wicked.

Leader   Because you have made the Lord your refuge,
the Most High your dwelling place,

Community   **no evil shall befall you,**

	no scourge come near your tent.
Leader	For he will command his angels concerning you to guard you in all your ways.
Community	**On their hands they will bear you up, so that you will not dash your foot against a stone.**
Leader	You will tread on the lion and the adder,
Community	**the young lion and the serpent you will trample under foot.**
Leader	Those who love me, I will deliver; I will protect those who know my name.
Community	**When they call to me, I will answer them; I will be with them in trouble, I will rescue them and honor them.**
Leader	With long life I will satisfy them,
Community	**and show them my salvation.**

There is a brief silence after the psalm before reading or presenting the audio version of the following reflection.

Reflection   "Welcoming Others into the Resurrection"
                                    by Timothy J. Ray

A period of silence is observed after the reflection for private meditation, with or without music. Afterward, the leader continues the service — proceeding either to the Eucharistic Prayer or to the Prayers and Blessings after the optional hymn.

Hymn (optional)

Eucharistic Prayer

If the community wishes to share the Eucharist, the table is prepared during the hymn. If there is no hymn, the table should be prepared in silence — slowly and deliberately. Then, the leader begins the Eucharistic Prayer.

Leader   Thanks be to you, Holy Father of Glory,
              father-kind, ever-loving, ever-powerful,
              because of all the abundance, favor and deliverance
              you bestow on us in our need.

193

Community	**May your name be praised forever,** **in the heavens above and here on earth.**
Leader	Whatever Providence befalls us as your children, in our portion, in our lot, in our path, give to us with it the riches of your hand and the joyous blessing of your mouth.
Community	**May your kingdom be seen to flourish** **through the joy of your people, always grateful.**
Leader	In the steep common path of our calling, be it easy or uneasy to our flesh, be it bright or dark for us to follow, your perfect guidance will be upon us.
Community	**Provide for us in all our needs,** **material and spiritual, this day and every day.**
Leader	Be a shield to us from the wiles of the deceiver, from the arch-destroyer with his arrows pursuing us, and in each secret thought our minds get to weave, guide and protect us.
Community	**Do not allow us to be tossed about by temptations** **and protect us from all evils that would do us harm.**
Leader	O Loving Christ, who was hanged upon a tree, each day and each night we remember your covenant; in our lying down and rising up, we yield ourselves to your cross, in our lives and our deaths, we seek in you our peace. Each day, may we remember the source of the mercies bestowed on us, gently and generously; each day, may we become fuller in love with you. My brothers and sisters, with St. Paul, I say to you: "I received from the Lord what I also handed on to you, that the Lord Jesus on the night when he was betrayed took a loaf of bread, and when he had given thanks, he broke it and said, 'This is my body that is for you. Do this in remembrance of me.' In the same way he took the cup also, after supper, saying, 'This cup is the new covenant in my blood. Do this, as often you drink it, in remembrance of me.' For as often as you eat this bread and drink the cup, you proclaim the Lord's death until he comes." (1 Corinthians 11: 23-26)

O Gracious God, *(making the sign of the cross)* your Spirit come upon us, and upon this bread and wine,

so that it might illumine our understanding, kindle our will, incite our love, strengthen our weakness, and enfold our desires.

Community **O Generous Lord,**
cleanse our hearts, make holy our souls,
confirm our faith,
keep safe our minds, encompass our bodies about
so that in our own hearts, we may feel your presence.

Leader O Holy Spirit, of greatest power,
come down upon us and subdue us;
from your glorious mansion in the heavens.
The knee that is stiff, O healer, make pliant,
the heart that is cold, make warm beneath your wing;
guide the soul that is wandering from your path
and it shall not die.
Each thing that is foul, may you cleanse,
each thing that is hard, may you soften with your grace,
each wound that is causing us pain, may you make whole.
Now to the Father who created each creature,
now to the Son who paid ransom for his people,
now to the Holy Spirit, comforter of might:
shield and protect us from every wound.

Community **Encompass the beginning and the end of our race,**
give us courage to sing in glory,
in peace, in rest, in reconciliation.

Leader Come share in the table of the Lord,
source of love for those who cherish his kindness,
source of solace for those who need his forgiveness,
source of hope for those who fear his judgement.
Come share in the table of the Lord.

Community **Where no tear shall be shed,**
where death comes no more. Amen.

The community shares the Eucharist in silence. Afterward, the table is cleared during the hymn. If there is no hymn, the members of the community use this time for private prayer.

195

Hymn (optional)

Then, the leader continues the service.

Prayers and Blessings

Leader	Praise to the Father, praise to the Son, praise to the Spirit.
Community	**The three in one.**

All stand.

Leader	Let us pray for the coming of the Kingdom, in the words our Lord taught us:
All	**"Our Father in heaven,** **hallowed be your name.** **Your kingdom come.** **Your will be done,** **on earth as it is in heaven.** **Give us this day our daily bread.** **And forgive us our debts,** **as we also have forgiven our debtors.** **And do not bring us to the time of trial,** **but rescue us from the evil one."** (Matthew 6: 9-13)
Leader	Thanks be to you, Eternal Father, for you have enwrapped our bodies and our souls, safeguarding us in the sanctuary of your love …
Community	**… and sheltering us under the mantle of your care.**
Leader	O Holy God, guide us with your wisdom, chastise us with your justice, help us with your mercy, protect us with your strength. In our dreams…
Community	**… arouse holy ambitions.**
Leader	In our repose…
Community	**… strengthen us for your service.**

Leader	In our hearts…
Community	**… nurture love for all your creatures.**
Leader	In our minds…
Community	**… implant saintly thoughts.**
Leader	In our deeds…
Community	**… may others see your kindness.**
Leader	In our words…
Community	**… may others hear your mercy.**
Leader	In our wishes…
Community	**… may others feel your compassion.**
Leader	In our reason…
Community	**… may others discern your wisdom.**
Leader	Divine Majesty,
	fill us with your goodness,
	shield us with your shade,
	and change us with your grace.
Community	**Amen.**
Leader	In the silence of your heart,
	bring your special needs or concerns before God.
	If you wish us to join in your prayers for these needs,
	speak them aloud, saying when you are finished,
	"For this I pray."

Members of the community offer their particular prayers. The community's response to these individual petitions is:

**May God's blessing be yours,
and well may it befall you.**

When these personal prayers are finished, the leader offers the final blessing.

Leader	May God our Creator
	guard you from hurt and
	protect you from harm
	in the nearness of his love.
	May Christ our Savior
	shield you from mischance and
	shelter you from grief
	in the nearness of his love.
	May the Guiding Spirit
	keep you from ill and

197

	bring you to the land of peace
	in the nearness of his love.
	Praise to the Father,
	praise to the Son,
	praise to the Spirit.
Community	**May the three in one bring us to the peace of eternity. Amen.**
Leader	Praise to the Father,
	praise to the Son,
	praise to the Spirit.
Community	**The three in one.**
Leader	*(making the sign of the cross)*
	The guarding of the God of life be on you,
	the guarding of the loving Christ be on you,
	the guarding of the Holy Spirit be on you,
	aiding and enfolding you
	each day and night of your lives.
Community	**May God, the three in one, encompass us all, shielding us on sea and on land, in day and in night, guarding each step and each path we travel. Amen.**

Hymn (optional)

The members of the community sit or kneel after the service concludes, as they prefer. Silence is observed to allow private prayer or meditation. Individuals should leave quietly as the Spirit moves them.

IX • THE PROMISED LAND OF THE SAINTS & THE RETURN HOME

The members of the community enter and pray in silence. After the community is fully assembled, the prelude should be presented.

Prelude   "The Promised Land of the Saints & The Return Home" (*from* The Voyage of Saint Brendan, *translated by John J. O'Meara*)

After leaving the island of Paul the Hermit, Saint Brendan and his companions sail to the south and return to some of the places they had visited before. After celebrating Easter and Pentecost, Saint Brendan and his brothers are guided to the Promised Land of the Saints — and then commanded to return home.

A period of silent meditation follows the reading before the leader begins the penitential prayers.

Penitential Prayers

A bell rings and the members of the community kneel. If anyone cannot kneel, they should remain seated with their head bowed.

Leader	We bend our knees
All	*(making the sign of the cross)*
	in the eye of the Father who created us,
	in the eye of the Son who purchased us,
	in the eye of the Spirit who cleansed us.
	Amen.

All stand.

Leader	Lord Jesus Christ,
	give us the grace of repentance;
	give us the grace of earnestness;
	give us the grace of submission.
Community	**Give us the strength and courage to confess our guilt**
	as earnestly as were this the moment of our death.

Leader	Lord Jesus,
	Bless and protect us beneath your glorious mantle.
	There is no plant in the ground, nor form in the strand,
	that is not full of your virtue.
	Lord Jesus, have mercy on us.
Community	**Lord Jesus, have mercy on us.**
Leader	Christ Jesus,
	Guard and secure us behind the strength of your shield,
	There is no life, in the sea or river, in air or on land,
	that does not proclaim your goodness.
	Christ Jesus, have mercy on us.
Community	**Christ Jesus, have mercy on us.**
Leader	Lord Jesus,
	Help and teach us to trust in your constant care.
	There is nothing in the firmament,
	nor beneath sun and moon,
	that is not full of your blessing.
	Lord Jesus, have mercy on us.
Community	**Lord Jesus, have mercy on us.**
Leader	Lord Jesus Christ,
	with the Father who created us and the Spirit that cleansed us,
	Purify our hearts, make holy our souls and confirm our faith,
	keep safe our minds and compass our bodies all about.
	Enfold us…
Community	**… and surround us.**
Leader	Guide our speech…
Community	**… and our thoughts.**
Leader	Guard us in our sleeping…
Community	**… and in our waking.**
Leader	Nurture us in our watching…
Community	**… and in our hoping.**
Leader	Shield us in our lives…
Community	**… and grant us peace in eternity.**
Leader	Holy God,
	Father, Son and Spirit,
	pour down upon us from heaven
	the rich blessing of your forgiveness.
	Be patient with us and grant to us

	the fear of God, the love of God, and your affection
	so we may do your will on earth at all times …
Community	**… as the angels and saints do in heaven.**
Leader	Holy God,
	Father, Son and Spirit,
	pour down upon us from heaven
	the rich blessing of your peace.
	Peace between nations …
Community	**… peace between neighbors.**
Leader	Peace between kindred …
Community	**… peace between lovers.**
Leader	Peace between persons injured …
Community	**… peace between foes.**
Leader	Holy God,
	Father, Son and Spirit,
	help us to love and bless your creation,
	all that we see, all that we hear, all that we touch.
	Let us share your peace with our fellow creatures at all times,
	living as signs of forgiveness and reconciliation on the earth …
All	**… as the angels and saints do in heaven:**
	without malice, without jealousy, without envy,
	without fear, without terror of anyone under the sun.
	And may the Father, the Son and the Spirit
	kindle in our hearts the flame of love to our neighbors,
	to our foes, to our friends, to our kindred all,
	to the brave, to the knave, to the thrall.
Leader	The peace of the Father of Joy,
	the peace of Christ the Lamb,
	the peace of the Spirit of Grace, be with you.
Community	**The peace of the Father of Joy,**
	of Christ the Lamb, and of the Spirit of Grace,
	be with us all.
Leader	Let us share a sign of peace with those present here
	as a testimony to the peace God offers to the world.

The members of the community share a sign of peace before sitting down. A brief period of silence follows before the reader begins the

Word of God.

The Word of God

Reader   I set the teachings of Christ before you;
                I set the guarding of God about you.
Community   **May it possess us and protect us all.**

Reader   A reading from the Gospel according to Saint John.

Jesus showed himself again to the disciples by the Sea of Tiberias; and he showed himself in this way. Gathered there together were Simon Peter, Thomas called the Twin, Nathanael of Cana in Galilee, the sons of Zebedee, and two others of his disciples. Simon Peter said to them, "I am going fishing." They said to him, "We will go with you." They went out and got into the boat, but that night they caught nothing.

Just after daybreak, Jesus stood on the beach; but the disciples did not know that it was Jesus. Jesus said to them, "Children, you have no fish, have you?" They answered him, "No." He said to them, "Cast the net to the right side of the boat, and you will find some." So they cast it, and now they were not able to haul it in because there were so many fish. That disciple whom Jesus loved said to Peter, "It is the Lord!" When Simon Peter heard that it was the Lord, he put on some clothes, for he was naked, and jumped into the sea. But the other disciples came in the boat, dragging the net full of fish, for they were not far from the land, only about a hundred yards off.

When they had gone ashore, they saw a charcoal fire there, with fish on it, and bread. Jesus said to them, "Bring some of the fish that you have just caught." So Simon Peter went aboard and hauled the net ashore, full of large fish, a hundred fifty-three of them; and though there were so many, the net was not torn. Jesus said to them, "Come and have breakfast." Now none of the disciples dared to ask him, "Who are you?" because they knew it was the Lord. Jesus came and took the bread and gave it to them, and did the same with the fish. This was now the third time that Jesus appeared to the disciples after he was raised from the dead.

The gospel of Jesus Christ, source of strength,
Source of salvation, source of healing grace.

Community   **May it be a mantle to our bodies.**

A brief silence follows the reading, until the leader begins the psalm.

Leader   Psalm 116, Verses 1 through 19.

I love the Lord, because he has heard
my voice and my supplications.

Community   **Because he inclined his ear to me,**
therefore I will call on him as long as I live.

Leader   The snares of death encompassed me;
the pangs of Sheol laid hold on me;
I suffered distress and anguish.

Community   **Then I called on the name of the Lord:**
"O Lord, I pray, save my life!"

Leader   Gracious is the Lord, and righteous;
our God is merciful.

Community   **The Lord protects the simple;**
when I was brought low, he saved me.

Leader   Return, O my soul, to your rest,
for the Lord has dealt bountifully with you.

Community   **For you have delivered my soul from death,**
my eyes from tears,
my feet from stumbling.

Leader   I walk before the Lord
in the land of the living.
I kept my faith, even when I said,
"I am greatly afflicted";

Community   **I said in my consternation,**
"Everyone is a liar."

Leader   What shall I return to the Lord
for all his bounty to me?

Community   **I will lift up the cup of salvation**

	and call on the name of the Lord,
Leader	I will pay my vows to the Lord
	in the presence of all his people.
Community	**Precious in the sight of the Lord**
	is the death of his faithful ones.
Leader	O Lord, I am your servant;
	I am your servant, the child of your serving girl.
	You have loosed my bonds.
Community	**I will offer to you a thanksgiving sacrifice**
	and call on the name of the Lord.
Leader	I will pay my vows to the Lord
	in the presence of all his people,
Community	**in the courts of the house of the Lord,**
	in your midst, O Jerusalem.
	Praise the Lord!

There is a brief silence after the psalm before reading or presenting the audio version of the following reflection.

Reflection   "Treasuring the Gifts of Pilgrimage"
                              by Timothy J. Ray

A period of silence is observed after the reflection for private meditation, with or without music. Afterward, the leader continues the service — proceeding either to the Eucharistic Prayer or to the Prayers and Blessings after the optional hymn.

Hymn (optional)

Eucharistic Prayer

If the community wishes to share the Eucharist, the table is prepared during the hymn. If there is no hymn, the table should be prepared in silence — slowly and deliberately. Then, the leader begins the Eucharistic Prayer.

Leader   Thanks be to you, Holy Father of Glory,
                     father-kind, ever-loving, ever-powerful,
                     because of all the abundance, favor and deliverance
                     you bestow on us in our need.

Community	**May your name be praised forever,**
	in the heavens above and here on earth.
Leader	Whatever Providence befalls us as your children,
	in our portion, in our lot, in our path,
	give to us with it the riches of your hand
	and the joyous blessing of your mouth.
Community	**May your kingdom be seen to flourish**
	through the joy of your people, always grateful.
Leader	In the steep common path of our calling,
	be it easy or uneasy to our flesh,
	be it bright or dark for us to follow,
	your perfect guidance will be upon us.
Community	**Provide for us in all our needs,**
	material and spiritual, this day and every day.
Leader	Be a shield to us from the wiles of the deceiver,
	from the arch-destroyer with his arrows pursuing us,
	and in each secret thought our minds get to weave,
	guide and protect us.
Community	**Do not allow us to be tossed about by temptations**
	and protect us from all evils that would do us harm.
Leader	O Loving Christ, who was hanged upon a tree,
	each day and each night we remember your covenant;
	in our lying down and rising up, we yield ourselves to
	your cross,
	in our lives and our deaths, we seek in you our peace.
	Each day, may we remember the source of the mercies
	bestowed on us, gently and generously;
	each day, may we become fuller in love with you.
	My brothers and sisters, with St. Paul, I say to
	you:
	"I received from the Lord what I also handed on to you,
	that the Lord Jesus on the night when he was betrayed
	took a loaf of bread, and when he had given thanks, he
	broke it and said, 'This is my body that is for you. Do
	this in remembrance of me.' In the same way he took
	the cup also, after supper, saying, 'This cup is the new
	covenant in my blood. Do this, as often you drink it, in
	remembrance of me.' For as often as you eat this bread
	and drink the cup, you proclaim the Lord's death until
	he comes." (1 Corinthians 11: 23-26)

O Gracious God, *(making the sign of the cross)*
your Spirit come upon us, and upon this bread and
wine,
so that it might illumine our understanding, kindle our
will, incite our love, strengthen our weakness, and
enfold our desires.

Community **O Generous Lord,**
cleanse our hearts, make holy our souls,
confirm our faith,
keep safe our minds, encompass our bodies about
so that in our own hearts, we may feel your presence.

Leader O Holy Spirit, of greatest power,
come down upon us and subdue us;
from your glorious mansion in the heavens.
The knee that is stiff, O healer, make pliant,
the heart that is cold, make warm beneath your wing;
guide the soul that is wandering from your path
and it shall not die.
Each thing that is foul, may you cleanse,
each thing that is hard, may you soften with your grace,
each wound that is causing us pain, may you make
whole.
Now to the Father who created each creature,
now to the Son who paid ransom for his people,
now to the Holy Spirit, comforter of might:
shield and protect us from every wound.

Community **Encompass the beginning and the end of our race,**
give us courage to sing in glory,
in peace, in rest, in reconciliation.

Leader Come share in the table of the Lord,
source of love for those who cherish his kindness,
source of solace for those who need his forgiveness,
source of hope for those who fear his judgement.
Come share in the table of the Lord.

Community **Where no tear shall be shed,**
where death comes no more. Amen.

*The community shares the Eucharist in silence. Afterward, the table is
cleared during the hymn. If there is no hymn, the members of the
community use this time for private prayer.*

Hymn (optional)

Then, the leader continues the service.

Prayers and Blessings

Leader	Praise to the Father,
	praise to the Son,
	praise to the Spirit.
Community	**The three in one.**

All stand.

Leader	Let us pray for the coming of the Kingdom,
	in the words our Lord taught us:
All	**"Our Father in heaven,**
	hallowed be your name.
	Your kingdom come.
	Your will be done,
	on earth as it is in heaven.
	Give us this day our daily bread.
	And forgive us our debts,
	as we also have forgiven our debtors.
	And do not bring us to the time of trial,
	but rescue us from the evil one."
	(Matthew 6: 9-13)
Leader	Thanks be to you, Eternal Father,
	for you have enwrapped our bodies and our souls,
	safeguarding us in the sanctuary of your love ...
Community	**... and sheltering us under the mantle of your care.**
Leader	O Holy God,
	guide us with your wisdom,
	chastise us with your justice,
	help us with your mercy,
	protect us with your strength.
	In our dreams...
Community	**... arouse holy ambitions.**
Leader	In our repose...
Community	**... strengthen us for your service.**

Leader	In our hearts…
Community	**… nurture love for all your creatures.**
Leader	In our minds…
Community	**… implant saintly thoughts.**
Leader	In our deeds…
Community	**… may others see your kindness.**
Leader	In our words…
Community	**… may others hear your mercy.**
Leader	In our wishes…
Community	**… may others feel your compassion.**
Leader	In our reason…
Community	**… may others discern your wisdom.**
Leader	Divine Majesty, fill us with your goodness, shield us with your shade, and change us with your grace.
Community	**Amen.**
Leader	In the silence of your heart, bring your special needs or concerns before God. If you wish us to join in your prayers for these needs, speak them aloud, saying when you are finished, "For this I pray."

Members of the community offer their particular prayers. The community's response to these individual petitions is:

May God's blessing be yours,
and well may it befall you.

When these personal prayers are finished, the leader offers the final blessing.

Leader	May God our Creator guard you from hurt and protect you from harm in the nearness of his love. May Christ our Savior shield you from mischance and shelter you from grief in the nearness of his love. May the Guiding Spirit keep you from ill and

	bring you to the land of peace
	in the nearness of his love.
	Praise to the Father,
	praise to the Son,
	praise to the Spirit.
Community	**May the three in one bring us to the peace of eternity.**
	Amen.
Leader	Praise to the Father,
	praise to the Son,
	praise to the Spirit.
Community	**The three in one.**
Leader	*(making the sign of the cross)*
	The guarding of the God of life be on you,
	the guarding of the loving Christ be on you,
	the guarding of the Holy Spirit be on you,
	aiding and enfolding you
	each day and night of your lives.
Community	**May God, the three in one, encompass us all,**
	shielding us on sea and on land, in day and in night,
	guarding each step and each path we travel. Amen.

Hymn (optional)

The members of the community sit or kneel after the service concludes, as they prefer. Silence is observed to allow private prayer or meditation. Individuals should leave quietly as the Spirit moves them.

X • KEEP US IN THE NEARNESS OF YOUR LOVE
A Liturgy of Memories & Blessings

The members of the community enter and pray in silence. After the community is fully assembled, the prelude should be presented.

Prelude   "The Burial of Saint Brendan"
                         by Padraig Colum

> Nearing death, Brendan knew his body would offer both spiritual and material gifts that some people would try to appropriate for their own benefit. In Padraic Colum's "The Burial of Saint Brendan," the saint seeks to ensure that — even in death — he will be able to glorify God for the good of all rather than profit the selfish few.

A period of silent meditation follows the reading before the leader begins the penitential prayers.

Penitential Prayers

A bell rings and the members of the community kneel. If anyone cannot kneel, they should remain seated with their head bowed.

Leader	We bend our knees
All	*(making the sign of the cross)*
	in the eye of the Father who created us,
	in the eye of the Son who purchased us,
	in the eye of the Spirit who cleansed us.
	Amen.

All stand.

Leader	Lord Jesus Christ,
	give us the grace of repentance;
	give us the grace of earnestness;
	give us the grace of submission.
Community	**Give us the strength and courage to confess our guilt**
	as earnestly as were this the moment of our death.
Leader	Lord Jesus,

	help us speak according to your justice,
	help us heed your laws and directives.
	Each day and night, help us know your chastening,
	so we may act justly toward you and toward others.
	Lord Jesus, have mercy on us.
Community	**Lord Jesus, have mercy on us.**
Leader	Christ Jesus,
	help us count the causes of your mercy,
	help us praise the features of your goodness.
	Each day and night, help us know your kindness,
	so we may act tenderly toward you and toward others.
	Christ Jesus, have mercy on us.
Community	**Christ Jesus, have mercy on us.**
Leader	Lord Jesus,
	help us know the depths of your love,
	help us live according to your wisdom.
	Each day and night, help us know your peace,
	so we may act humbly toward you and toward others.
	Lord Jesus, have mercy on us.
Community	**Lord Jesus, have mercy on us.**
Leader	Lord Jesus Christ,
	with the Father who created us and the Spirit that cleansed us,
	Purify our hearts, make holy our souls and confirm our faith,
	keep safe our minds and compass our bodies all about.
	Enfold us…
Community	**… and surround us.**
Leader	Guide our speech…
Community	**… and our thoughts.**
Leader	Guard us in our sleeping…
Community	**… and in our waking.**
Leader	Nurture us in our watching…
Community	**… and in our hoping.**
Leader	Shield us in our lives…
Community	**… and grant us peace in eternity.**
Leader	Holy God,
	Father, Son and Spirit,
	pour down upon us from heaven
	the rich blessing of your forgiveness.

	Be patient with us and grant to us
	the fear of God, the love of God, and your affection
	so we may do your will on earth at all times …
Community	**… as the angels and saints do in heaven.**
Leader	Holy God,
	Father, Son and Spirit,
	pour down upon us from heaven
	the rich blessing of your peace.
	Peace between nations …
Community	**… peace between neighbors.**
Leader	Peace between kindred …
Community	**… peace between lovers.**
Leader	Peace between persons injured …
Community	**… peace between foes.**
Leader	Holy God,
	Father, Son and Spirit,
	help us to love and bless your creation,
	all that we see, all that we hear, all that we touch.
	Let us share your peace with our fellow creatures at all times,
	living as signs of forgiveness and reconciliation on the earth …
All	**… as the angels and saints do in heaven:**
	without malice, without jealousy, without envy,
	without fear, without terror of anyone under the sun.
	And may the Father, the Son and the Spirit
	kindle in our hearts the flame of love to our neighbors,
	to our foes, to our friends, to our kindred all,
	to the brave, to the knave, to the thrall.
Leader	The peace of the Father of Joy,
	the peace of Christ the Lamb,
	the peace of the Spirit of Grace, be with you.
Community	**The peace of the Father of Joy,**
	of Christ the Lamb, and of the Spirit of Grace,
	be with us all.
Leader	Let us share a sign of peace with those present here
	as a testimony to the peace God offers to the world.

The members of the community share a sign of peace before sitting down. A brief period of silence follows before the reader begins the Word of God.

The Word of God

Reader   I set the teachings of Christ before you;
I set the guarding of God about you.

Community   **May it possess us and protect us all.**

Reader   A reading from the Gospel according to Saint John.

Jesus said:

"I am the true vine, and my Father is the vinegrower. He removes every branch in me that bears no fruit. Every branch that bears fruit he prunes to make it bear more fruit. You have already been cleansed by the word that I have spoken to you. Abide in me as I abide in you. Just as the branch cannot bear fruit by itself unless it abides in the vine, neither can you unless you abide in me. I am the vine, you are the branches. Those who abide in me and I in them bear much fruit, because apart from me you can do nothing. Whoever does not abide in me is thrown away like a branch and withers; such branches are gathered, thrown into the fire, and burned. If you abide in me, and my words abide in you, ask for whatever you wish, and it will be done for you. My Father is glorified by this, that you bear much fruit and become my disciples. As the Father has loved me, so I have loved you; abide in my love. If you keep my commandments, you will abide in my love, just as I have kept my Father's commandments and abide in his love. I have said these things to you so that my joy may be in you, and that your joy may be complete.

"This is my commandment, that you love one another as I have loved you."

The gospel of Jesus Christ, source of strength,
Source of salvation, source of healing grace.

Community   **May it be a mantle to our bodies.**

A brief silence follows the reading, until the leader begins the psalm.

Leader   Psalm 62, Verses 1 through 12.

                  For God alone my soul waits in silence;
                  from him comes my salvation.
Community   **He alone is my rock and my salvation,**
                  my fortress; I shall never be shaken.
Leader   How long will you assail a person,
Community   **will you batter your victim, all of you,**
                  as you would a leaning wall, a tottering fence?
Leader   Their only plan is to bring down a person of
                  prominence.
                  They take pleasure in falsehood;
Community   **they bless with their mouths,**
                  but inwardly they curse.
Leader   For God alone my soul waits in silence,
Community   **for my hope is from him.**
Leader   He alone is my rock and my salvation,
                  my fortress; I shall not be shaken.
Community   **On God rests my deliverance and my honor;**
                  my mighty rock, my refuge is in God.
Leader   Trust in him at all times, O people;
                  pour out your heart before him;
Community   **God is a refuge for us.**
Leader   Those of low estate are but a breath,
                  those of high estate are a delusion;
Community   **in the balances they go up;**
                  they are together lighter than a breath.
Leader   Put no confidence in extortion,
                  and set no vain hopes on robbery;
Community   **if riches increase, do not set your heart on them.**
Leader   Once God has spoken;
                  twice have I heard this:
                  that power belongs to God,
Community   **and steadfast love belongs to you, O Lord.**
                  For you repay to all
                  according to their work.

Depending upon the size of the prayer community, one of the following options should be chosen:

In a small group, where all participants in the prayer service would be able to contribute if they wished, the leader should invite the community to share reflections on their experiences during this sequence of prayer services by saying:

Leader   At the end of any journey, especially a spiritual one, it is important to consider where you have been, what you have done and who you have met during your travels. So, take a moment to reflect on your time traveling with Brendan and his companions.

Then, if you have any thoughts or prayers you would like to share, perhaps an image or a particular moment from your prayers, please share them now as remembrances or prayerful desires for your companions. Please remember to be brief so everyone who desires will have an opportunity to speak.

The members of the community share brief reflections or prayers from their experiences during the retreat. When appropriate, the leader ends these reflections by saying:

Leader   Let us reflect and pray in silence.

A period of silence is observed after the community members share their reflections, with or without music. Then, the leader continues the service — proceeding either to the Eucharistic Prayer or to the Prayers and Blessings after the optional hymn.

In a larger group, where it would be difficult for all participants to contribute their reflections, there is a brief silence after the psalm before reading or presenting the audio version of the following reflection.

Reflection   "Returning to Clonfert"
                         by Timothy J. Ray

Afterward, the leader continues the service.

Leader At the end of any journey, especially a spiritual one, it is important to consider where you have been, what you have done and who you have met during your travels. So, take a moment to reflect on your pilgrimage with Brendan and his companions.

Leader   So, let us reflect and pray in silence.

A period of silence is observed for private meditation, with or without music. Afterward, the leader continues the service — proceeding either to the Eucharistic Prayer or to the Prayers and Blessings after the optional hymn.

Hymn (optional)

Eucharistic Prayer

If the community wishes to share the Eucharist, the table is prepared during the hymn. If there is no hymn, the table should be prepared in silence — slowly and deliberately. Then, the leader begins the Eucharistic Prayer.

Leader   Thanks be to you, Holy Father of Glory,
father-kind, ever-loving, ever-powerful,
because of all the abundance, favor and deliverance
you bestow on us in our need.

Community   **May your name be praised forever,**
in the heavens above and here on earth.

Leader   Whatever Providence befalls us as your children,
in our portion, in our lot, in our path,
give to us with it the riches of your hand
and the joyous blessing of your mouth.

Community   **May your kingdom be seen to flourish**
through the joy of your people, always grateful.

Leader   In the steep common path of our calling,
be it easy or uneasy to our flesh,
be it bright or dark for us to follow,
your perfect guidance will be upon us.

Community   **Provide for us in all our needs,**
material and spiritual, this day and every day.

Leader   Be a shield to us from the wiles of the deceiver,
from the arch-destroyer with his arrows pursuing us,

and in each secret thought our minds get to weave,
guide and protect us.

Community **Do not allow us to be tossed about by temptations**
and protect us from all evils that would do us harm.

Leader O Loving Christ, who was hanged upon a tree,
each day and each night we remember your covenant;
in our lying down and rising up, we yield ourselves to
your cross,
in our lives and our deaths, we seek in you our peace.
Each day, may we remember the source of the mercies
bestowed on us, gently and generously;
each day, may we become fuller in love with you.

My brothers and sisters, with St. Paul, I say to
you:
"I received from the Lord what I also handed on to you,
that the Lord Jesus on the night when he was betrayed
took a loaf of bread, and when he had given thanks, he
broke it and said, 'This is my body that is for you. Do
this in remembrance of me.' In the same way he took
the cup also, after supper, saying, 'This cup is the new
covenant in my blood. Do this, as often you drink it, in
remembrance of me.' For as often as you eat this bread
and drink the cup, you proclaim the Lord's death until
he comes." (1 Corinthians 11: 23-26)

O Gracious God, *(making the sign of the cross)*
your Spirit come upon us, and upon this bread and
wine,
so that it might illumine our understanding, kindle our
will, incite our love, strengthen our weakness, and
enfold our desires.

Community **O Generous Lord,**
cleanse our hearts, make holy our souls,
confirm our faith,
keep safe our minds, encompass our bodies about
so that in our own hearts, we may feel your presence.

Leader O Holy Spirit, of greatest power,
come down upon us and subdue us;
from your glorious mansion in the heavens.
The knee that is stiff, O healer, make pliant,
the heart that is cold, make warm beneath your wing;

	guide the soul that is wandering from your path

guide the soul that is wandering from your path
and it shall not die.
Each thing that is foul, may you cleanse,
each thing that is hard, may you soften with your grace,
each wound that is causing us pain, may you make
whole.
Now to the Father who created each creature,
now to the Son who paid ransom for his people,
now to the Holy Spirit, comforter of might:
shield and protect us from every wound.

Community   **Encompass the beginning and the end of our race,
give us courage to sing in glory,
in peace, in rest, in reconciliation.**

Leader   Come share in the table of the Lord,
source of love for those who cherish his kindness,
source of solace for those who need his forgiveness,
source of hope for those who fear his judgement.
Come share in the table of the Lord.

Community   **Where no tear shall be shed,
where death comes no more. Amen.**

*The community shares the Eucharist in silence. Afterward, the table is
cleared during the hymn. If there is no hymn, the members of the
community use this time for private prayer.*

Hymn (optional)

Then, the leader continues the service.

Prayers and Blessings

Leader   Praise to the Father,
praise to the Son,
praise to the Spirit.

Community   **The three in one.**

All stand.

Leader   Let us pray for the coming of the Kingdom,
in the words our Lord taught us:

All	"Our Father in heaven,
	hallowed be your name.
	Your kingdom come.
	Your will be done,
	on earth as it is in heaven.
	Give us this day our daily bread.
	And forgive us our debts,
	as we also have forgiven our debtors.
	And do not bring us to the time of trial,
	but rescue us from the evil one."
	(Matthew 6: 9-13)
Leader	Thanks be to you, Eternal Father,
	for you have enwrapped our bodies and our souls,
	safeguarding us in the sanctuary of your love ...
Community	**... and sheltering us under the mantle of your care.**
Leader	We give you our whole soul, O God:
	our thoughts, our deeds, our words, our will,
	our understanding and our intellect.
	Everything we are sings your praises.
	We give you worship with our whole lives.
Community	**Keep us in the nearness of your love.**
Leader	We give you assent with our whole powers.
Community	**Keep us in the nearness of your love.**
Leader	We give you praise with our whole tongues.
Community	**Keep us in the nearness of your love.**
Leader	We give you honor with our whole utterances.
Community	**Keep us in the nearness of your love.**
Leader	We give you reverence with our whole understanding.
Community	**Keep us in the nearness of your love.**
Leader	We give you offering with our whole thoughts.
Community	**Keep us in the nearness of your love.**
Leader	We give you praise with our whole being.
Community	**Keep us in the nearness of your love.**
Leader	We give you love with our whole devotion.
Community	**Keep us in the nearness of your love.**
Leader	We give you kneeling with our whole desires.
Community	**Keep us in the nearness of your love.**
Leader	We give you love with our whole heart.
Community	**Keep us in the nearness of your love.**
Leader	We give you affection with our whole sense.

Community	**Keep us in the nearness of your love.**
Leader	We give you our existence with our whole mind.
Community	**Keep us in the nearness of your love.**
Leader	We beseech you, O God,
	keep us from all ill, hurt and harm,
	protect us from mischance, grief and despair,
	and guide us into the land of your peace.
Community	**Amen.**
Leader	In the silence of your heart,
	bring your special needs or concerns before God.
	If you wish us to join in your prayers for these needs,
	speak them aloud, saying when you are finished,
	"For this I pray."

Members of the community offer their particular prayers. The community's response to these individual petitions is:

May God's blessing be yours,
and well may it befall you.

When these personal prayers are finished, the leader offers the final blessing.

Leader	May the Father, Son and Spirit enfold you on every side,
	never forsaking or forgetting you,
	nor letting evil come near you,
	in each step of the journey before you.
	God the Father go with you at every pass,
	Christ our Lord be with you on every hill,
	The Spirit of Grace guide you across every stream.
	May the Triune God protect and keep you
	from every challenge and sorrow,
	from every evil and anguish …
Community	**… offering a mantle for both our bodies and our souls.**
	Amen.
Leader	Praise to the Father,
	praise to the Son,
	praise to the Spirit.
Community	**The three in one.**
Leader	*(making the sign of the cross)*
	The guarding of the God of life be on you,
	the guarding of the loving Christ be on you,

the guarding of the Holy Spirit be on you,
aiding and enfolding you
each day and night of your lives.

Community   **May God, the three in one, encompass us all,
shielding us on sea and on land, in day and in night,
guarding each step and each path we travel. Amen.**

Hymn (optional)

*The members of the community sit or kneel after the service concludes,
as they prefer. Silence is observed to allow private prayer or meditation.
Individuals should leave quietly as the Spirit moves them.*

Returning Home

God calls each of us to become instruments of love and hope to those around us — cultivating our "better angels" through service and prayer — but this also may require us to confront those people or social forces that might obstruct this vocation.

"The Burial of Saint Brendan"

by Padraic Colum

Nearing death, Brendan knew his body would offer both spiritual and material gifts that some people would try to appropriate for their own benefit. In Padraic Colum's "The Burial of Saint Brendan," the saint seeks to ensure that — even in death — he will be able to glorify God for the good of all rather than profit the selfish few.

On the third day from this (Saint Brendan said)
I will be where no wind that filled a sail
Has ever been, and it blew high or low:
For from this home-creek, from this body's close
I shall put forth: make ready, you, to go
With what remains to Cluan Hy-many,
For there my resurrection I'd have be.

But you will know how hard they'll strive to hold
This body o' me, and hold it for the place
Where I was bred, they say, and born and reared.
For they would have my resurrection here,
So that my sanctity might be matter shared
By every mother's child the tribeland polled
Who lived and died and mixed into the mould.

So you will have to use all canniness
To bring this body to its burial
When in your hands I leave what goes in clay;
The wagon that our goods are carried in —
Have it yoked up between the night and day,
And when the breath is from my body gone,
Bear body out, the wagon lay it on;

And cover it with gear that's taken hence —
"The goods of Brendan is what's here," you'll say
To those who'll halt you; they will pass you then:
Tinkers and tailors, soldiers, farmers, smiths,
You'll leave beside their doors — all those thwart men

224

For whom my virtue was a legacy
That they would profit in, each a degree —

As though it were indeed some chalice, staff,
Crozier or casket, that they might come to,
And show to those who chanced upon the way,
And have, not knowing how the work was done
In scrolls and figures and in bright inlay:
Whence came the gold and silver that they prize,
The blue enamels and the turquoises!

I, Brendan, had a name came from the sea —
I was the first who sailed the outer main,
And past all forelands and all fastnesses!
I passed the voiceless anchorets, their isles,
Saw the ice-palaces upon the seas,
Mentioned Christ's name to men cut off from men,
Heard the whales snort, and saw the Kraken!

And on a wide-branched, green, and glistening tree
Beheld the birds that had been angels erst:
Between the earth and heaven 'twas theirs to wing:
Fallen from High they were, but they had still
Music of Heaven's Court: I heard them sing:
Even now the island of the unbeached coast
I see, and hear the white, resplendent host!

For this they'd have my burial in this place,
Their hillside, and my resurrection be
Out of the mould that they with me would share.
But I have chosen Cluan for my ground
A happy place! Some grace came to me there:
And you, as you go towards it, to men say,
Should any ask you on that long highway:

"Brendan is here, who had great saints for friends:
Ita, who reared him on a mother's knee,
Enda, who from his fastness blessed his sail:
Then Brighid, she who had the flaming heart,
And Colum-cille, prime of all the Gael;

Gildas of Britain, wisest child of light."
And saying this, drive through the falling night.[*]

As you reflect on this poem, take a moment to contemplate the graces and blessings you received from your spiritual journey with Saint Brendan and consider whether any of them might need to be protected against being misused, either by other people or by your own temptations. Then, in prayer, ask God to preserve the integrity of these spiritual gifts as well as your own handling of them.

---

[*]   Padraic Colum, *The Poet's Circuits: Collected Poems of Ireland* (Dublin: Dolmen Press, 1981), pages 58-59.

Returning to Clonfert

some thoughts on Brendan's companions

While returning home to Clonfert from his journey brought Brendan renown, we hear nothing further of his companions. With a certain sadness, we realize that they are not even named in the telling of Brendan's journey. These companions rode on the back of the leviathan, were fed by God's special emissaries and saw angels singing as birds while traveling to the Land of the Saints with their abbot. And surely, just as Brendan did, they also took some souvenirs of that place — bits of fruit or precious stones — and brought them home where they may have shared them with others or quietly treasured them in private. Yet, we never hear any more of them after their return to Clonfert — whether they left the monastery again as missionaries or pilgrims, whether they chose to live as hermits or whether they quietly returned to the routines of monastic life. While Brendan is crowned with glory, his companions fade into the mists of anonymity.

Still, we know these holy companions received their share of graces during their travels. Inspired by Barrind's story and their love for Brendan, they generously and enthusiastically offered to join their abbot on his pilgrimage. But only through prayer would they have been able to remain faithful to that commitment during their difficult journey. Brendan's companions learned self-control and patience by working together within the tight confines of their boat, and their abbot's wisdom — shown in so many strange and dangerous situations — strengthened their ability to submit gently to his commands. They became kinder and more compassionate when they saw God's mercy towards terrible sinners or witnessed the deaths of their friends. Finally, they experienced a joyful sense of peace as they walked in the Land of the Saints before returning home. These are all fruits of God's holy Spirit, the hallmarks of a saintly life.

Nevertheless, while the spiritual gifts these monks received during their travels must have benefited their community in many significant ways, the contributions of these saintly companions remain hidden with their names. In all likelihood, Brendan's companions were respected — perhaps even admired — in their community after their return home. But much of this recognition probably came from their association with the monastery's famous and saintly abbot, and at least some of those who came to them for blessings and spiritual guidance would have been seeking a surrogate for the saint. Still, even if these monks lived in the shadow of a great spiritual adventure, their lives would never have been reduced to this one event. God does not waste his gifts, and each of these hidden saints received the graces they needed to help build the kingdom of God through their own choices and actions.

So, it remains vitally important that we recognize the contributions of the many hidden saints who kept the Celtic spiritual traditions alive over the centuries. We certainly learn from the example and teachings of famous Celtic saints like Brendan, Brigid, Columba, Ita or Patrick — finding inspiration in the adventures and achievements of these great men and women — but we also need to recognize the spiritual vitality that surrounded these exemplary individuals, an aura of sanctity produced by generations of anonymous saints who practiced and preserved the Celtic traditions of prayer in private. These seemingly common and ordinary people (both in the ancient Celtic world and during the centuries after the Celtic churches faded into history) possessed an uncommon and exceptional spiritual life that helped empower the revival of Celtic spirituality in the last century or so, showing that the blessings and graces received through these ways of prayer were not limited to the better-known Celtic saints.

Recognizing the important contributions of these hidden saints also reminds us to acknowledge those people in our own lives who have shown us the face of Christ through their quiet gestures of kindness or faith — the hidden saints who humbly continue to build God's kingdom without fanfare — and encourages us to act with greater humility and generosity as we share the spiritual gifts we receive with others. Through their humble and unaffected testimonies, these men and women challenge us to accept the spiritual gifts and graces we receive to help build the kingdom of God and to share them with others, knowing that God's desires are being fulfilled through our actions and choices even when we are ignored or dismissed.

As you conclude your journey with Brendan and his companions, it is important that you devote some time to reviewing the gifts — both large and small — you received during your own prayerful pilgrimage and reflecting on which ones you might want to share with others as you strive to build the kingdom of God, even if you receive scant recognition for your efforts.

Consider where these gifts might lead you, whether in service to familiar communities or in search of new and unknown places to serve God. Then, in prayer, ask God to nurture these gifts and preserve these holy desires.

Resources for Prayer and Worship

(1)   Digital Materials
for use with these reflections and prayer services

(2)   Resources for Prayer
• On Holy Ground:
rituals for creating a sacred space
• Making a Morning Caim:
a prayerful consideration of the coming day
• An Evening Prayer of Remembrance:
venerating God's presence in the passing day

(3)   Resources for Worship
• "Sing and Make Melody to the Lord":
sources and suggestions for music during worship
• Print-Ready Programs for Worship,
prepared in various sizes and formats

Introduction

The following subsections provide a link to online digital materials designed to accompany the reflections and prayer services in this book as well as present rituals intended to help you develop consistent habits of prayers, directions for two prayers designed to heighten your awareness to God's activity in your life, and materials intended to help you create powerful communal prayer services.

Digital Materials

This page provides a link to online resources for the spiritual reflections and prayer services in this book. These include audio recordings of the readings from *The Voyage of Saint Brendan*, their companion reflections and the two Celtic examens (included in this section) as well as pre-formatted programs for the prayer services.

Resources for Prayer

The documents in this subsection address the technical aspects of creating a mental and spiritual space for your prayer through personal rituals as well as instructions for two prayerful reviews of your day (called examens) using traditional Gaelic prayers from Alexander Carmichael's *Carmina Gadelica*.

"On Holy Ground" suggests three short rituals that you might use to consecrate your prayer. These spiritual gestures will create a mental "common space" that unifies the different times and places in which you pray, strengthening your ability to create good prayer habits and easing your entry into the silence and solitude of contemplation.

The two Celtic examens highlight God's active presence in your day. The first examen, intended to be used in the morning, presents a Celtic *caim* (or encircling prayer) in which you look forward to the coming day while asking God to encircle and protect the expected events of your day and the people you might meet during them. The second examen, prayed at night before going to bed, uses the rhythmic repetition of a traditional Gaelic prayer to create a litany of gratitude based on the events and people you encountered during your day.

Resources for Worship

This subsection provides materials and suggestions that will help you conduct the prayer services in your community. These include guidelines for using music during the services as well as print-ready programs.

"Sing and Make Melody to the Lord" suggests hymnals and other musical collections that you might use during the services as well as provides advice on selecting and presenting these songs in your community.

Finally, "Print-Ready Programs for Worship" provides ready-made programs for your prayer services in various sizes as well as suggestions for adapting these programs to the particular needs or desires of your community.

Digital Materials

for use with these reflections and prayer services

The digital resources for this book may be found at:

http://www.resources.silentheron.net

These include:
- audio recordings of the readings from *The Voyage of Saint Brendan* and their companion reflections (from the first section)
- audio recordings of the guided versions of the Celtic examens (found in this section)
- print-Ready Programs for Worship (described in this section)

Resources for Prayer

rituals for creating a sacred space

The consequences of incorporating personal rituals into our prayer often exceed our expectations. The consistent use of private rituals helps us develop bodily habits that allow us to more quickly put aside our daily concerns and enter into a prayerful conversation with our Creator. But these rituals also remind us that we are invoking protection and guidance while seeking communion with a loving God. With each successive act of ritual, we invite God to consecrate our time with him and reconfirm our desire that he transform us into signs of his presence in the world.

With these goals in mind, you may find one or more of the following three rituals (using traditional Gaelic prayers selected from Alexander Carmichael's *Carmina Gadelica*) helpful:

#1 — A Trinitarian Act of Humility

Note: For this ritual, place three candles at the focal point of your prayer space — along with an image of the Trinity (e.g., a triskele or an icon), if you like. You also will need some matches or a long lighter.

• After relaxing into your prayer space, light the candles while reciting this prayer:
I am bending my knee
(lighting the first candle)
in the eye of the Father who created me,
(lighting the second candle)
in the eye of the Son who died for me,
(lighting the third candle)
in the eye of the Spirit who cleansed me,
in love and desire.
• After completing your prayer, as you prepare to leave your prayer space, extinguish the candles in the same order you originally lit them while repeating the following prayer:
I am bending my knee
in the eye of the Father who created me,

(extinguishing the first candle)
in the eye of the Son who died for me,
(extinguishing the second candle)
in the eye of the Spirit who cleansed me,
(extinguishing the third candle)
in love and desire. Amen.

#2 — A Personal Caim (Encircling Prayer)

Note: This ritual does not require any objects, but you may want to use a crucifix or other image of Jesus as the focal point of your prayer space.

• After becoming comfortable, open your hands — palms up — in front of you or pick up and hold the image of Jesus. Then, looking at your palms or the image, offer the following prayer:
O Lord, who brought me from the rest of last night
Unto the joyous light of this day,
Bring me from the new light of this day
Unto the guiding light of eternity.
• Now, allowing an image to form in your imagination as you slowly say:
The shape of Christ be towards me,
The shape of Christ be from me,
The shape of Christ be before me,
The shape of Christ be behind me,
The shape of Christ be over me,
The shape of Christ be under me,
The shape of Christ be with me,
The shape of Christ be around me.
• When you are finished, return the image of Jesus to its place or move your hands to where you will hold them during prayer.
• After you finish your prayer, pick up and hold the image of Jesus or open your hands in front of you as you pray:
O Lord, bring me from the new light of this day
Unto the guiding light of eternity.
Oh! from the new light of this day
Unto the guiding light of eternity. Amen.
• Wait a moment in silence after the prayer. Then, close your hands or replace the image of Jesus before leaving.

#3 — A Veneration of the Cross

Note: In this ritual, the focal point for your prayer space should include a candle placed before a cross or crucifix. You also will need some matches or a lighter.

• After calming yourself, make the sign of the cross while saying:
In the name of the King of life,
In the name of the Christ of love,
In the name of the Holy Spirit,
The triune of my strength.
• Then, light the candle before continuing with this prayer:
May the cross of the crucifixion tree
Upon the wounded back of Christ
Deliver me from distress,
From death and from spells.

The cross of Christ without fault,
All outstretched toward me;
O God, bless me!
• After concluding your prayer period, repeat the following prayer while you extinguish the candle:
May the cross of the crucifixion tree
Upon the wounded back of Christ
Deliver me from distress,
From death and from spells.

The cross of Christ without fault,
All outstretched toward me;
O God, bless me!
• Then, make the sign of the cross as you say:
In the name of the King of life,
In the name of the Christ of love,
In the name of the Holy Spirit,
The triune of my strength. Amen.

Making a Morning Caim

a prayerful consideration of the coming day

[1]   Focus on this present moment and allow all other concerns or problems to fade from your consciousness. Then, become aware of your desire to know the fullness of God's love for you — and to feel his continuing compassion and guidance — as you quietly affirm God's redemptive presence in you and in the world around you.

[2]   Consider your life. Bring to mind the times when you do not reflect God's goodness, the times when you squander or misuse the gifts he has given to you, and the times when you feel abandoned by God. Become aware of your desire to live in God's goodness as well as your desire to properly use the many gifts he has given you.

[3]   Pray for the grace to see God's action in your life more clearly, to understand his desires for you more accurately, to respond to his guidance to you more generously. Pray also that others in the world might see, understand and respond to God's guidance in their lives.

[4]   Now, imagine the coming day, seeing God's love enfolding and encircling every situation. Feel God's love touch you in the depths of your being, expressing his desire to share his creation with you in the coming day. Ask God to bless your day, the people and creatures you will meet in it, and those who are close to your heart.

• Then, see God in all the events and people of the coming morning. Feel his loving presence surrounding, protecting and guiding you as you imagine the moments when you expect to be alone during this morning and when you expect to be with other people. Feel God's love pervade your home, your work and your travels as you ask him to encircle the events and people of this morning with his love, saying:

The compassing of God be on you,
The compassing of the God of life.

• Imagine the events and people of the coming midday. Again, feel God's presence surrounding, protecting and guiding you as you see the moments when you expect to be alone and when you expect to be with other people. As you ask him to encircle the events and people of this midday with his love, saying:

The compassing of Christ be on you,
The compassing of the Christ of love.

• Envision the coming afternoon, seeing God's presence in the times when you are alone and when you are with others. Hear his voice speak to you in all these events and people as you ask God to encircle them with his love, saying:

The compassing of Spirit be on you,
The compassing of the Spirit of Grace.

• Finally, see the coming evening. Feel God's love pervade the moments when you expect to be alone and when you expect to be with other people before asking him to encircle them with his love, saying:

The compassing of the Three be on you,
The compassing of the Three preserve you,
The compassing of the Three preserve you.

[5] As you allow these images to ebb and flow in your consciousness, make a mental note of your emotional responses to the people and events you expect to encounter during the coming day, quietly affirming your desire to live in God's goodness. Then, become aware of your need for God's continuing care and guidance so you may properly use the many gifts he has given you in these circumstances — and in the unexpected events of this day.

[6] When you are ready, conclude by offering this traditional prayer:

God, bless to me the new day,
Never vouchsafed to me before;
It is to bless your own presence
　　That you have given me this time, O God.
　　Bless my eyes,
　　may my eyes bless all they see;
　　I will bless my neighbor,
　　May my neighbor bless me.
God, give me a clean heart,
let me not from sight of your eye. Amen.

An Evening Prayer of Remembrance

venerating God's presence in the passing day

[1]   Become completely focused on this present moment and allow all other concerns or problems to dissolve from your consciousness. Become aware of God's goodness and of the many gifts that God has given to you, quietly acknowledging God's sustaining power in your life and in the world around you.

[2]   Consider your life. Bring to mind the times when you do not reflect God's goodness, the times when you squander or misuse the gifts God has given to you, and the times when you feel abandoned by God. Become aware of your desire to live in God's goodness and quietly affirm your desire to properly use the many gifts God has given you, asking for God's continuing guidance to help you achieve this goal.

[3]   Become aware of the need — both in you and in the world around you — for God's healing and redemptive presence.

    • Open yourself to that divine presence as you ponder and pray the words of this traditional prayer:

I am bending my knee

    In the eye of the Father who created me,
    In the eye of the Son who purchased me,
    In the eye of the Spirit who cleansed me,

In friendship and affection.

    • Then, pray for the grace to see God's action in your life more clearly, to understand God's desires for you more accurately, and to respond to God's guidance to you more generously. Pray also that others in the world might see, understand and respond to God's guidance in their lives.

[4]   Now, review this day in your memory, allowing yourself to feel God's presence in its events and emotions.

    • Remember waking this morning. Recall whether you awoke easily or with difficulty, calling to mind how you felt — whether you were happy, sad, relaxed or tense. Make a mental note of whether you felt God close to you or distant from you. Take a moment to consider these things, acknowledging the shaping presence of God in the beginning of the day, as you say:

I am bending my knee

In friendship and affection.

• Recall your preparations for the day. Remember whether you dressed quickly or slowly, calling to mind your thoughts and feelings. Ask yourself whether God was on your mind as you prepared for this day. Take a moment to consider any feelings that these memories evoke in you, acknowledging the shaping presence of God in them, as you say:

I am bending my knee
In friendship and affection.

• Bring to mind your morning. Recall those moments when you were alone and when you were with other people. Recall the emotions you felt during the morning hours, allowing specific feelings to connect to the things you did as well as the things about which you thought or talked. Ask yourself how God was present to you this morning. Take a moment to consider these images and feelings, acknowledging the shaping presence of God in them, as you say:

I am bending my knee
In friendship and affection.

• Call to mind what you did at midday, remembering those moments when you were alone and when you were with other people, becoming aware of any emotions associated with specific things you did or things about which you thought or talked. Ask yourself about the ways in which God was present to you or on your mind at midday. Take a moment to consider these images and feelings, acknowledging the shaping presence of God in them, as you say:

I am bending my knee
In friendship and affection.

• Remember your afternoon, recalling those moments when you were alone and when you were with other people. Recall the emotions you felt during the afternoon, particularly if they are connected to specific things you did or about which you thought or talked. Ask yourself how God was present to you this afternoon. Take a moment to consider these images and feelings, acknowledging the shaping presence of God in them, as you say:

I am bending my knee
In friendship and affection.

• Recall your evening, remembering those moments when you were alone and when you were with other people. Become aware of any emotions you felt during the evening hours as you consider the things you did as well as the things about which you thought or talked.

Ask yourself how God revealed his presence to you this evening. Take a moment to consider these images and feelings, acknowledging the shaping presence of God in them, as you say:

I am bending my knee
In friendship and affection.

• Consider the present moment. Become aware of your feelings and your current sense of God's presence. Take a moment to consider these feelings, acknowledging the shaping presence of God in this moment, as you say:

I am bending my knee
In friendship and affection.

[5]   Allow all the images and memories to flow freely in your consciousness, feeling God's presence in them. Make a mental note of your emotional responses to these images and memories as they ebb and flow. Then, become aware once again of your desire to live in God's goodness as you quietly affirm your desire to properly use the many gifts he has given you and ask for his continued guidance as you try to achieve this goal.

[6]   When you are ready, conclude with this traditional prayer:

Through your own Anointed One, O God,
Bestow upon us fullness in our need.

> *Love towards God,*
> *The affection of God,*
> *The smile of God,*
> *The wisdom of God,*
> *The grace of God,*
> *The fear of God*

To do in the world of the Three,
As angels and saints
Do in heaven;

> *Each shade and light,*
> *Each day and night,*
> *Each time in kindness,*

Give us your Spirit. Amen.

Resources for Worship

"Sing and Make Melody to the Lord"

sources and suggestions for music during worship

This book presents a distinctive prayer service using the traditional Gaelic prayers collected in Alexander Carmichael's *Carmina Gadelica*. Even in translation, the prayers gathered in Carmichael's collection have a potent immediacy that allows a person praying them in the present to hear the voice of past generations united by their desire for union with God. To preserve this spiritual union between previous and present communities, the musical selections used in the prayer services need to retain the simplicity and prayerful rhythms of the traditional Scottish prayers joined together in *A Journey to the Land of the Saints*.

Sources for Music

Fortunately, there are a number of published collections of Celtic hymns and songs that may be used during the prayer services presented in this book. In particular, three collections by the Iona Community (and its Wild Goose Resource Group) are well-suited to the topics and themes of the prayer services in *A Journey to the Land of the Saints* — the *Iona Abbey Music Book*, *Heaven Shall Not Wait* and *Psalms of Patience, Protest and Praise* (which contains interpretations of some of the psalms used in the prayer services). In addition to these books from the Iona Community, Ray Simpson (the Founding Guardian of the Community of Aidan and Hilda) has gathered a broad range of 255 hymns in his *Celtic Hymn Book*. Finally, a number of individual musicians and composers (such as George Bayley, Roddy Cowie and Larry Shackley) have published or posted their own collections of Celtic/Gaelic-inspired music for prayer and worship that may be found through online searches.

Choosing and Using Songs for Your Worship

As you consider the songs and hymns for your prayers services, you will need to reflect on their place within your worship. You have the choice of singing on two or three occasions during the prayer services, depending on whether you use the Eucharistic Prayer — at the end of the Word of God section and at the conclusion of the prayer services as well as at the end of the optional Eucharistic Prayer (when it is used). Each of these moments have their own particular character and this should be respected in the songs you choose.

For instance:

• After the Word of God, it might be best to select a song that echoes the gospel reading or psalm used in that particular service — reaffirming the message of these scriptural passages at the heart of your reflections.

• On the other hand, a general thematic song would re-encapsulate the core message of your shared prayers at the end of the service before the members of your community disperse.

• At the end of the Eucharistic Prayer, however, you may choose either to reassert the central reading of the service by using a gospel-based song or to "set the tone" for the service's final prayers and blessings by selecting a thematic song.

With these considerations in mind, you may want to refer to the following table listing the themes and scriptural passages in these prayer services as you select the songs that are most appropriate for your community.

Prayer Service	Themes	Gospel Reading	Psalm
I	listening for God's voice	John 4: 3-26	Psalm 19
II	finding Christ in all things	John 1: 35-51	Psalm 139
III	sharing in the love of the Trinity	John 2: 1-11	Psalm 27

IV	Becoming a loved sinner	John 9: 1-41	Psalm 33
V	living as citizens of heaven	John 6: 1-27, 35-40	Psalm 103
VI	discerning God's presence	John 11: 1-3, 17-46	Psalm 40
VII	embracing the cross of Christ	John 18:28, 38 - John 19:18	Psalm 22
VIII	seeking the place of resurrection	John 20: 1-18	Psalm 91
IX	treasuring the gifts of pilgrimage	John 21: 1-14	Psalm 116
X	returning home from your journey	John 15: 1-12	Psalm 62

After selecting the songs that are best-suited to your community, you will need to decide the best way to present the songs during the prayer services. It would be best for the community to sing the songs during the services, but this will require that you find ways to introduce the music and invite communal singing. If this is not possible, you might create a small ensemble of musicians and singers to create a contemplative atmosphere during the services, allowing them to perform the songs for your community.

Finally, you might consider offering the songs used during the prayer services as a resource for private prayer. This will allow individuals to deepen their private prayer by returning to songs that were particularly important to them during the services, connecting them to particular readings or prayers as the seeds planted in the services begin to germinate in each person in their own unique ways.

Print-Ready Programs for Worship

prepared in various sizes and formats

Following the instructions provided at the beginning of the resources section, you will find folders containing print-ready programs for the prayer services prepared as PDF documents. These are labelled according to the paper size you will need to print these programs (e.g., "Letterhead(US)-PDF", "A4-PDF", etc.).

• Each of these folders include two subfolders, one containing programs with the Eucharistic Prayer and the other containing programs without it. This will give you the option of including or excluding the Eucharistic Prayer during your prayer services.

• To create the appropriate programs for your community, you should print double-sided copies of the documents and make certain they are properly collated before being folded and stapled together.

• While these programs refer to hymns and other music that may be presented during the prayer services, they do not contain the words or titles of these selections. So, any music used during the services will need to be provided separately or inserted into .docx versions of the programs (in the manner described below).

Note: _For help in finding and selecting songs for your prayer services, please consult "Sing and Make Melody to the Lord" in these resource pages._

In addition, there is a folder containing PDF versions of the programs, giving you the option of distributing these documents electronically. Like the other versions of the pre-formatted programs, this folder contains subfolders offering the option of including or excluding the Eucharistic Prayer during your services.

For groups wishing to modify these programs, some versions are provided in the .docx format (e.g., "Letterhead(US)-docx", "A4-docx", etc.). These documents may be revised to include biblical selections and psalms from other translations, to add the words for hymns, or to provide information about the musical selections used during the prayer services.

• To revise the biblical citations in these programs, find and replace the selections (presented in red print) in the Word of God, the Eucharistic Prayer, and the Prayers and Blessings sections. Then, if necessary, adjust the print color and indentation of the new selections before printing and preparing your programs using the paper size of your choice.

Note: While you may change the scriptural citation in the Eucharistic Prayer using these techniques, it is not recommended since this selection is interwoven with the surrounding text. Changing the citation might disrupt the rhythms of the prayers in that section and prove distracting to your community.

• If you want to include the words of hymns or to provide information about the music used for meditation, you will need to insert the wording into the document and format it to match the surrounding text. Then, you will be able to print the programs for your prayer services before formatting them using the paper size of your choice.

Note: If you are adding musical material but not changing the biblical citations in the programs, you will need to find and change the color of the bible verses before printing and formatting your programs.

Printed in Great Britain
by Amazon